Social Entrepreneurship and Innovation in Rural Europe

Social Entrepreneurship and Innovation in Rural Europe investigates how social entrepreneurship advances social innovation in rural Europe and contributes to fighting social and economic challenges in these regions.

Based on longitudinal data collected in four European countries, this book explains how social enterprises enact their business model based on an entrepreneurial reconfiguration of resources they obtain from their network relations, and how their activities empower local communities, driving change and eventually innovation. In these activities, the entrepreneurial mindset and the role as intermediary between different groups and domains of society help to reframe challenges into opportunities. The argument in this book develops from a description of what social enterprises report to do to an analysis of how they do it, and results in an explanation of why they take these actions. In doing so it gradually broadens the view from a focus on the social enterprises themselves to their interactions and network partners and, finally, to their positioning in societal fields. The presented model complements network theory with the concept of strategic action fields. This book reveals the crucial role of social entrepreneurship in innovation in rural regions, and the rich insights provided have far reaching implications for research, practice, and policy.

This book will appeal to everyone interested in the interface of social entrepreneurship, innovation, and regional/rural development, either on a practical or academic level.

Ralph Richter is a senior researcher and lecturer in Regional and Urban Sociology. At the Leibniz Institute for Research on Society and Space (IRS) in Erkner/ Germany he has conducted the EU funded research project "Social Innovation in Structurally Weak Rural Regions" (RurInno).

Matthias Fink is founding head of the Institute of Innovation Management at the Johannes Kepler University Linz, Austria and a Professor for Innovation and Entrepreneurship at ARU Cambridge, UK. In addition, he is academic director of two MBA programs at LIMAK Austrian Business School.

Richard Lang is Assistant Professor at the Institute of Innovation Management at Johannes Kepler University Linz, Austria, and an Honorary Senior Research Fellow at the School of Social Policy at University of Birmingham, UK.

Daniela Maresch is an Associate Professor at the University of Southern Denmark (DK) and an Associate Senior Researcher at the Institute of Innovation Management (IFI) at the Johannes Kepler University Linz (A).

Routledge Studies in Social Enterprise & Social Innovation

Series Editors
Jacques Defourny, Lars Hulgård, and Rocio Nogales

A Social Enterprise seeks to achieve social, cultural, community economic or environmental outcomes; whilst remaining revenue generating business. A Social Innovation is said to be a new idea or initiative to a social problem that is more effective, efficient, sustainable, or just than the current process and which sees the Society it is operating in receive the primary value created rather than a private organization or firm.

Routledge Studies in Social Enterprise & Social Innovation looks to examine these increasingly important academic research themes as a central concept for social theories and policies. It looks to examine and explore the activities of social participation among civil society organisations, SMEs, governments, and research institutions. Publishing the breakthrough books of the new frontiers of the field as well as the state-of-the-nation defining books that help advance the field.

Social Enterprise in Asia
Theory, Models and Practice
Edited by Eric Bidet and Jacques Defourny

Theory for Social Enterprise and Pluralism
Social Movements, Solidarity Economy, and Global South
Philippe Eynaud, Jean-Louis Laville, Luciane Dos Santos, Swati Banerjee, Flor Avelino, Lars Hulgård

Social Enterprise in Latin America
Theory, Models and Practice
Edited by Luiz Inácio Gaiger, Marthe Nyssens and Fernanda Wanderley

Social Entrepreneurship and Innovation in Rural Europe
Ralph Richter, Matthias Fink, Richard Lang, and Daniela Maresch

For more information about this series, please visit: www.routledge.com/ Routledge-Studies-in-Social-Enterprise--Social-Innovation/book-series/RSESI

Social Entrepreneurship and Innovation in Rural Europe

Ralph Richter, Matthias Fink,
Richard Lang, and Daniela Maresch

Routledge
Taylor & Francis Group

NEW YORK AND LONDON

First published 2020
by Routledge
605 Third Avenue, New York, NY 10017

and by Routledge
2 Park Square, Milton Park, Abingdon, Oxon, OX14 4RN

First issued in paperback 2021

Routledge is an imprint of the Taylor & Francis Group, an informa business

Library of Congress Cataloging-in-Publication Data
A catalog record for this book has been requested

ISBN 13: 978-0-367-78602-1 (pbk)
ISBN 13: 978-0-8153-7997-3 (hbk)

Typeset in Sabon
by Apex CoVantage, LLC

Contents

Tables and Figures

Tables

Figures

Preface

This timely book makes an insightful contribution to the developing nexus between social entrepreneurship research and rural studies. There has been considerable academic and policy interest in social entrepreneurship over the last 20 years. As in most new areas, early work was particular focused upon conceptual and definitional issues (Dees, 1998; Mair & Martí, 2006; Martin & Osberg, 2007). While there is still no single accepted definition of social entrepreneurship (and probably never will be), there has been movement in both academic and practitioner circles[1] away from restrictive notions of social entrepreneurship, focusing on heroic individuals, and towards a broader and more inclusive conceptualization, whereby social entrepreneurship involves recombining resources in order to achieve social change (Zahra et al., 2009). This approach accepts that social entrepreneurship is contextually dependent (Kerlin, 2013; Teasdale, 2012), since social problems vary across time and context as do the resources available to social entrepreneurs.

This broadening of the field opened up possibilities for understanding how social entrepreneurship varies geographically, with a particular focus on how social entrepreneurs are embedded in different communities and how they rely on networks, trust and reputation (Littlewood & Khan, 2018). In recent years there have been a small number of academic publications focusing on social entrepreneurship in rural communities (Eversole et al., 2014; Farmer et al., 2012; Farmer et al., 2008; Johnstone & Lionais, 2004; Munoz et al., 2015; Steinerowski & Steinerowska-Streb, 2012; Zografos, 2007), with particular emphasis on the unique social challenges faced in rural communities, and how social enterprises, by virtue of their embeddedness in local networks, might be well placed to respond to particular challenges posed by the withdrawal of services from rural communities. Interestingly, a small number of geographers (Munoz, Farmer and Steiner), originally based in Scotland, are responsible, through various collaborations, for many of these articles. As these geographers (or at least two of them) left rural Scotland they took a focus on rural social entrepreneurship with them.

Subsequently, the emergent field of rural social entrepreneurship research is beginning to attract a critical mass following a special issue of the *Journal of Rural Studies* (see Steiner et al. 2019), dedicated streams at major conferences such as the International Social Innovation Research Conference, and most pertinent to this book, the award by the European Union's Horizon 2020 Scheme for the Research Programme: Social Innovation in Structurally Weak Rural Regions (RurInno).

Ralph Richter, Matthias Fink, Richard Lang and Daniela Maresch make a valuable and welcome contribution to the development of a rural social entrepreneurship research field through this book. For the authors, rurality refers not simply to the locality where social enterprises are based, but also the nature of the challenges they address. For me the key contribution is the novelty of the approach taken. This novelty falls into three areas. First, the book is unusual in that it brings the voices of rural social entrepreneurs to the fore, most notably in Chapter 4, where themes developed over the course of the research are discussed in conversation with practitioners. Second, the book draws upon cases of social enterprises in different countries to develop a multi-level framework that conceptualizes social enterprises as acting as vertical links between regimes and communities, and thus paving the way for social change. Third, the authors engage in cross-case analysis through the lens of strategic action fields (Fligstein & McAdam, 2012) to develop an understanding of how social entrepreneurs strategically position themselves across different fields in order to attract resources/achieve social change. Together these key contributions to the wider literature provide a fine-grained insight into how social enterprises act at the interface between structure and agency to reconfigure resources obtained from wider networks and empower local communities to drive social change.

Simon Teasdale, Glasgow Caledonian University

Note

1 Note, for example, the change in emphasis by Ashoka from supporting unique individuals to the concept of 'everyone a changemaker'.

References

Dees, J. G. (1998). Enterprising nonprofits. *Harvard Business Review*, 76(1), 54–67.
Eversole, R., Barraket, J. and Luke, B. (2014). Social enterprises in rural community development. *Community Development Journal*, 49(2), 245–261. https://doi.org/10.1093/cdj/bst030
Farmer, J., Hill, C. and Muñoz, S-A. (2012). *Community Co-Production: Social Enterprise in Remote and Rural Communities*. Cheltenham: Edward Elgar Publishing.
Farmer, J., Steinerowski, A. and Jack, S. (2008). Starting social enterprises in remote and rural Scotland: Best or worst of circumstances? *International Journal of Entrepreneurship and Small Business*, 6(3), 450–464.

Fligstein, N. and McAdam, D. (2012). *A Theory of Fields.* New York: Oxford University Press.

Johnstone, H. and Lionais, D. (2004). Depleted communities and community business entrepreneurship: Revaluing space through place. *Entrepreneurship & Regional Development*, 16(3), 217–233. https://doi.org/10.1080/089856204 2000197117

Kerlin, J. A. (2013). Defining social enterprise across different contexts: A conceptual framework based on institutional factors. *Nonprofit and Voluntary Sector Quarterly*, 42(1), 84–108. https://doi.org/10.1177/0899764011433040

Littlewood, D. and Khan, Z. (2018). Insights from a systematic review of literature on social enterprise and networks: Where, how and what next? *Social Enterprise Journal*, 14(4), 390–409. https://doi.org/10.1108/SEJ-11-2018-068

Mair, J. and Martí, I. (2006). Social entrepreneurship research: A source of explanation, prediction, and delight. *Journal of World Business*, 41(1), 36–44. https://doi.org/10.1016/j.jwb.2005.09.002

Martin, R. L. and Osberg, S. (2007). Social entrepreneurship: The case for definition. *Stanford Social Innovation Review*, Spring, 28–39.

Munoz, S-A., Steiner, A. and Farmer, J. (2015). Processes of community-led social enterprise development: Learning from the rural context. *Community Development Journal*, 50(3), 478–493. https://doi.org/10.1093/cdj/bsu055

Steiner, A., Farmer, J. and Bosworth, G. (2019). Rural social enterprise—evidence to date, and research agenda. *Journal of Rural Studies*. https://doi.org/10.1016/j.jrurstud.2017.12.021

Steinerowski, A. A. and Steinerowska-Streb, I. (2012). Can social enterprise contribute to creating sustainable rural communities? Using the lens of structuration theory to analyse the emergence of rural social enterprise. *Local Economy*, 27(2), 167–182. http://dx.doi.org/10.1177/0269094211429650

Teasdale, S. (2012). What's in a name? Making sense of social enterprise discourses. *Public Policy and Administration*, 27(2), 99–119. https://doi.org/10.1177/0952076711401466

Zahra, S. A., Gedajlovic, E., Neubaum, D. O. and Shulman, J. M. (2009). A typology of social entrepreneurs: Motives, search processes and ethical challenges. *Journal of Business Venturing*, 24(5), 519–532. https://doi.org/10.1016/j.jbusvent.2008.04.007

Zografos, C. (2007). Rurality discourses and the role of the social enterprise in regenerating rural Scotland. *Journal of Rural Studies*, 23(1), 38–51. https://doi.org/10.1016/j.jrurstud.2006.04.002

Acknowledgments

This book is an outcome of the EU funded research project RurInno ("Social Innovation in Structurally Weak Rural Regions"). The authors are very grateful to the project coordinator Professor Gabriela Christmann and to the Leibniz Institute for Research on Society and Space (IRS) in Erkner/Germany for supporting this research. Especially, we would like to acknowledge with gratitude the input and effort contributed by the social entrepreneurs and the social enterprise staff members involved in this study as well as the many interview partners. Thank you for having shared your insights and experiences. Special thanks go to Karina Böhm for her excellent support and to Jan Zwilling for his efforts in public relations, both from the IRS. We would also like to thank the team of the Institute of Innovation Management (IFI) at the Johannes Kepler University Linz/Austria for their support during the secondments and especially to Johannes Gartner for his efforts in the data collection. Moreover, we would like to acknowledge the series editors of Routledge Studies in Social Enterprise & Social Innovation, Rocio Nogales, Lars Hulgård, and Jacques Defourny for considering this book for your series and the anonymous reviewers for their very helpful comments and advice. We are grateful to the European Union for funding the project under the Horizon 2020 MSCA RISE 2015 funding scheme (Grant agreement No. 691181).

Introduction

Action matters! Social entrepreneurship fosters innovation in rural Europe because of the action social entrepreneurs take and the action they make others take. Neither social nor entrepreneurial mission impact on the region unless they result in activity. Neither policies nor strategic spatial planning make a change in a region unless they are translated into action. What makes a change in a place is what is done in the place (McMullen & Shepherd, 2006; Frese, 2009; Frese & Gilnik, 2014; Phillips et al., 2015). This action focus on social entrepreneurship helps to overcome several confusions in social entrepreneurship research regarding the definition of what it is, the role and identity of the individual and its embeddedness, the role of the organization and its legal form as well as the divide between the American and the European schools of thought (e.g. Mair & Marti, 2006; Martin & Osberg, 2007; Defourny & Nyssens, 2010; Bacq & Janssen, 2011; Doherty et al., 2014). While we heavily build on the rich literature that has emerged from these discourses, our focus is not so much on contributing another theoretical piece on the foundation of social entrepreneurship as a field of research. Rather, we push the discourse forward by focusing on what those who call their venture a social enterprise actually do and how this action impacts the place in terms of innovation.

Action is needed, especially in rural Europe. Rural regions are defined following the OECD (2006) approach, which is based on regional settlement structure. In this definition, areas are classified as rural if they have population densities of below 150 inhabitants per square kilometre, and do not contain a major urban centre. A local community is considered rural if it is located in a rural region. This approach is consistent with most individual country definitions of rurality (OECD, 2006). The continued marginalization of structurally weak rural regions threatens the social and territorial cohesion in the European Union. Disadvantaged rural areas offer fewer opportunities for higher education and highly skilled jobs, and are economically less productive than urban or intermediate regions. They are faced with intense outmigration and a brain drain of young, well skilled residents. Not least, rural communities are particularly affected by the demographic change, which burdens the social security systems and local health infrastructure given the higher concentration of older residents (Bosworth & Glasgow, 2012; EC, 2013; Christmann, 2014; Lang et al., 2014; Steiner & Atterton, 2015). Not only does this highlight the significance of studying social entrepreneurship in rural communities, but it has also led to the increasing problematization of sociocultural traditions in rural regions by scholars and policymakers (North & Smallbone, 2006; OECD, 2006, 2011). While the significance of agriculture in Europe and many OECD countries has been decreasing dramatically, often local institutional settings have remained the same, thus, potentially hindering the emergence of new forms of entrepreneurship (Pezzini, 2001; Fornahl, 2003; Marti et al., 2013). Recent research by Lafuente and colleagues (2010) emphasizes this issue by demonstrating that local values and levels of acceptance of entrepreneurship in rural contexts reduce entrepreneurs' motivation to locate their new knowledge-based businesses in rural regions. A similar argument is put forward by Fornahl (2003), who sees many rural areas as 'entrepreneurial laggards' due to their sociocultural institutional framework, which does not promote effective entrepreneurial activity. A key institutional factor exerting a negative influence on venture development by rural economic agents is the lack of entrepreneurial role models in rural regions (Fornahl, 2003; Lafuente et al., 2007). Generally speaking, this raises the importance of location sensitive institutional approaches for developing our contextual understanding of entrepreneurial behaviour (Welter, 2011; Jennings et al., 2013). This book addresses, in particular, the critical role of institutions for rural entrepreneurship.

Great hope is placed in social entrepreneurs, as they are considered to be change agents who can break unfavourable routines through social innovation (Estrin et al., 2013; Lang et al., 2014; Kibler et al., 2015). Recent literature has highlighted the innovative and problem-solving capacity of social entrepreneurs as promising actors who tackle the socioeconomic problems of structurally weak rural regions and induce sustainable change (e.g. Defourny & Nyssens, 2010; McCarthy, 2012; Munoz et al., 2015; Steiner & Teasdale, 2018). The individual and organizational levels, as well as the action and process perspectives, are strongly interlinked as social entrepreneurship is the process through which social entrepreneurs develop ventures that act as social enterprises (Defourny & Nyssens, 2008). Thus, from an action perspective, all three terms—social entrepreneurship, social entrepreneur, and social enterprise—reflect the same phenomenon that unfolds an impact in a community through entrepreneurial action taken.

Social enterprises deliver offerings to communities neglected by the market—due to their limited profitability, and the state—due to the limited reach of their positive external effects (Santos, 2012) by pursuing proactive, innovative and risky business models (Guth & Ginsberg, 1990;

Zahra & Covin, 1995; Wiklund & Shepherd, 2005) that mobilize a variety of resources, ranging from donations and voluntary work to government subsidies, and income from market operations. These resources are embedded in the social entrepreneurs' relationships that span across different levels of the network hierarchies (Richter, 2017; Lang & Fink, 2018) and across the boundaries of the market, state and civil society realm (Brandsen et al., 2005). By communicating credible attachment to the place, social entrepreneurs can mobilize these resources, which, recombined in a Schumpeterian sense, provide the social entrepreneur the basis for innovative approaches that address the specific needs of rural communities (Lang & Fink, 2018, Richter, 2018). The activity of social enterprises can foster innovation in the place on two levels. First, in participatory community development processes (Teasdale, 2012) new social capital emerges from new relationships. Second, the activities moderated by the social enterprise may result in offerings that are new and valuable—i.e. innovative (Garcia & Calantone, 2002)—for the local community and even beyond. Thus, the potential of social entrepreneurship for innovation in rural regions emerges from the actions taken in the place. These actions are new to the place and in case they address social challenges better than before, they are adopted by the locals and, thus, induce social innovation (Bock, 2012, 2016; Neumeier, 2012, 2016).

In this book we investigate how social entrepreneurship advances (social) innovation in rural Europe and contributes to fighting social and economic challenges in these regions. Specifically, we explain how social enterprises enact their business model based on an entrepreneurial reconfiguration of resources they obtain from their network relations, and how their activities empower local communities. Both directly drive change and eventually innovation in the place and beyond. In these activities, the entrepreneurial mindset helps to reframe challenges into opportunities. Our reasoning is driven by the idea that intentions and actions result from an interplay between structure and agency. Thus, in building a consistent theoretical foundation for our arguments, we complement network theory with the concept of strategic action fields (Fligstein & McAdam, 2011, 2012). The argument in this book develops from a description of what social enterprises report to do, to an analysis of how they do it and results in an explanation of why they take these actions. In doing so we gradually broaden the view from focusing on the social enterprises themselves to their interactions and network partners and, finally, to their positioning in societal fields. This journey reveals the crucial role of social entrepreneurship in innovation in rural regions. The rich insights of this journey have far reaching implications for research, practice and policy.

Dialogue between practitioners and researchers is the key concept of this book. The concept of reconstructing the practices of social enterprises in a conversation between those active in the field and social entrepreneurship scholars was already the basis for the EU-funded research programme that generated the rich data presented here. This conversation was realized in a combined research and training project comprising eight months of on-site field research by four researchers in four social enterprises and six months of secondments by members of the social enterprises at two research institutions. While the long-term investigation in four European countries enabled the researchers to gain deep insights of social enterprises across different rural contexts and to gather rich empirical data, the practitioners used their stay at research institutions to critically reflect on their practices together with the researchers. This intensive conversation is consequently mirrored in the sequence of the subsequent chapters.

In Chapter 1 we set the stage for the analysis in later chapters. We start the conversation on the side of the practitioners. The selected cases are located in structurally disadvantaged rural areas in Ireland, Greece, Austria and Poland. The case descriptions are written from the perspective of an insider. They are based on data gathered from semi-structured interviews, events observed in participatory observations and documents published by the enterprise. Thus, the case descriptions represent a reconstruction of the cases' self-picture as a social enterprise along the lines of the three EMES dimensions of social enterprises, namely (1) the social mission, (2) the entrepreneurial mission, and (3) the governance structure (Defourny & Nyssens, 2013). We complement the descriptions with basic information on the socio-economic profile of the context in which the cases are embedded and an overview of the challenges that rural communities face in the respective countries, as well as the activities the social enterprises have unfolded to meet these challenges.

The perspective switches from the practitioners to the researchers in Chapters 2 and 3. In Chapter 2, we set out to develop a multilevel network model that integrates and extends the frameworks recently put forth by Richter (2017) and Lang and Fink (2018). In this analytical framework, we integrate different literature streams and condense their key insights to conceptualize the role of enterprises in the multilevel network arena of rural contexts. We specifically draw on a social capital approach (Putnam et al., 1993) that provides an interesting analytical perspective from which to study the embeddedness of social enterprises in the rural context (Granovetter, 1985; Johnstone & Lionais, 2004; Lang & Roessl, 2011; Welter, 2011; Kibler et al., 2015). The second subchapter is devoted to the research methods and data collection. We provide an overview of (1) the methodology and research design, (2) the selection of cases, (3) applied methods and (4) data processing and analytical methods. Subsequently, four subchapters present the single case analyses explaining how the social enterprise mobilizes the resources and reconfigures them to develop novel answers to social challenges and make a change.

In the third chapter, we engage in a cross-case analysis to identify similarities and differences among the four cases. The chapter builds on the insight from the previous chapters that the four case enterprises are operating in a larger organizational space characterized by institutional hybridity. Such organizations reflect a mix of rationales, values and practices of the three traditional societal domains: the state, the market and the community (Brandsen et al., 2005). Chapter 3 applies the Strategic Action Field Theory (Fligstein & McAdam, 2011, 2012) to explore the field positioning strategies of our case organizations. An initial step is to understand the particular configuration of fields in which the organizational case studies are embedded. (Re-)positioning represents a longer-term strategy of actors and is also triggered by events in the external environment. We further distinguish actual from symbolic positioning in fields (Gorski, 2012; Macmillan et al., 2013). Both types of positioning require the 'social skill' of entrepreneurs, i.e. "a highly developed cognitive capacity for reading people and environments, framing lines of action, and mobilizing people" (Fligstein & McAdam, 2011, p. 7).

In Chapter 4 the practitioners respond to the findings of the single- and cross-case analysis. Their voice is presented in the format of an interview. It responds to the analytical perspective of the researchers and provides a holistic and reflected view of the spirit that drives the investigated social enterprise.

Chapter 5 brings together the lines of argumentation developed in the subsequent chapters. It integrates the outcomes of the analysis conducted against the background of the reconstruction of the social enterprises' self-picture, their role in the multi-level network and their positioning strategies in strategic action fields. Thus, the discussion section cumulates the insights from our journey that developed along the questions of what characterizes the activities of rural social enterprises, how the rural context enables and limits their activities, how rural social enterprises innovate, what their field positioning strategies are, and how they deal with the different institutional logics in these fields? From these insights on the role of social entrepreneurship for innovation in rural Europe, we deduct implications that are directly relevant to future research, practice and policy.

Especially invited to read beyond this point is everyone interested in the interface of (social) entrepreneurship, (social) innovation and regional/rural development, either on a practical or academic level. Due to the concept of a conversation between practitioners and researchers, we believe that a main audience for this research-based book will be threefold:

Academic scholars (researchers, teachers and students at all levels and around the globe) in the fields of (community-based) social innovation and entrepreneurship, new venture creation and finance, third sector studies, non-profit and public management, European studies, international/regional/rural development as well as international relations with a focus on intra-European know-how exchange. These subjects are commonly part of curricula both at universities and business schools.

Policy-makers who design the general conditions for social and economic development in rural regions can gain a better understanding of the interplay between society, politics and businesses on the level of the communities, but also on regional, national and supranational administrative levels. This book provides them with useful information on the potentials and barriers of diverse interventions in the local social and economic structure. Thus, this book is most relevant to their every-day business.

Practitioners owning, managing, consulting or working (in) social ventures and/or who pursue social innovation in rural regions benefit from the clear focus and the explicit nature of the recommendations for action and the practically relevant results provided in this book.

References

Bacq, S. and Janssen, F. (2011). The multiple faces of social entrepreneurship: A review of definitional issues based on geographical and thematic criteria. *Entrepreneurship & Regional Development*, 23(5–6), 373–403.

Bock, B. B. (2012). Social innovation and sustainability: How to disentangle the buzzword and its application in the field of agriculture and rural development. *Studies in Agricultural Economics*, 114, 57–63.

Bock, B. B. (2016). Rural marginalisation and the role of social innovation: A turn towards nexogenous development and rural reconnection. *Sociologia Ruralis*, 56(4), 552–573.

Bosworth, G. and Glasgow, N. (2012). Entrepreneurial behaviour among Rural In-migrants. In J. Vergunst, M. Shucksmith, D. Brown, S. Shortall, and M. Warner (Eds.): *Rural Transformations and Rural Policies in the UK and US*. London: Routledge.

Brandsen, T., van de Donk, W. and Putters, K. (2005). Griffins or chameleons? Hybridity as a permanent and inevitable characteristic of the Third Sector. *International Journal of Public Administration*, 28, 749–765.

Christmann, G. B. (2014). Social entrepreneurs on the periphery: Uncovering emerging pioneers of regional development. *disP-The Planning Review*, 50(1), 43–55.

Defourny, J. and Nyssens, M. (2008). Social enterprise in Europe: Recent trends and developments. *Social Enterprise Journal*, 4, 202–228. https://doi.org/10.1108/17508610810922703

Defourny, J. and Nyssens, M. (2010). Conceptions of social enterprise and social entrepreneurship in Europe and the United States: Convergences and divergences. *Journal of Social Entrepreneurship*, 1(1), 32–53.

Defourny, J. and Nyssens, M. (2013). Social innovation, social economy and social enterprise: What can the European debate tell us? In Frank Moulaert, et al. (Eds.): *The International Handbook on Social Innovation* (40–52). Cheltenham, UK and Northampton, MA: Edward Elgar.

Doherty, B., Haugh, H. and Lyon, F. (2014). Social enterprises as hybrid organizations: A review and research agenda. *International Journal of Management Reviews*, 16(4), 417–436.

Estrin, S., Mickiewicz, T. and Stephan, U. (2013). Entrepreneurship, social capital, and institutions: Social and commercial entrepreneurship across nations. *Entrepreneurship Theory and Practice*, 37(3), 479–504.

European Commission (EC). (2013). *Rural Development in the EU*—Statistical and Economic Information—Report 2013, Brussels.

Fligstein, N. and McAdam, D. (2011). Toward a general theory of strategic action fields. *Sociological Theory*, 29(1), 1–26.

Fligstein, N. and McAdam, D. (2012). *A Theory of Fields*. London: Oxford University Press.

Fornahl, D. (2003). Entrepreneurial activities in a regional context. In D. Fornahl and T. Brenner (Eds.): *Cooperation, Networks and Institutions in Regional Innovation Systems* (38–57). Cheltenham, UK: Edward Elgar.

Frese, M. (2009). Towards a psychology of entrepreneurship—an action theory perspective. *Foundations and Trends in Entrepreneurship*, 5(6), 437–496.

Frese, M. and Gilnik, M. M. (2014). The psychology of entrepreneurship. *Annual Review of Organizational Psychology and Organizational Behaviour*, 1(1), 413–438.

Garcia, R. and Calantone, R. (2002). A critical look at technological innovation typology and innovativeness terminology: A literature review. *Journal of Product Innovation Management: An International Publication of the Product Development & Management Association*, 19(2), 110–132.

Gorski, P. S. (2012). Bourdieusian theory and historical analysis: Maps, mechanisms, and methods. In P. S. Gorski (Ed.): *Bourdieu and Historical Analysis* (327–367). Chapel Hill: Duke University Press.

Granovetter, M. (1985). Economic action and social structure: The problem of embeddedness. *American Journal of Sociology*, 91(3), 481–510.

Guth, W. D. and Ginsberg, A. (1990). Guest editors' introduction: Corporate entrepreneurship. *Strategic Management Journal*, 11 [Special Issue], 5–15.

Jennings, D., Greenwood, R., Lounsbury, D., et al. (2013). Institutions, entrepreneurs, and communities: A special issue on entrepreneurship. *Journal of Business Venturing*, 28(1), 1–9.

Johnstone, H. and Lionais, D. (2004). Depleted communities and community business entrepreneurship: Revaluing space though place. *Enterpreneurship and Regional Development*, 16, 217–233. https://doi.org/10.1080/08985 62042000197117

Kibler, E., Fink, M., Lang, R. and Muñoz, P. (2015). Place attachment and social legitimacy: Revisiting the sustainable entrepreneurship journey. *Journal of Business Venturing Insights*, 3, 24–29. DOI: 10.1016/j.jbvi.2015.04.001

Lafuente, E., Vaillant, Y. and Rialp, J. (2007). Regional differences in the influence of role models: Comparing the entrepreneurial process of rural Catalonia. *Regional Studies*, 41(6), 779–795.

Lafuente, E., Vaillant, Y. and Serarols, C. (2010). Location decisions of knowledge-based entrepreneurs: Why some Catalan KISAs choose to be rural. *Technovation*, 30(11), 590–600.

Lang, R. and Fink, M. (2018). Rural social entrepreneurship: The role of social capital within and across institutional levels. *Journal of Rural Studies*. https://doi.org/10.1016/j.jrurstud.2018.03.012

Lang, R., Fink, M. and Kibler, E. (2014). Understanding place-based entrepreneurship in rural central Europe—a comparative institutional analysis. *International Small Business Journal*, *32*, 204–227. https://doi.org/10.1177/0266242613488614

Lang, R. and Roessl, D. (2011). Contextualizing the governance of community co-operatives: Evidence from Austria and Germany. *Voluntas*, *22*, 706–730. https://doi.org/10.1007/s11266-011-9210-8

Macmillan, R., Taylor, R., Arvidson, M., Soteri-Proctor, A. and Teasdale, S. (2013). *The Third Sector in Unsettled Times: A Field Guide*, Third Sector Research Centre Working Paper 109, University of Birmingham.

Mair, J. and Marti, I. (2006). Social entrepreneurship research: A source of explanation, prediction, and delight. *Journal of World Business*, *41*(1), 36–44.

Marti, I., Courpasson, D. and Barbosa, D. (2013). Living in the fishbowl. Generating an entrepreneurial culture in a local community in Argentina. *Journal of Business Venturing*, *28*(1), 10–29.

Martin, R. L. and Osberg, S. (2007). Social entrepreneurship: The case for definition. *Stanford Social Innovation Review*, *5*(2), 28–39.

McCarthy, B. (2012). From fishing and factories to cultural tourism: The role of social entrepreneurs in the construction of a new institutional field. *Enterpreneurship and Regional Development*, *24*, 259–282. https://doi.org/10.1080/08985626.2012.670916.

McMullen, J. S. and Shepherd, A. (2006). Entrepreneurial action and the role of uncertainty in the theory of the entrepreneur. *Academy of Management Review*, *31*(1), 132–152.

Munoz, S-A., Steiner, A. and Farmer, J. (2015). Processes of community-led social enterprise development: Learning from the rural context. *Community Development Journal*, *50*, 478–493. DOI: 10.1093/cdj/bsu055

Neumeier, S. (2012). Why do social innovations in rural development matter and should they be considered more seriously in rural development research? Proposal for a stronger focus on social innovations in rural development research. *Sociologia Ruralis*, *52*(1), 48–69.

Neumeier, S. (2016). Social innovation in rural development: Identifying the key factors of success. *The Geographical Journal*, 1–13.

North, D. and Smallbone, D. (2006). Developing entrepreneurship and enterprise in Europe's peripheral rural areas: Some issues facing policy-makers. *European Planning Studies*, *14*(1), 41–60.

Organisation for Economic Co-operation and Development (OECD). (2006). *The New Rural Paradigm: Policy and Governance*, Working Paper on Territorial Policy in Rural Areas, Paris: OECD.

Organisation for Economic Co-operation and Development (OECD). (2011). *OECD Rural Policy Reviews: England, United Kingdom 2011*. Paris: OECD Publishing.

Pezzini, M. (2001). Rural policy lessons from OECD countries. *International Regional Science Review*, *24*(1), 134–145.

Phillips, W., Lee, H., Ghobadian, A., O'Regan, N. and James, P. (2015). Social innovation and social entrepreneurship: A systematic review. *Group & Organization Management*, *40*(3), 428–461.

Putnam, R. D., Leonardi, R. and Nanetti, R. Y. (1993). *Making Democracy Work: Civic Traditions in Modern Italy*. Princeton, NJ: Princeton University Press.

Richter, R. (2017). Rural social enterprises as embedded intermediaries: The innovative power of connecting rural communities with supra-regional networks. *Journal of Rural Studies*. https://doi.org/10.1016/j.jrurstud.2017.12.005

Richter, R. (2018). The Janus face of participatory governance: How inclusive governance benefits and limits the social innovativeness of social enterprises. *Journal of Entrepreneurial and Organizational Diversity (JEOD)*, 7(1), 61–87.

Santos, F. M. (2012). A positive theory of social entrepreneurship. *Journal of Business Ethics*, 111(3), 335–351.

Steiner, A. and Atterton, J. (2015). Exploring the contribution of rural enterprises to local resilience. *Journal of Rural Studies*, 40, 30–45.

Steiner, A. and Teasdale, S. (2018). Unlocking the potential of rural Social Enterprise. *Journal of Rural Studies*.

Teasdale, S. (2012). What's in a name? Making sense of social enterprise discourses. *Public Policy and Administration*, 27, 99–119. https://doi.org/10.1177/0952076711401466

Welter, F. (2011). Conceptual challenges and ways forward. *Entrepreneurship Theory & Practice*, 35(1), 165–184.

Wiklund, J. and Dean, S. (2005). Entrepreneurial orientation and small business performance: A configurational approach. *Journal of Business Venturing*, 20, 71–91.

Zahra, S. A. and Covin, J. G. (1995). Contextual influences on the corporate entrepreneurship-performance relationship: A longitudinal analysis. *Journal of Business Venturing*, 10, 43–58.

1 Rural Social Entrepreneurship and Innovation in Practice

Case Descriptions

To set the stage for the analysis in later chapters, in this case description we dig into the history and summarize in detail what we learned about the company. Specifically, we outline four cases that provide an overview of the challenges that rural communities face in the respective countries, and the activities the social enterprises have created to meet these challenges. This initial overview is followed by in-depth descriptions of the cases, which are based on the three EMES dimensions of social enterprises: (1) the social mission, (2) the entrepreneurial mission, and (3) the governance structure.

According to Defourny and Nyssens (2013), the social mission of social enterprises manifests itself in three criteria. First, social enterprises originate in civil society initiatives and "evolve in collective dynamics" (Defourny & Nyssens, 2013, p. 46) rather than being the project of a single leader. Second, "they aim to benefit the community" (ibid.) or society as a whole and not only the interests of an exclusive group. Third, the profit distribution in social enterprises is limited in order "to avoid a profit-maximizing behaviour" (ibid.). However, social enterprises are not only characterized by their social mission, but also by an entrepreneurial dimension. This entrepreneurial mindset distinguishes them from other organizations that strive for positive social impact. By executing entrepreneurial activities, social enterprises differ, for example, from public sector organizations, which typically implement delegated tasks. Defourny and Nyssens (2013) define three criteria that are indicative of the entrepreneurial dimension of social enterprises: (1) producing and selling goods and services, (2) taking entrepreneurial risks, and (3) employing paid workers. Lastly, social enterprises cannot be distinguished from their commercial counterparts only by their social and entrepreneurial mission but also by a more inclusive governance structure (Defourny & Nyssens, 2013). The governance of social enterprises is characterized by a high degree of autonomy (instead of operating on behalf of other institutions), decision-making that is independent from capital ownership (unlike voting powers related to financial shareholding), and having stakeholders involved in decision-making (instead of governing in an autocratic way).

The case descriptions are written from the perspective of an insider and are therefore based on descriptions gathered from semi-structured interviews, from participatory observations, and from documents published by the enterprise.

Empowering Rural Communities: How a Social Enterprise Provides Help for Self-Help in the Irish Hinterland

The Irish case reflects many of the aspects typical of a social enterprise. At the same time, it is very different from the other three cases, because it fills in the gaps of the institutional environment left by the Irish state, which is only rudimentarily present in rural regions. Thus, the Irish social enterprise emerged to compensate for the institutional voids. It covers many of the services that are typically delivered by the state in continental Europe. In this respect, it is an attempt to establish an entrepreneurial fast-track to social and regional development by leapfrogging the establishment of a modern welfare state. To enable a detailed understanding of the specific aspects of the Irish social enterprise, we first introduce the setting in which it is embedded and we identify the challenges it faces and the answers it provides to these challenges. We also describe its business model and offer a detailed description of the case along the three dimensions of social enterprises.

Challenges in Rural Ireland

Ireland is overwhelmingly rural according to recent statistical data (EC, 2017). About 90 percent of the Irish territory is predominantly rural. Only the greater Dublin area meets the European classification of "urban". Nearly one third of the Irish live in rural areas. In comparison, across the EU, rural regions account for just 19.1 percent of the total population. Ireland is the most rural economy in Europe and has the most extreme divergence in economic output between urban and rural areas anywhere across the continent. With a GDP factor of 104.6 (100 corresponds to the EU average), rural Ireland is only half as strong as urban Ireland, which has a GDP factor of 207.9. Compared to the EU average, rural Ireland has a strong secondary sector (35.9 percent of the GDP). Irish rates of unemployment, employment, and risk of poverty and social exclusion are quite similar in rural and urban regions. Interestingly, more people are employed (70.8 percent) in rural Ireland and fewer are unemployed (7.7 percent) than on average in the EU. The risk of poverty and social exclusion for the population in rural Ireland is very close to the EU average of 25.5 percent.

Looking back, the 1980s was a decade of extremely high unemployment in Ireland, with an all-time high of 17.3 percent in December 1985.

In addition, the country faced high levels of emigration with 70,600 persons leaving Ireland in 1989. A series of governments and sequent elections contributed to further undermining the economic development. This caused the government to increase borrowing and impose tax rates as high as 60 percent. Additionally, after joining the European Exchange Rate Mechanism (ERM) in 1979, Ireland had an overvalued currency that was not rectified until the 1986 devaluation. This extensive period of economic downturn especially impacted the viability of rural communities in Ireland. Rural areas were challenged as they lacked human capacity and infrastructure and offered few economic opportunities to their residents.

In early 2000, investments by multi-nationals such as Facebook and Google were running at a high, but new jobs tended to focus on a zone of investment within an hour's drive of Dublin. According to a rural development expert:

> In the last elections the government had the slogan 'Keep the recovery going.' That was grand in Dublin. But outside Dublin there was no recovery. The new government brought in the rhetoric of 'Fixing rural Ireland.' Now, the reality is that the majority of public investments still goes to Dublin.
>
> (Regional development expert, personal communication, December 13, 2016)

The concentration of investments in urban areas has put rural areas at risk of slipping further behind. This is particularly true as investments in physical infrastructure such as roads, railways and airports have focused on addressing urban bottlenecks created by growth rather than on rural areas. The economic development and investment imbalance at a national level continues to be a challenge for rural Ireland.

The strongest impacts of the downturn were evident in smaller towns, where job losses in construction and locally traded services were significant. Small enterprises were badly hit, as evident in the numbers of closed premises, the depressed property prices, and the derelict buildings in many Irish villages. In the Mid-West rural region spanning around a scenic mountain range and located between the towns of Cork and Limerick the recession in the 1980s and the recent downturn following the financial crises in 2008 revealed underlying and persistent structural weaknesses and disadvantages across the area. This was reflected by the higher-than-Irish-average unemployment rates, increased out-migration levels, and increased business closures. The male employment rate in the region fell from 63.1 percent in 2006 to just 46.7 percent in 2011. During the same period, the disposable income of average households dropped by 12 percent in rural Mid-West Ireland and poverty rates increased significantly. When coupled with reduced service levels in the public and private sectors, this development caused a high level of stress for households and businesses.

The impact of the recession varied spatially within rural Mid-West Ireland. The locations closer to Limerick experienced the lowest income decline, while areas further south were more seriously affected. For instance, in just one Social Welfare Office serving the area of a local village, the number of persons who were registered as unemployed rose from 811 in 2006 to 2,756 in 2011—representing a 240 percent increase. Moreover, rural Mid-West Ireland also has areas of concentrated intergenerational disadvantages in some housing estates as well as hidden social exclusion in more spatially dispersed rural areas. To some extent, the period of economic growth and the boom in the early 2000s merely masked the underlying structural weaknesses typical of rural areas in Mid-West Ireland. These disadvantages include demographic imbalance, a lack of economic diversification, and inadequate infrastructure—all of which continue to provide challenges for this region.

In the rural Mid-West region, agriculture and food production predominate and are an intrinsic part of people's lives and the economy. In the late 1990s, it was estimated that as much as 67 percent of the workforce were directly or indirectly dependent on the agricultural sector, working mainly in dairy and beef enterprises and their associated food processing industries (OECD, 2001). The region has a dominant secondary sector with two of Ireland's largest milk processors located in small, local towns. However, since 2000, the number of people employed in the agri-food sector has declined due to the restructuring of industrial production, which led to job losses in agri-processing and in other traditional manufacturing industries. The area lost approximately 1,200 jobs between 2000 and 2008. This was due mainly to restructuring but also to a decline in the number of full-time farmers and an increase in part-time farming. The number of milk suppliers in the area decreased from 2,260 to 1,640 between 2000 and 2008. In the post milk quota era, the local dairy-based agricultural economy experienced a dramatic reduction in farm incomes. The Irish Creamery Milk Supplier Association has highlighted a nearly 40 percent fall in dairy prices since 2014, which led to a decrease in average annual farm incomes by up to €35,000 (Central Statistic Office, 2016), aggregating to a loss in farm incomes in rural Mid-West Ireland of an estimated €1.35 billion. Since the mid- to late-1990s, the urban boom in Ireland's construction, retail, and services sectors has partly compensated for the impact of these structural adjustments, particularly for part-time farmers who now commute to a second job. The structural change has further moved the economic power toward the urban centers. A regional policy expert summarized the challenges:

> *We need to diversify economy, create jobs and have a strong education system with access for everybody.*
>
> (Regional policy expert, personal
> communication, December 13)

These developments call for governmental policies that support Ireland's rural areas.

However, local public authorities traditionally have little input regarding the delivery of core services to communities in rural Ireland. Political representation and administration in the region have traditionally been concentrated in cities such as Limerick and Cork. Rural communities are remotely controlled by authorities located in these urban centers. Consequently, the CEO of the social enterprise stresses that *"implementation usually differs from what the evidence was. And that is where it starts to go wrong"* (CEO of social enterprise, personal communication, April 28, 2016). He also asserts that the national government has so far not appropriately addressed the challenges of rural Ireland:

> *We've had a minister for diaspora and a minister for social enterprise, but with no budget. What's the point? Until the government takes it really seriously – what it means to do business in rural Ireland – there won't be any change. To support the growth of indigenous enterprises you need infrastructure. You need roads, rail, broadband, and communications. These are all things rural Ireland doesn't have.*
>
> (CEO of social enterprise, personal communication, December 15, 2016)

While rural Mid-West Ireland faces major structural challenges, it is important to recognize that this region is less peripheral than other rural regions in Ireland, particularly those in the West and North-West. Moreover, the region has considerable human and natural resources and a history of using them to promote economic and social development. This is the point of leverage for social enterprises such as the regional development company that we investigated in the Irish case. The regional development company covers an area divided into two administrative areas: (1) South and East Limerick and (2) North-East Cork. The regional population of over 860,000 is spread out over 54 communities. The headquarters of the regional development company is in a small village in County Limerick. The social enterprise also has four outreach offices in small villages distributed across Mid-West Ireland.

In summary, rural development companies emerged in Ireland to fill the gap that public authorities left in the rural hinterland. Their business models focus on the provision of core public services such as delivering regional, national, and EU funding programs aimed at social, economic, and environmental development, enhancing employability among the unemployed, supporting micro-sized and small businesses and promoting rural Mid-West Ireland as a tourist destination. In the words of the social enterprise's CEO: *"Our activities focus on community development, enterprise support, and employment"* (CEO of social enterprise, personal communication, April 28, 2016).

How the Social Enterprise Fights the Challenges

The regional development company was founded in 1988 and had 40 employees in 2016. Between 2009 and 2015 the company supported nearly 800 people in gaining employment and provided social inclusion activities to over 3,300 children and young adults (O'Hara & O'Shaughnessy, 2015). Over time, the staff of the regional development company has played several different but complementary roles, including that of a researcher, an identifier of needs/gaps/solutions, an animator, deliverer, supporter, facilitator, encourager, implementer, project leader, and project partner. The company has been involved in several different activities, including developing networks, partnerships and collaborative projects, and the brokerage of additional resources and programs. It closely cooperates with the local and national authorities in the development of regional development plans.

In each of these roles and activities, the focus is on the client, be it the community, an individual or a business, and the regional development company is committed to ensuring that the needs of the client are met, either by the company itself or together with one or more of its partners. These partners can be local authorities or government departments, such as the Office of Public Works, the Department of Social Protection, the Department of Agriculture, and the Department of Tourism and Heritage. The partners engage with the regional development company through various networks. For example, a member of Teagasc (the state agriculture advisory agency) is a director on the board of the regional development company. At the same time, several staff members participate in networks such as the Village Partnerships and the Family Resource Centre. The CEO of the regional development company stressed: "*We work as multi-disciplinary, multi-program, multi-area service provider*" (CEO of social enterprise, personal communication, April 28, 2016).

The regional development company has acquired a lot of knowledge and developed considerable competencies from the management and successful implementation of national and European programs, which can now be applied to other programs and regions. This experience is complemented by a track record of delivering tangible results, establishing strong links with client groups and developing key partnerships with a range of community groups, social partners, local authorities, and statutory agencies. The regional development company uses its resources to facilitate and enhance the implementation of local development strategies in communities. This approach maximizes the benefits to communities, individuals, and businesses, thereby leading to economically, socially, and environmentally sustainable results across the local development strategy area.

In their activities, Irish rural development companies take a participative approach. They help the communities help themselves and enhance social cohesion across communities by facilitating community-led local development activities. This is also true for the company under investigation. From its incorporation, it has recognized the importance of engagement with clients and communities, referred to as *animation*. Animation comprises coaching, guiding, and supporting individuals and communities to increase their potential contribution to the development of the area. As the CEO explains:

> *We would never say 'we did', because at the end of the day, we facilitate the community to build their capacity and achieve. It's really about the community having the capacity to do it. The communities, the businesses, and the individuals lead the development and implement it, and we're there in a supportive and facilitation role.*
>
> (CEO of social enterprise, personal communication, April 28, 2016)

Thus, the regional development company supports participative bottom-up community initiatives without forcing its own ideas on the communities. Once communities recognize a common need and search for ways to address it, the regional development company comes into play, providing expertise in mediating community activation and mentoring application processes for suitable funding schemes. The company is very clear about the fact that the impetus must remain with the communities. This keeps community members engaged, makes them take ownership of the process, and makes rural communities more inclusive.

The idea behind the participatory approach is to ensure that communities have a sense of ownership of their area and feel they can influence economic and social change in their relevant communities. As the CEO of the social enterprise explained: "*We foster participating democracy – communities having a voice and people having a voice and getting their voices heard at various platforms*" (CEO of social enterprise, personal communication, April 28, 2016). This idea is also mirrored in the mission of the organization: the regional development company aims at working in partnership to foster a proactive and inclusive society it is eager to preserve heritage and culture, and it embraces change and exploits new opportunities. In addition, its goal is to make it possible for those living and working in the area to realize their social, cultural, environmental, and recreational expectations. The mission of the company is thus to effectively bring about change irrespective of whether the outcome is the establishment of new businesses or an improvement in the quality of life.

The activities of the regional development company have unfolded in various forms and have had a diverse impact on positive sustainable social and economic change in the region. Over the years, the company has supported budding entrepreneurs through its "Start Your Own Business" program. It has also successfully delivered successive government social inclusion programs. In these programs, the regional development company engages those who are most disadvantaged and excluded from society by working with the residents in some of the disadvantaged housing estates in the area. It also has created two food units. These food units create an enterprising space for food businesses that bring local employment to the area. In addition, a program called "The Jobs Club" supports jobseekers through workshops that focus on the preparation of CVs and cover letters and the improvement of interview skills.

In addition to these hands-on activities, the regional development company also brings communities together to develop a socio-economic plan for their area. These plans are essential for community development. In collaboration with University College Dublin it has also developed the ADOPT model. The emphasis of this model is pre-development training, animation, capacity building, and networking.

All activities are linked to the implementation of the company's strategy to develop, empower, and include communities, to embrace new opportunities, to reduce inequalities, and to drive positive, sustainable, social and economic change. Consequently, Mid-West Ireland should become an attractive location to live in, to conduct business, and to visit. However, recent government reforms endanger the approved business model of rural social enterprises delivering public services. One of these government reforms was to replace contracts for the provision of public services with tenders. While this reform ensures transparency and prevents the distribution of funds from becoming path-dependent, it simultaneously impairs planning and carries the risk of a race to the bottom. In addition, the government created opportunities for rural communities to receive direct state support with fewer administrative hurdles. This allows rural communities to bypass rural development companies and undermine their role as intermediaries between funding schemes and rural communities. Finally, the Irish LEADER budget shrank considerably from €425 million (program period 2007–2014) to €250 million (2014–2020) due to a reduction of co-financing by the Irish government. The regional development company responded to this challenging situation by diversifying its services and funding sources.

In legal terms, the regional development company is a limited company with charitable status. It is a partnership of the community and of the voluntary sector, social partners, local government, and statutory agencies. The company is run by the CEO with a management team that consists of a community development manager, financial controller, and a corporate manager. The company currently has about 40 employees. Its aim is to retain these employees. As the CEO explained:

Over time, we have managed to retain staff fairly constantly. We can move them between diverse projects. So, we are able to balance people out . . . If any particular fund comes to stop, then the staff has to go. That old organizational knowledge is lost. And the next time the program comes in again, you're starting from scratch.

(CEO of social enterprise, personal communication, December 15, 2016)

The board of the regional development company is comprised of 20 voluntary directors from social partners (farming, trade unions), local government (elected members/officials), statutory agencies (education, food, forestry, the Gardaí), and community representatives. Each director serves a term of three years with a maximum of three terms if re-elected. There are also five subcommittees within the board (economics, environment and agriculture; community; audit, finance and governance; HR and strategy) whose role is to advise and guide the plans and strategies of the company. There are also several advisory councils that act as a consultative forum and comprise non-board members.

In summary, the regional development company evolved from a period of economic difficulty with high levels of unemployment and rural decline. Some of the challenges Mid-West Ireland faces are unemployment, demographic imbalance, lack of economic diversification, and inadequate infrastructure. Initiated by governmental agencies, a group of local community members came together to develop a sustainable plan for their region. At first the group only included voluntary members, but soon it evolved into a limited company with charitable status that was able to leverage several funding programs to implement an integrated development plan. The company professionalized its operations when it received funding from the LEADER 1 Program, which required the company to implement a complex development program and respond to detailed European funding requirements. At the same time, this challenge created the conditions for more inclusive and multi-level decision-making (national, regional, and local actors) and multi-stakeholder involvement (involving formal and informal political institutions and non-governmental actors). The business model that resulted from these developments focuses on working with local groups from the rural area and concentrates on empowering and progressing disadvantaged communities and citizens. To do so, the regional development company employs a participatory approach in the areas of community development, employment, and enterprise supports.

The CEO stressed the importance of regional development companies:

For a good quality of life in rural Ireland you need services, you need jobs, and you need reasons for young people to stay. You need policies to promote that and you need activities to make that happen. If authorities aren't doing these things, communities need to do them themselves. If communities weren't doing those things, you would have nothing in rural Ireland, because government policy has been to close schools, close post offices, and close fire stations. The huge urban centers have been invested in and now are quality places to live. Without quality life in rural Ireland, nobody will be there apart from an isolated old population. Our organization is in the position to help and support communities to deliver and build the services that they themselves need. We can broker in funding, but it is the communities who need to become active.

(CEO of social enterprise, personal
communication, April 28, 2016)

The Social Mission

Being a social enterprise implies having a social mission that manifests itself through the following criteria: (1) social enterprises originate in civil society initiatives, (2) they aim to benefit the community or society, and (3) they have limited profit distribution that avoids profit-maximizing behavior. In what follows, we describe the Irish case based on these three criteria.

To evaluate the first criterion of the social mission it is helpful to review the history of the Irish case and assess whether the initiative that resulted in the regional development company was launched by a group of citizens or civil society organizations. The initiative started in 1987 when the local branch of the state tourism body convened a meeting to explore the future of the area. Participants in this meeting were representatives from the State Agriculture Advisory Agency, Rent an Irish Cottage (one of the largest tourism office in Mid-West Ireland), the Irish Farmers' Association, and the communities located in the region. One year later, a planning committee was established. The committee comprised members from the community and the public and private sector who had a broad range of experience. The planning committee was established with support from the State Agriculture Advisory Agency and Macra Na Feirme (the representative organization of young farmers). In the following years, increasingly more local coordinating groups came on board throughout Mid-West Ireland.

The first manager of the regional development company was a local. When she started the job in 1989, she already had vast experience in agritourism. She was the driving force of the regional development company. The manager was able to generate income from the successful implementation of European and national funding programs. This income ensured the sustainability of the organization. Regarding the involvement of citizens and the civil society in the initiation and development of the organization it is important to note that, right from the beginning, she built strong partnerships with local, regional, national, and international actors. Therefore, the regional development company was able to ensure an integrated approach to support communities in developing action plans and identifying a range of projects that would deliver economic diversification and enhance quality of life in Mid-West Ireland.

The current CEO of the regional development company defined the motives behind the development of the organization and its status:

> We are an independent entity, but we started out at arm's length from the government. We are delivering on behalf of the government and not for any private enterprise.
>
> (CEO of social enterprise, personal communication, December 15, 2016)

Thus, the company was initiated top-down by national agencies, but with strong involvement from local associations and representatives from the local communities. With the management entrusted to a local, the local communities quickly took ownership of the novel organization and actively participated in its further development. The strong role of citizen groups and civil society organizations is evident in the organizational structure and the business model. While the CEO runs the everyday business, he is dependent on the board, which comprises several representatives from local community groups and civil society organizations. The business model taps the creativity and initiative of local community groups that emerge around specific issues. The regional development company takes on the role of the facilitator and supports local community groups in developing and implementing solutions to the community's needs. The activities offered by the regional development company range from giving advice and moderating a participative community development process to brokering funding from the regional, national, and European levels. Additionally, the employees of the regional development company voice the perspective of the local communities into discussions and decision-making processes at the regional and national level since they represent the communities in various boards. As the CEO reported in an interview, "*We sit on a lot of representative bodies in Ireland*" (CEO of social enterprise, personal communication, April 28, 2016).

The social mission implies not only that the social enterprise is rooted in a civil society initiative but also that it is driven by social responsibility to the community or society as a whole and not just by the interests of an exclusive group. In the Irish case, the mission revolves around the idea of empowering communities to develop places that are attractive to live in. The focus on communities is emphasized by the company's mission statement:

> We are working in partnership to develop empowered and inclusive communities that inspire and embrace new opportunities, drive positive sustainable social and economic change and reduce inequalities

thereby making Mid-West Ireland an attractive location in which to live, do business and work.

(Founder of social enterprise, personal communication, December 12, 2016)

The focus on the needs of communities rather than of single individuals or small, exclusive groups also stems from the roots of local development companies. As discussed above, these companies were originally established to provide public services that were not being delivered by the state. These services typically benefit a broader group of clients. However, the regional development company does more than fill the gaps left by the regional and national government; it has also developed a business model that focuses on the identification and support of new opportunities for communities in Mid-West Ireland. From the interviews, it has become apparent that the management and the staff of the regional development company feel responsible and accountable for the communities they represent. The CEO illustrated this idea:

In our interventions with the people we focus on the difference you make to clients and the difference you make to communities.

(CEO of social enterprise, personal communication, April 28, 2016)

Accordingly, even though the regional development company allocates its resources on a program-by-program basis (and each of these programs has a different focus), they all contribute to enhancing the quality of life in the local communities. For example, the social inclusion and economic development programs both address a different aspect of community development, but they still depend upon each other. The social inclusion program was created to develop a strategy for personal development and the progression of individuals and households within a district. However, a holistic solution can only be achieved with economic support, such as progression into employment or advice and subsidies for firms. Even community landscaping projects have been shown to foster the engagement and cooperation of locals in community development. Throughout its history, the regional development company has been innovative in identifying the needs of communities and creating solutions to address these needs from within the communities themselves.

Regarding the criterion of having a limited profit distribution, the regional development company applies the concept of the double bottom line, which uses positive social impact as a second performance measure besides financial performance. The management is aware that in order to be sustainable and improve the quality of life in the local communities the company needs to perform well economically. The regional development company has been strikingly successful in accessing and leveraging funding. It has sourced funding from the Department of Environment, community and local governments (LEADER and SICAP), the Department of Education and Skills (local training initiatives), the Department of Social Protection (Rural Social Scheme, Community Work Placement Initiative, The Jobs Club), and the Department of Children and Youth Affairs (Family Support Worker Project). In addition, it is very strategic and effective in sourcing funds from other public and private sector sources. The regional development company identifies and accesses funding sources for projects or identifies other service providers who can provide funds for and/or lead particular initiatives.

The ability to identify such providers is facilitated by extensive and effective networking and shared experience from other joint projects. It often means that the regional development company adds value to public funding by facilitating projects that would not have happened otherwise or that are greatly enhanced by the company's support. In total, the regional development company's turnover was over €5.7 million in 2015. While 92.5 percent of those funds were invested in facilitation, capacity building, education, and training and developing individuals, communities, and businesses, only 7.5 percent were spent on overhead and administrative costs. The regional development company does not distribute profits. As the CEO explained:

> *We are a social enterprise with charitable status. Nobody has shares. We're not commercially oriented. We reinvest back into what we are doing rather than anybody taking money out.*
> (CEO of social enterprise, personal communication, April 28, 2016)

The assessment of the Irish case based on the three aspects of the social mission of social enterprises shows a rather clear picture. While the Irish company leverages its economic performance to facilitate positive social impact and clearly focuses on the improvement of communities rather than exclusive groups, the initiative from which the company emerged was originally launched top-down by governmental organizations. However, representatives from community groups were involved from the outset. Furthermore, very early in the development of the company, the civil society took control of the management and the strategy by having local CEOs, staff, and members on the various boards that steer and advise its activities. Thus, the social dimension typical for a social enterprise according to the EMES definition is easily identifiable in the Irish case.

The Entrepreneurial Dimension

Social enterprises follow a social and an entrepreneurial mission. In the following, we will assess how thoroughly the Irish company follows the entrepreneurial dimension based on the following three criteria: (1) producing and selling goods and services, (2) taking entrepreneurial risks, and (3) employing paid workers.

The regional development company continuously provides a broad variety of services to the local communities along three lines. First, they conduct several activities funded by major funding schemes. The rural development program (LEADER) promotes sustainable development in rural areas to improve the quality of life and the diversification and development of the rural economy. The Social Inclusion Community Activation Program tries to reduce poverty and promote social inclusion. This is done by empowering communities to work together with the goals of community development, education, training, and (self-) employment. The Rural Social Scheme aims to provide services that benefit the rural community by harnessing the skills and talents available among low-income farmers. The Community Work Placement Initiative is an activation initiative for those who are unemployed and receive social welfare. This program provides suitable working opportunities for people who are unemployed, thereby improving work readiness while carrying out beneficial work within communities. The Jobs Club offers support to jobseekers through individualized and group initiatives, including workshops for preparing CVs and cover letters and for improving interview skills. Local training initiatives are targeted to people under the age of 35 who do not have any formal education. These initiatives include training and work experience for participants, helping them to progress to employment or further education.

The second line of activities is organized around separate social enterprises that developed as spin-offs out of the regional development company. For example, there is an outdoor recreation and environmental education social enterprise that focuses on designing and delivering activities and events to participants. The regional development company also operates two food units in small towns in the region. These food units facilitate and support the establishment and growth of local micro food business. Furthermore, another spin-off offers social enterprise support, which includes financial management, company secretarial training, and compliance products and services for other social enterprises. Another example of a spin-off of the regional development company is the community center in Groom, County Limerick, which features a coffee shop, a library, and an event venue.

The third line of activities comprises a variety of smaller projects, including the Family Supports Initiative, the Enterprise Start Up Project, and the Towards Occupation Program. In this line of activities, the regional development company also supports two community houses in villages in the Counties Limerick and Cork. The Community Houses are managed by their residents, with support from the regional development company. They provide a basis for offering educational and recreational activities to all sectors of the community. In addition to providing a meeting space, one of the houses has a fully equipped training room with nine computers. The training room makes it possible for courses to be delivered in-house to the target groups from the local and surrounding areas.

A large share of the second and third line of activities is financed through national and European funding schemes on a project-by-project basis. Thus, the regional development company does not sell its services to private businesses, individuals, or households, but delivers these services on behalf of funding bodies. However, the Irish authorities have recently and dramatically changed the organization of these funding schemes to have more market-based logic. Traditionally, a contracting system was used, under which the government directly contracted development companies to deliver specific services that addressed a community need. This system gradually transformed into a tendering system. In the tendering system, the development companies must bid for tenders with explicit quantified targets for specific aspects of community development.

Besides the provision of goods and services on the market the entrepreneurial dimension of social enterprises also manifests in the significant level of economic risk associated with their core activities. The business model of the Irish company entails three types of entrepreneurial risk. The first one is the risk of its individual programs failing. For example, the regional development company took significant risk in developing a pilot program in a small village in County Limerick, and another village in County Cork, to provide in-home care services for elderly persons and persons with disabilities. Due to the project's pilot character and the large investments (e.g. in developing and defining the market and building a reputation), it was a high-risk, high-gain project. If the program had failed, the regional development company would have lost most of its investments in the tailor-made infrastructure. Luckily, the pilot was successful, and a company limited by guarantee and with charitable status was established in 1998.

The second type of risk faced by the Irish company is the risk of failing in the competitive tendering processes used to distribute national and EU funds among the local development companies. These tendering processes are open to international competitors and involve difficult, target-based performance measures. Choosing service providers based on quantitative performance measures avoids the issue of path-dependency, but largely ignores the track record of companies and does not fully consider the quality of their services. The CEO of the regional development company stressed the challenges involved in the tendering process:

> *The distribution of funds is moving towards competitive tendering. Everybody is just counting. There is no record of the quality of the progress made in community development. So, the challenge we have as an organization is to demonstrate our value for money.*
>
> (CEO of social enterprise, personal communication, December 15, 2016)

As a result, there is no guarantee that the organization will be successful in winning a contract for a specific program the next time around. The consequences of this can be significant. According to the CEO:

> *If the money stops flowing in because we do not win the tender, we would not have the money to pay the staff. We had to go through redundancies recently, which wasn't nice, but necessary in order to move from one to the next program period.*
>
> (CEO of social enterprise, personal communication, December 15, 2016)

The third risk is related to environmental uncertainty caused by a malfunction or delay in the governmental processes. As the distribution of funds depends on decisions made by governmental bodies, funds available for the work of the regional development company can vary significantly at short notice. For example, the Rural Development Program 2007–2013 allocated over €18 million to the Irish social enterprise, whereas the Rural Development Program 2014–2020 has allocated only around €5.6 million. This is a 68 percent reduction. The CEO highlighted the challenges of government agencies delaying funding decisions:

> *Right now, we are living on a month-to-month basis because at the end of the day we are no state agency.*
>
> (CEO of social enterprise, personal communication, December 15, 2016)

Closely linked to the criterion of economic risk is the criterion of paid work in organizations. Paid work implies fixed costs that in turn generate economic risk if there is no stable flow of income. Paid work also ensures sustainability in the activities of the social enterprise because these organizations cannot rely on voluntary work for their core activities indefinitely. The Irish company is run by a manager who is employed by the company full-time. Over the last few years, the company has employed (on average) 40 people. These employees undertake the core activities of the regional development company, but they are supported by volunteers.

Participatory Governance

Social enterprises typically differ from their commercial counterparts not only by having a double bottom line, but by having a more participatory governance. Three criteria characterize this form of governance: (1) a high degree of autonomy, (2) decision-making independent of capital ownership, and (3) having stakeholders involved in decision-making. We will now look at how these criteria manifest in the Irish social enterprise.

In the case of the regional development company, the degree of autonomy is high both in terms of the organization's independence from other institutions and in terms of internal leadership practices. Even though the regional development company is an autonomous organization, it is dependent on financial resources distributed by the government. However, this dependency is put into perspective by considering the diverse portfolio of programs and funding schemes in which the company is active. Due to this diversification, the social enterprise could avoid a reduction of funds from national bodies following government reforms aimed at consolidating the sector.

Regarding the internal governance structure in the regional development company employees work in teams and have considerable individual scopes. They are expected to be skillful in adapting to changing conditions and anticipating trends in identifying funding opportunities, and in producing project proposals. Staff members are active in their local communities and see themselves as advocates for community development. Some of them have joined the regional development company after being self-employed or working for their family businesses, and they bring those experiences to their roles. Some employees have been inspired by this entrepreneurial drive and have started their own businesses as spin-offs of the social enterprise.

As to the second criterion, the decision-making power in the Irish company is not based on capital ownership. The regional development company is a limited company with charitable status. It is a partnership of the community and the voluntary sector, social partners, local government, and statutory agencies. This partnership is also reflected by the company's operating structure. The day-to-day business in the company is run by the CEO, who is supported by a management team, who are the line managers for the other employees. Strategic decisions are taken by the board, which comprises voluntary directors elected for a three-year period from social partners, local government, statutory agencies, and community representatives. These board members are very engaged with the work of the social enterprise and regard it as being critical to the social and economic opportunities of citizens in the region and the sustainability of communities. Many of the board members are from the region, which has a strong tradition of community-based, self-help activities rooted in the cooperative movements Muintir Na Tire and Macra Na Feirme. There are also five subcommittees within the board. The role of these subcommittees is to advise and guide the plans and strategies of the company. There are also several advisory councils that act as a consultative forum and that comprise non-board members.

Thus, the decision-making power in the Irish company follows the principle of representative democracy. Many board members are representatives of the local communities. They have decision-making power regardless of capital ownership in the company.

Social enterprises are further characterized by the participatory nature of their governance. This criterion reflects the degree of involvement of internal and external stakeholders in strategy definition and decision-making. As outlined above, the regional development company evolved from a government agency's initiative that brought several communities together to identify common opportunities and challenges. The common link between the participating communities at this stage was being situated in the shadow of a scenic mountain range. From the beginning, the regional development company had a core team of employees, but it also relied to a large extent on voluntary contributions. The volunteers were truly devoted to supporting a successful model of sustainable local development. From the outset, this model aimed at fostering a dynamic process in which the social enterprise facilitates community and citizen development through an interactive process of animation, capacity building, engagement, partnership, planning, review, and evaluation. As the geographical area expanded outside of the small region, there was the added difficulty of creating sustainable commitment for the region from new communities. However, as the organization engaged with these communities and as key successes were achieved, the brand of the regional development company was accepted, and parochial rivalries were put aside.

While all groups affected by the activities of the regional development company participate in leadership and strategy definition through their decision-making power as members of the board, the activities are developed with strong participation from the communities as well, as the CEO explained:

> *Our activities are evolving from what we're hearing from communities where communities and individual people you're dealing with tell us their needs . . . If people have challenges, they quite often have solutions that they just might need help with. Your activities are evolving because you're listening to the people in the communities and you try to find what support is out there in order to drive that initiative.*
>
> (CEO of social enterprise, personal communication, April 28, 2016)

Regarding the involvement of internal stakeholders there is no institutionalized form of internal participation in the Irish company. The organizational culture is rather informal. Thus, the employees can easily approach the CEO or other members of the management team. However, they do not have a formal say in strategy definition or management decisions.

Looking at the three aspects of the governance dimension of social enterprises, the Irish company reflects a mixed picture. It is legally and managerially independent from other institutions but financially dependent on national and EU funding. The decision-making is participatory regarding the external stakeholders but not regarding the internal stakeholders. However, everyone affected by the activities of the regional development company can be engaged in the company by participating in one of the various boards that steer or consult the activities of the company.

Awakening of Innovative Agriculture: How Social Cooperatives Foster the Resilience of Small Farmers in Greece

The Greek case is complex in many aspects, because the firm appears to have several identities. Like the Janus of Greek mythology, it shows different faces on different occasions to different audiences. However, across all its identities, the Greek firm positions itself as a social enterprise. This becomes clear when taking a detailed look at the specific aspects of social enterprises. In this section, we first introduce the setting in which the Greek case is embedded, and we identify the challenges it faces and the answers it provides to these challenges. We also describe its business model and offer an in-depth description of the case along the three dimensions of social enterprises.

Challenges in Rural Greece

Recent statistics (EC, 2017) show that rural regions in Greece are highly relevant because they account for about two thirds of the territory and one third of the population. This is clearly above the average of the EU, where rural regions cover 44.1 percent of the territory and give home to 19.1 percent of the population. The importance of rural areas is a consequence of the dispersion of the Greek territory across many islands and the rough mountains in the north. In Greece, agriculture is still a relevant sector, employing 11.9 percent of the working population, which is significantly higher than the 2.5 percent in the EU15 (EC, 2017). However, the agricultural sector is characterized by small family farms with rather inefficient production. Thus, farming contributes little to the rural GDP.

Rural Greece is economically weak. With a GDP factor of 57.1, predominantly rural areas have about two thirds the strength of predominantly urban areas (which have a GDP factor of 90.5), which also fall short of the EU average of 100 percent (EC, 2017). Employment in predominantly rural Greek areas (55.6 percent) is slightly below the EU average of 66 percent (EC, 2017). In contrast to the EU, employment rates are higher in predominantly rural areas than in urban centers in Greece (50.7 percent). Employment rates increase with education: 61 percent of adults with a post-secondary, non-tertiary qualification in Greece are employed, as are 67 percent of people with a bachelor's or equivalent degree, 79 percent of people with a master's or equivalent degree, and 91 percent of people with a doctoral or equivalent degree. However, only 2 percent of the population in Greece have earned a master's degree

(EC, 2017). Self-employment is traditionally strong in Greece. A share of 29.5 percent of the working population was self-employed in 2016 (EC, 2017). However, this share fell by 11 percent between 2011 and 2016. Unemployment is a key issue in Greece (EC, 2017). In predominantly rural areas, 19.4 percent of the working-age population are registered as jobseekers; in urban centers 25.6 percent are registered. Among those aged between 15 and 24 years, these numbers reach an alarming 47.4 percent in rural areas and 45.8 percent in urban centers. Thus, youth unemployment is a major challenge in rural Greece. Correspondingly, the risk of poverty and social exclusion is higher in Greece than it is on average in the EU. Around one third of the Greek population faces this risk, irrespective of whether they live in rural or urban regions.

Greece was badly hit by the post-2008 financial crisis. The Greek state was saved from bankruptcy by massive loans provided by the European Central Bank and the International Monetary Fund over a period of eight years. However, these institutions and the other Euro zone countries required the Greek government to introduce severe austerity policy measures, including substantial cuts in pensions and a dramatic reduction in the public sector and public investments. These measures were accompanied by increased consumer taxes and a more effective regime of tax collection. Together, these measures led to a recession, which reduced the disposable income of Greek households and increased unemployment rates, especially among the younger population. Many Greeks left their home country. The Greek population shrank by 3.1 percent between 2011 and 2016, with the urban centers (4.7 percent) being hit more than twice as hard as the rural regions (2.3 percent) (EC, 2017). In addition, many young Greeks returned home to their families in the villages and small towns in the peripheral areas because they could not afford the high costs of living due to reduced incomes or the job losses in the urban centers. While in Greece the share of elderly people above 65 years of age is among the highest in the EU, this group grew only half as fast in rural areas as it did in urban centers. At the same time, the working-age population shrank by 2.6 percent in urban centers but only by 1.0 percent in rural Greece (EC, 2017). Thus, during the financial crisis, rural regions were less affected by the brain drain than urban regions, shifting the talent pool towards rural regions.

Phthiotis, a region in central Greece, is a predominantly agricultural rural region with approximately 21,000 farmers. Its agricultural products include cotton, corn, wheat, clover, olives, pomegranates, cherries, pistachios, walnuts, and vegetable cultivations in green houses. For many years, the region focused on the production of tobacco leaves. Traditionally, the cultivation of tobacco provided a considerable share of the income of the small family farms in the region. The recent downturn of the local tobacco industry threatened the survival of the family farms and, coincidentally, opened the door to innovation in farming.

Due to the decreased demand for tobacco, Phthiotis farmers searched for new cultivations and products that could generate more income for them and provide more value to the consumers. They realized that to achieve this goal, agricultural production needed to become more sustainable and more integrated along the value chain. The horizontal integration of the value chain, however, required farmers to join forces and pool their resources. Fortunately, the farmers in the Phthiotis region already had experience working together in tobacco cooperatives. At the same time, they needed to adopt an entrepreneurial perspective to successfully innovate and develop new products and services that span the full value chain. As one local farmer put it:

> *We have to refocus from being farmers to being businessmen who deliver sustainable products from the field to the shelf.*
>
> (Member of the cooperative, personal communication, March 14, 2017)

The economic downturn during the financial crises has posed major challenges to the Greek economy and more broadly to Greek society. The main challenges are linked to unemployment and the risk of poverty and social exclusion. Interestingly, the Greek rural areas provide a promising mix of resources to fight these challenges. The farmers in the Phthiotis region can build on their history of intensive collaboration to jointly innovate the agricultural sector toward sustainable, high-value products. With skilled businesspersons returning to their hometowns in rural regions also, the much-needed entrepreneurial mindset is available to innovate in the local economic ecosystem. As a local expert in agriculture explained:

> *Tobacco brought death, first to the customers and then to the region. We need sustainable farming products that bring back life to the region and ultimately to the customers.*
>
> (Expert in agriculture, personal communication, March 31, 2017)

How the Social Enterprise Fights the Challenges

The stevia cooperative investigated in Greece was founded in 2012 in the prefecture of Phthiotis. The starting point of the stevia cooperative was the downturn of the local tobacco cultivation, which highlighted the pressing need for new ways of producing and cultivating crops in the area. At that time, former tobacco growers, new farmers, and scientists were intensively looking for new products that would fit the region's climate and environmental conditions to generate income. During this time, the first experimental stevia cultivations were conducted in the region in cooperation with Greek agronomists and regional universities. The successful outcome of these experiments motivated the farmers to discuss how to best seize the potentials offered by the cultivation of stevia.

More former tobacco farmers from the region became aware of the stevia plant. They realized that with this crop they could leverage the expertise they gained from tobacco cultivation, as stevia can be grown and processed similarly to tobacco. At the same time, they saw a growing demand for health products (superfoods) in the national and international markets. Stevia fit this trend perfectly, as it is a natural sugar substitute that is 300 times sweeter than sugar but without calories. Stevia is even suitable for the growing number of customers suffering from diabetes.

In 2016, the stevia cooperative produced 70 tons of dried stevia leaves (in 2015, it produced 50 tons). At that time, it had seven employees, and more than 70 farmers were members of the cooperative. The farms of the cooperative's members are located mostly in a valley, where the climate and environmental conditions are ideal for the stevia plant because it requires high temperatures, adequate rainfall and plenty of sunshine and because it cannot endure longer periods of severe frost. Looking at all activities of the stevia cooperative along the value chain the social enterprise directly and indirectly supported 280 locals until 2016.

The members of the stevia cooperative have set themselves a clear goal. They want to be a customer-oriented, agri-food business that covers all production stages of developing and producing stevia sugar for regional, national, and international markets. To reach this goal, the stevia cooperative educates its farmers in cultivation methods, supports the modernization of harvesting, collecting, and processing leaves, and markets the extracted stevia sugar. Instead of only producing the raw product, the stevia cooperative aims at covering the whole value chain from the plant to the final product. The underlying idea is to direct the value added throughout the value chain to the small farmers, to preserve jobs in a region to fight youth unemployment, and to improve the economic resilience of the region as a whole. As the CEO of the stevia cooperative explained:

> *I told the farmers: form a cooperative. Please cultivate the leaves and sell them to a third party in France. Take back the raw material from France and package and market the final product. By doing so, you can take some extra money because you cover the full value chain – from field to fork!*
>
> (CEO of cooperative, personal communication, May 11, 2016)

Today, the stevia cooperative is among the few stevia producers in Europe. Expansion plans revolve around building up capacities to process the stevia leaves in the region instead of shipping them to

France and buying back the raw stevia. The processing plant would be an investment of approximately €10 million. Cutting out the French factory from the value chain would substantially increase the local value creation, as illustrated by an example offered by the CEO of the stevia cooperative:

> *The cooperative buys a kilo of leaves for €2 from the farmers and sells it to the French processor for €2.3. One kilo of raw stevia is bought back for €9, and depending on the packaging and the quantity, it sells on the market for €15 to €17.*
>
> (CEO of cooperative, personal communication, April 1, 2017)

Thus, the current practice of outsourcing extraction is costly.

Farmers in the Phthiotis region tend to be risk averse and conservative regarding innovation and investments, which are necessary to develop innovations from the idea stage to the market. The locals did not know initially what the stevia cooperative wanted to achieve. When they learned the vision of the organization, they thought it would be very difficult if not impossible to realize. Thus, the new business initiative faced a lack of confidence and massive mistrust from the local population and public decision-makers. To them, the idea of trying something new and innovative (that had neither been tested in the fields nor in the Greek or European markets) was frightening. The consequence was a lack of external support for the cooperative.

However, this lack of external support mobilized internal support from the members of the cooperative. For instance, a new building was financed solely by the members of the cooperative. The building offers storage for leaves, a meeting room, and an office space. Being organized as a cooperative helped the company gain strength through internal cohesion and to build up legitimacy in the community. Internally, the intensive communication that resulted from the participatory organization of a cooperative ensured that all members shared the same ideas about the product as well as the strategy and led to stronger relations among the members. Additionally, there are many meetings that deal with the establishment of future collaborations with other companies. These collaborations concern, for instance, the cultivation and processing of stevia as well as the creation and monitoring of the micro-climate necessary for the stevia plants to prosper. The cooperative has also established various contacts with people from regional, national, and international authorities. In addition, it participates in the regional agri-food collaboration, which offers a mutual exchange of knowledge between local players regarding current trends in the agri-food sector. The contacts also open the door for the stevia cooperative to participate in national and international exhibitions and fairs. In these exhibitions and fairs, the stevia cooperative offers and gains new insights and valuable network contacts. Taken together, the activities of the cooperative have intensified communication both within the organization and between the cooperative and its relevant stakeholders from business, science, and politics.

Over time, more information about the cooperative and stevia spread throughout the local community. When the first products (which come in well-designed packages) were ready for sale, the local community became more supportive and started to believe that the activities and efforts of the stevia cooperative led to tangible results. From this point on, increasingly more people asked about the product, what it was, and why it was different and new. With more intensive communication, more locals were convinced that stevia offered new opportunities to the region. The successful move into stevia production and the foundation of the social enterprise have also prompted local farmers to change their mindsets and practices. While in the past, farmers preferred to produce and sell only raw products, the stevia cooperative has initiated an upward integration of the value chain, which empowers farmers to play an important role in the new market for stevia. The economic impact of the cooperative on its members and the local community is too early to judge, as it is still in the process of entering the market. However, the stevia cooperative has already helped its members to enhance efficiency and to reduce costs by sharing machines and knowledge. They have also started to learn to speak with one voice in negotiations with suppliers and customers.

The starting point of the cooperative was a common interest among local farmers. They all faced challenges related to the downturn of tobacco farming, relatively small patches of farmland and the complexity of developing new crops and products. As they wanted to address these challenges as a group, they decided to rely on an organizational model they already knew, so they formed a cooperative. However, in this new venture, they chose a special form of cooperative that highlights the benefits for the community over and above the benefits for its individual members. The newly established social cooperative is dedicated to the cultivation and production of stevia as a final product to be sold to food retailers and households. A member of the management board of the cooperative highlighted the fundamental ideas behind the organizational form:

> *People are stronger together, and in rural regions it is a traditional agricultural business model that is used to develop the local communities in all aspects. Our social mission is the wellbeing of our members and the prosperity of the region as a whole.*
> (Board member of cooperative, personal communication, April 1, 2017)

The stevia cooperative consists of the general assembly, the board of directors, the supervisory committee, and the CEO. The general assembly comprises the 82 cooperative members. Most members have farming backgrounds. Besides annual meetings, additional meetings take place during the year if specific decisions with far reaching consequences for the cooperative must be made. Additionally, the board of directors, which has five members, discuss, organize, and plan the affairs, projects, and operations of the cooperative in its monthly meetings. The board of directors consists of a president, a vice-president, a secretary, a cashier, and a representative of the members. The supervisory committee has three members and monitors the board of directors. The CEO translates the strategic decisions of the board of directors and the general assembly into practice. Specifically, he is responsible for managing the operations of the cooperative in the areas of quality management, research and development, marketing, logistics, and accounting.

In a nutshell, the stevia cooperative has innovated local agriculture by introducing stevia as a new crop and by vertically integrating the value chain in the agri-food business. To do this, it joins forces within the community, offering expert professional management in return. The aim of the stevia cooperative is to provide a better and more sustainable income for local farmers by creating jobs and increasing the local value added. Ultimately, the business aims to strengthen the local economy and society, which was heavily affected by the recession in 2008.

The Social Mission

The social mission dictates that social enterprises "evolve in collective dynamics," "aim to benefit the community," and "avoid a profit-maximizing behavior" (Defourny & Nyssens, 2013, p. 46). We will now have a look at the Greek cooperative regarding these criteria.

The initiative that resulted in the foundation of the stevia cooperative was launched by a group of local farmers. The starting point was a dramatic economic downturn due to a considerable decline in tobacco farming in the region and the negative effects of the financial crisis in Greece. The resulting recession intensified the demand for social enterprise services such as the support of disadvantaged people. The dramatic reduction of the public sector fostered necessity entrepreneurship. However, due to the austerity policy, the Greek state has had limited leeway to support social enterprises in their aim to support local communities. As a cooperative, the Greek company's development was less affected by the austerity policy, because it is financed by cooperative shares and the voluntary contributions of its members.

Well before the establishment of the cooperative, the local farmers started to meet in a small village in the region to discuss their options to counter the dramatic reduction of their income. One of the outcomes of the farmers' meeting was the insight that they must join forces to gain strength. Consequently, a five-member committee was formed to establish a cooperative.

The founding president of the stevia cooperative (a farmer and former president of tobacco growers at the national level) played a key role in gathering farmers from the region. He leveraged his network with research institutions to promote a shift away from tobacco and toward alternative crops such as stevia. During this time, the current vice-president of the cooperative (an agronomist) was also very engaged in promoting the vision of a cooperative devoted to the production of stevia to local farmers and officials. While the president focused on the political level, the vice-president concentrated on the practical level by providing suggestions to solve the issues related to the cultivation of stevia on former tobacco farms. Soon the committee realized that they were lacking entrepreneurial skills and business expertise. Thus, they approached an entrepreneur and financial expert who had international experience but who was born and raised in the region. They convinced him to join the initiative as its CEO. The CEO described the importance of his community roots in gaining the trust of local farmers, saying:

> *For the farmers, I was the local guy. I was the boy from the village. You know him. His parents are there, his grandfather, his mother, we know all of them.*
>
> (CEO of cooperative, personal communication,
> May 11, 2016)

He soon became the key figure in the cooperative's business development at the local, national, and international levels. After the establishment of the cooperative two academically trained agronomists were employed to further develop stevia cultivation techniques. They also deal with the back-office work and handle the day-to-day management of the organization.

The activities and intensive communication between the cooperative representatives and the people from the region motivated more local farmers to join. At present, the stevia cooperative has 82 members and employs three people from the local community. As is typical of social enterprises, its operations heavily rely on voluntary support from the members of the cooperative. The organization tries to combine the traditional model of cooperatives and the community-based values they stand for with a more businesslike approach in order to succeed in the competitive agri-food markets. Thus, the initiative for the foundation of the stevia cooperative not only emerged from the local community but its current operations also heavily rely on the support of the local community.

Historically, many cooperatives have emerged during economic crises because they provide a way of joining to address challenges that local communities face. However, a common mistake of earlier cooperatives in the region was not offering benefits to its member-employees. The stevia cooperative claims to do this differently. Its president has extensive experience in developing cooperatives and strongly believes that the cooperative can be successful only when it unites local actors who work together toward a joint vision and keep the common good for the community in mind. The aim of the cooperative is defined as continuous joint and risky entrepreneurial venture that produces stevia and that strongly supports and exercises participative governance, development through education and training, cooperation among cooperatives, and concern for the community.

The cooperative follows this aim and offers expertise to the local community regarding farming and business opportunities related to agri-food and its neighboring sectors. For instance, the social enterprise is supporting the establishment of a new energy production cooperative by using municipal pruning in collaboration with the local municipality and a regional university. The idea was first communicated during a workshop in 2013 and is based on successful examples of such cooperatives in other EU countries. For this initiative, the stevia cooperative has organized educational meetings, workshops, and day conferences in order to diffuse knowledge and information. At present, the cooperative collaborates with Greenpeace to produce green energy, and it offers pellets for heating to schools in the region.

Generally, the company's management is convinced that the cooperative is a way to address many problems in the local community, including (youth) unemployment and low rural incomes. It expects that there will be more job opportunities and income for the local community as the business grows. Currently, however, most of the cooperative's profits are reinvested in the growth of the operation, especially in production and processing facilities and in entering new markets.

Under the articles of association, the profits of the cooperative are distributed to the members of the cooperative according to their share in the production of stevia leaves or other input in the operations, such as management efforts. As the CEO explained:

> *The profits of the cooperative are distributed to the members depending on their share in the production of leaves. I think that's fair. If you produce a lot of leaves, you get a lot of money. For my work, I get a specific percentage of the sales.*
>
> (CEO of cooperative, personal communication,
> April 1, 2017)

The remaining profits are reinvested into the sustained growth of the organization.

During the start-up phase, the distribution of profits was very limited and even the compensation for stevia leaves was delayed by years. Thus, the first distribution of profits in 2017 was vital to encourage the members of the cooperative. The management of the stevia cooperative is convinced that people's mistrust in new and innovative ventures is even stronger in rural regions. The rural mindset is conditioned to think in cycles of seed and harvest with a maximum time horizon of one year. Thus, local farmers needed to see quick results to believe in the success of new activities.

The Entrepreneurial Dimension

The social mission of social enterprises is typically complemented by an equally important entrepreneurial dimension based on three criteria: (1) producing and selling goods and services, (2) taking entrepreneurial risks, and (3) employing paid workers. In what follows, we address these criteria for the Greek case.

The stevia cooperative is predominantly concerned with cultivating, processing, and selling stevia. The products are dried stevia leaves, pure stevia, and crystal stevia. The aim is sustainable growth that is financed mainly internally and that enables the cooperative to gradually span the whole value chain, from stevia seeds to the final product. In addition to the production of stevia, the cooperative also provides training to its members and other members of the local community. These services are provided in cooperation with regional universities and business partners. Usually, the courses take place in a public building provided to the cooperative by regional authorities. Typically, in these courses, agronomists from the local community and researchers from regional universities would teach local farmers how to cultivate crops on small to medium-sized farms in safer and more efficient ways. These trainings often include field trips to the stevia fields of the social enterprise. Besides enhancing the cultivation techniques of the existing members of the cooperative, these trainings also aim to motivate additional local farmers to change their production from traditional farming products, such as cotton, to stevia.

Interestingly, the individual items of the cooperative's product and service portfolio are interrelated. For instance, its education and training initiatives focus on cultivation procedures and quality standards regarding stevia. Therefore, these initiatives indirectly improve efficiency in cultivation, product quality, and ultimately profit. At the same time, the management receives training on marketing skills, for example, or on promoting the stevia cooperative and its products. These free services for the cooperative members and the local community are financed by selling stevia.

For its portfolio of products and services, the stevia cooperative has four distinct groups of customers. First, in line with the underlying idea of cooperatives, the members of the cooperative and the regional community are the most important customer group. Second, the cooperative has industrial customers who use pure stevia as an input in their production processes. Third, customers also include wholesalers and retailers in the food and health sector, which list the final stevia product for sale. Finally, individual customers who buy crystal stevia directly from the cooperative form the fourth group of customers.

The business model of the stevia cooperative implies substantial economic risk. Refocusing the production from traditional crops such as tobacco, cotton, and olives to stevia calls for substantial, specific investments. Given the uncertain future demand for the sugar substitute, farmers who invest in stevia production face the threat of sunk costs. Stevia is new to consumers. Many potential customers have not heard of stevia and do not know how to use it. The stevia plant itself is also rather new to the local farmers, and it is still unclear how it will develop in the region's micro climate in the long term. The business model builds on substantial economies of scale and a steep learning curve with respect to harvesting, drying, defoliating, and transporting the stevia leaves and processing raw stevia into the final product. These existential threats are even exacerbated by the unclear legal situation regarding the use of stevia in the food industry. Although the EU has already given the green light in late 2011 for the use of steviol glycosides as an additive (EU Regulation 1131/2011), other regions of the world still protect their sugar producers from this innovation.

In light of these risks, the members of the stevia cooperative have decided to limit their economic risks to their shares in the cooperative, their voluntary input, and their individual investments in their farms while refraining from taking loans from a bank or a state-run business-promotion agency. This conservative attitude toward risk limits the growth potential of the cooperative. As the CEO critically pointed out:

> *They won't take a loan to develop the cooperative because they don't have the entrepreneurial spirit. They don't have the entrepreneurial mindset to understand that if you want to sell something you should invest first. They want to earn a lot of money from day one.*
> (CEO of cooperative, personal communication, April 1, 2017)

Thus, the economic risk for the members of the cooperative is limited, but given the small scale of their farms, it is nevertheless substantial.

As to the criterion of employing paid workers, the stevia cooperative is a small company in terms of headcount. The cooperative has 82 members but employs only three staff. The operations of the business heavily rely on voluntary support provided by the members of the cooperative. As the CEO explained:

> *The members of the board cannot be paid. The two girls are employed full time and another person works part-time for the cooperative. The rest is done by our members.*
> (CEO of cooperative, personal communication, April 1, 2017)

To sum up, the social cooperative scores high in the entrepreneurial dimension, as its business model involves the continuous effort to market products and services. These activities imply a considerable degree of economic risk for those involved. Moreover, the social enterprise also relies on paid work over and above the voluntary work of its members.

Participatory Governance

Participatory governance requires a high degree of autonomy and decision-making independent from capital ownership but with strong involvement from stakeholders. Again, we will discuss the Greek company along the lines of these three aspects to evaluate its degree of participatory decision-making.

While the cooperative enjoys a high degree of independence from public funds and state aid, it is strongly dependent on bureaucratic procedures. Especially in the agri-food business, firms must adhere to several regulations, and their processes and products must undergo intensive controls by state authorities. Thus, the social enterprise suffers from frequently slow public administrative processes. It is also dependent on publicly funded research and development institutions such as universities. The inefficient administration also hampers access to these institutions and their knowledge base.

The CEO acknowledges the subsidies and in-kind support that the stevia cooperative receives from the local and regional government. At the same time, he also emphasizes that political decision-makers in Greece traditionally refrain from giving substantial support, especially to successful ventures:

> *The national government subsidizes us with some money. And the local governor supports us. But I don't think that we have great support from the officials. I think politicians see me as threat. In Greece if you succeed in business, the next day you are a politician. At the last exposition in Athens, they put us in the worst place. They literally hid us!*
>
> (CEO of cooperative, personal communication, April 1, 2017)

Regarding the aspect of autonomy, the stevia cooperative is thus comparatively independent in its decision-making. This is particularly true compared to other players in the agri-food sector who face the same administrative burden but cannot rely on internal financing from members of a cooperative.

In cooperatives, decision-making follows the principal of "one member, one vote." The members of the cooperative are organized in the general assembly, which appoints the members of the board of directors, which is monitored by the supervisory board. The general assembly also makes all key decisions, such as the termination or merger of the cooperative, and it dis/approves the annual financial report.

In day-to-day business, the board of directors is the main decision-making body. It initiates, develops, and decides the strategies and practices of the cooperative. The board of directors is also responsible for selecting and supervising the CEO. As the professional manager, the CEO is an addition to the traditional model cooperative. This addition emphasizes the entrepreneurial mission of the social enterprise. The CEO is responsible for carrying out the decisions made by the board of directors. However, as the members of the board of directors have an agricultural background whereas the CEO has a background in business and finance, in practice the CEO often takes over a considerable share of the decision-making power formally ascribed to the board of directors. The CEO described this situation with a metaphor:

> *If I leave them, they are going to die . . . Just before they die, you can provide the oxygen. I have the oxygen!*
> (CEO of cooperative, personal communication, April 1, 2017)

At the same time, the CEO knows that his power only exists so long as he does not exercise it against the will of the board of directors, or the general assembly. He stressed the need for intensive communication and a broad consensus as follows:

> *I always discuss my plans with the cooperative. Always! I want to be fair. I don't cheat them. I have discussed my plans many times.*
> (CEO of cooperative, personal communication, April 1, 2017)

Due to the principle that each member has one vote in the general assembly, a cooperative is a generic way to organize joint economic activity in a participatory way. The general assembly of the stevia cooperative is dominated by farmers on the one hand and a strong CEO with specific competences in entrepreneurship and business on the other hand. Each member of the cooperative and the board of directors as well as the CEO bring with them strong networks that enable the cooperative to activate resources from outside the group of locals directly involved in the firm. The CEO described his network as follows:

> *I have a very good circle of friends who help me, and I'm trying to help them. For example, the service association of the Greek industry asked me to participate in a think tank that they have built on agri-food. They appreciate my different perspective on cooperatives, my knowledge on the grass level. I am also part of the agri-food*

accelerator of the National Bank of Greece, NBG Seeds. Such contacts are of great value for me and I can use them for the cooperative.
(CEO of cooperative, personal communication,
April 1, 2017)

However, when the stevia cooperative was started, other stakeholders (such as customers, political decision-makers, or non-farming members of the community) were not involved in its governance. While the members of the social enterprise were selected to include the key opinion leaders among the farming community, this showed that the non-farming community should be represented in the governance of the cooperative to gain legitimacy in the local community. Consequently, the stevia cooperative has recently started to take members on board who do not have a farming background but are concerned with the stevia business in some other way.

The Greek case provides a mixed picture when looking at the three criteria of the governance dimension of social enterprises. Despite being dependent on bureaucratic procedures, it is financially independent from public funds and state aid. Due to the principle that each member of the cooperative has one vote irrespective of his or her financial stake, the decision-making is participatory for the internal stakeholders. External stakeholders, however, have only recently started to join the stevia cooperative.

Enabling Brain Gain: How a Social Cooperative Enables Experimentation and Knowledge Exchange in Austrian Villages

In many aspects, in the opinion of the members of the organization, the Austrian company in this study is a role model for a social enterprise. It has a strong entrepreneurial component, and it follows a social mission of fostering rural development by attracting talented people living in rural communities, which is why we will refer to the enterprise as "the brain gainers." However, its entrepreneurial and social missions are addressed in different parts of the organization rather than jointly. Separating contradictory activities is a typical approach in organizations to maintain the capacity to act. Compared to an ambidextrous approach, a split organization can reduce the potential for innovation. For the organization this organizational separation creates a double bottom that strengthens the competitiveness of the social enterprise. When competing with non-profit organizations they can claim to be one of them, but to be entrepreneurial as well. When competing with for-profit organizations, again they can claim to be one of them, but to have a social mission as well. We take a detailed look at specific aspects of the Austrian social enterprise, and begin by introducing the setting in which the company is embedded and identifying the challenges it faces and the answers it provides to these challenges. We also describe the business model, and offer an in-depth description of the case along the three dimensions of social enterprises.

Challenges in Rural Austria

In Austria, rural regions are of comparably high relevance. About 75.2 percent of the territory is predominantly rural and about 40.7 percent of Austrians live in rural areas. Both values clearly exceed the respective figures for the European Union (EU) where about 44.1 percent of the territory is rural and about 19.1 percent of the population lives in rural regions (EC, 2017). The importance of rural areas is a consequence of the specific topology of the Alp Mountains, which cover large parts of the country and allow for only a low population density. Agriculture is still a relevant sector, employing about 4.1 percent of the working population (the respective share in the 15 more industrialized EU member states is 2.5 percent) (EC, 2017). It is characterized by small family farms and contributes little to the rural gross domestic product (GDP). As in many industrialized countries, the economy of predominantly rural Austrian regions is shaped by the secondary and tertiary sector, which employ 22.5 percent and 73.6 percent of the rural workforce respectively. These regions have a comparatively strong economy and high employment rates. With a GDP factor of 105.3 (100 corresponds to the EU average) predominantly rural Austrian regions clearly exceed the average of all rural regions in Europe, which have a GDP factor of 72.9 (EC, 2017). While one in four inhabitants of rural areas (25.5 percent) is at risk of poverty or social exclusion across the entire EU, the respective figure is much lower (13.9 percent) in Austria.

Although predominantly rural regions in Austria perform well economically, they continually lose young and well-educated people like many other rural regions in Europe do. Between 2011 and 2016 these regions experienced a decrease of 0.6 percent in children 14 years old and younger and an increase of 1.3 percent in people older than 65 years (EC, 2017). A qualitative study conducted by the Austrian Conference on Spatial Planning (ÖROK) reveals that bigger cities in Austria attract young people due to better career perspectives and a better provision of goods and services. In particular, people with tertiary education are much more attracted to cities than to rural regions (ÖROK, 2015).

The consequence of this attractiveness is a brain drain in rural areas. The Austrian social enterprise under investigation has also observed brain drain. In an interview, one of the founders of the enterprise discussed a study they had conducted on demographic change:

> *At that time, we made a study on demographic change that was alarming . . . We did not only investigate the reasons why young*

people leave rural areas in the search for experiences but also why they do not return.

(Member of social enterprise, personal communication, March 9, 2016)

In another interview a regional development expert agreed that out-migration is a problem, particularly for remote, rural communities:

If we ask them [communities] about their motivation to implement an Agenda 21 process, they simply want to counteract the loss of people. However, there are differences within districts . . . some communities do not face this problem while others, particularly those at the outskirts of our district, are heavily affected . . . I believe that many young people who go to Vienna or Linz do not have any incentive to come back because there are no offers that . . . enable exchange or provide possibilities for networking.

(Regional development expert, personal communication, October 7, 2016)

Another interview partner observes that especially peripheral regions face the risk of losing women because women are more affected by structural issues, such as a lack of part-time jobs, than men. In rural areas, men, however, often benefit from the networks provided by various clubs, such as football clubs:

Clubs are an important anchoring point, particularly for men. For women, structures and opportunities count. Thus, if structures disappear in rural areas women are among the first to leave and as a consequence, men suffer. If women leave, rural areas die.

(Member of social enterprise, personal communication, March 10, 2016)

However, most rural areas in Austria are far from dying. Many interviewees emphasized the diversity of rural regions and that not all of them suffer from population decreases, ageing, or a lack of well-educated people. They believe that limited geographical distance, access to motorways and railway lines, a potential for tourism, an availability of quality jobs, and the provision of goods and services are crucial requirements for the prosperity of rural regions. The municipality where the investigated social enterprise is located, for example, has been less affected by demographic change and structural problems because the municipality benefits from direct access to the motorway and from several manufacturing companies that operate in the area, among which are world-leading engineering companies. Consequently, the municipality has experienced a population increase in recent decades. Interviewees described the municipality as transitioning from a village shaped by agriculture into a village with modern industries:

> *We are a village next to the motorway. The motorway is important for the business park, but there are two worlds that collide. I find it is a difficult transition zone . . . the interplay between both creates a certain tension.*
> (Member of the local support group of the social enterprise, personal communication, October 5, 2016)

On the one hand, the establishment of new firms enables the municipality to generate high tax revenues and thus have increased financial room to maneuver. On the other hand, interviewees observed that the transformation reduces the residents' attachment to the place. In times of increasing spatial mobility, children are often sent to schools in bigger towns instead of being enrolled in the local school. Since school years are important in the development of social and emotional bonds with the local community, these pupils are less likely to return to their home villages:

> *Those who leave the village for school at the age of ten, lose social bonds and will rarely return later in life.*
> (Local policy maker, personal communication, October 6, 2016)

How the Social Enterprise Fights the Challenges

Listening to the members of the social enterprise, there is little doubt that the main aim of the brain gainers is to meet the challenges that occur in rural regions. One of these challenges is the lack of talented people:

> *Our aim is to create support activities which help creative people in rural areas to fulfill themselves, to be active, and to act entrepreneurially, thus, not to follow the old approach, which is out-migration to urban areas in the search of cool locations and networks.*
> (Member of social enterprise, personal communication, March 10, 2016)

The brain gainers find it important to search for solutions and to take perspectives that are different from the established ones. While other experts in the field of regional development discuss ways to prevent brain drain, the Austrian social enterprise wants to foster *brain gain*. In doing so, rural areas must create opportunities for self-fulfillment that entice creative people to work and live there rather than simply discouraging people from leaving.

The social enterprise uses open technology labs to attract talented people to rural areas. These technology labs provide space to work and meet, and they are equipped with technical devices such as 3D printers, virtual reality glasses, and repair tools. Anyone can use the technology labs to experiment, meet creative people, and share knowledge. The social enterprise was the first organization in Austria to establish open technology labs in rural areas. Previously, such labs only existed in cities. The focus of these labs is technology education. Due to the technical equipment provided and the support offered by experienced persons, young and old people alike find a place to test new ideas, repair things, and have fun. Open technology labs support the acquisition of technical knowledge and skills, and they foster the development of prototypes, which can be starting points for professional careers and new businesses.

An important principle of open technology labs is to share knowledge. For example, a retired person in the company's lab is skilled in wood-turning. After having practiced this hobby for years at home, the man now has the opportunity to lead workshops and share his skills with others in the open technology lab. Besides technology education, the open labs also host free events and courses that would otherwise rarely take place in rural communities. The brain gainers stressed the importance of openness and providing a space without barriers:

> *We realized that there is a huge desire for open spaces. This is particularly important for groups that are not organized in clubs. Suddenly, they found a place to meet.*
> (Member of social enterprise, personal communication, March 10, 2016)

By offering open spaces, the social enterprise also counteracts the lack of public spaces and the vacancy of buildings in rural areas. Communities that experience a decline in population often possess vacant buildings, and they have no idea what to do with them. Open technology labs offer a solution for this challenge. They provide space that is open to all interested persons or groups and thereby offer a meaningful use of previously vacant buildings and rooms.

The Austrian social enterprise has also developed an initiative to foster children's interest in technology and natural science. The initiative is an exhibition with several stations that invite kids to play and experiment with water power, magnetism, over-sized Lego bricks, turning machines for wax figures, 3D printing, and disassembling electronic devices. The exhibition intends to *"gain interest of pre-school kids for technology"* (Member of social enterprise, personal communication, March 9, 2016) in a playful way and to pave the way for possible careers in the fields of technology, engineering, and natural sciences (skilled workforces in these fields are in high demand in rural areas). The exhibition is often booked by rural communities, (pre-) schools, and companies (offering, for example, summer events for their employees' children). The brain gainers regard the exhibition as a means of strengthening the educational opportunities in rural communities. They hope that the program will make children more likely to attend local schools, and to develop social bonds and a personal attachment to their home villages.

While the exhibition is set up and run by members of the social enterprise, open technology labs in rural areas are inspired but not implemented by the social enterprise itself. The establishment of new open technology labs is in the hands of local teams that operate remotely. The social enterprise supports new labs when at least three conditions are met. First, the lab must be run by a minimum of five persons (called *"the magic five"*), as this is regarded as the smallest group size to realize and operate an open technology lab in a sustainable way. Second, the municipality must support the lab by providing the space and the basic infrastructure (e.g. heating, toilettes, Wi-Fi) for free. The provision of the space must be legitimized by a democratic decision in the local council. Third, the team running the new lab must accept the social enterprise's charter, which is a list of shared principles such as maintaining openness and diversity, participatory governance and trust, and the search for social change and humanism. Apart from these requirements the relationship between the social enterprise and the team running the new lab is rather loose. The brain gainers provide inspiration and support but do not guide or control the new labs. This approach – fostering the diffusion of open technology labs in rural areas by offering the idea and delegating the realization to local teams – is seen as *process innovation*. In contrast, *product innovation* would involve retaining the realization of the innovative idea or product completely in the hands of the enterprise. Innovation transfer by way of this process innovation is summarized by the motto of the social enterprise: *"We make nothing: we make things happen"* (Member of social enterprise, field note, March 9, 2016).

The organizational model underneath the rural open labs is a double structure comprised of a social enterprise at its core and a network of associated local teams. The social enterprise first operated as an association. When the tasks of the association became more complex and it became necessary to hire employees, the persons involved realized that they needed a different organizational model to support their business activities. At the same time, they wished to retain the democratic principles upon which the association was based. Therefore, they founded a cooperative in 2014 that guarantees decision-making rights to each member. In addition, they wanted to combine the self-determination that they enjoyed as individual entrepreneurs with the security of employment. Hence, the cooperative they set up allows them to be members and employees of the cooperative simultaneously. The resulting model of a self-employment cooperative was the first of its kind in Austria and was awarded with a social innovation prize. For the cooperative's members, this model is a way to counteract the labor alienation observed in post-industrialized, Western societies. The members identify with the principles of the new work movement (Bergmann, 1977, 2014), which promotes a work model with equal shares of gainful employment, self-sufficient work, and creative work that people *"really, really want"* (Bergmann, 2017, p. 121).

The cooperative has been the umbrella organization of the rural open technology labs even though these labs are run independently by local teams. The cooperative still promotes the idea of rural open technology labs, supports their diffusion with an outreach team, and fosters an exchange of knowledge within the network of local teams by organizing annual meetings. Many local teams try to safeguard the future existence of their labs by establishing associations. Today, almost 30 of these rural open technology labs exist in four European countries.

In sum, the Austrian social enterprise searches for solutions to meet the challenges that rural Austria faces. These challenges comprise a lack of creative and well-educated people and the difficulty of attracting these people to live in the countryside. To meet these challenges the social enterprise has developed rural open technology labs. By developing these labs, the social enterprise has also been able to address other challenges in rural areas, such as a lack of public spaces and the existence of vacant buildings. On a more personal level, the members of the social enterprise wanted to address a lack of satisfying, self-determined work. They therefore founded a self-employment cooperative that promises its members both the security of gainful employment and the self-determination and self-fulfillment of being an entrepreneur.

The Social Mission

A social mission comprises three criteria: (1) an initiative launched by a group of citizens or a civil society organization, (2) an explicit aim to benefit the community, and (3) limited profit distribution. In what follows, we describe the Austrian social enterprise along these criteria.

The Austrian social enterprise has its roots in a small group of people who wanted to make their rural environment an attractive place for talented people. In 2008, the members of this group worked in the field of regional and sustainable development, partly as employees and partly as entrepreneurs. They had the idea to establish rural open technology labs. Based on this idea, they developed a project and applied for public funding. However, the proposal was not successful, so the open technology labs were not yet established. At the same time, the idea of open technology labs attracted the attention of the mayors of two rural communities in Upper Austria. With their support and the help of interested persons from the civil society the first two open technology labs were established. A lack of public funding paved the way for a bottom-up strategy that is still applied today:

> *On the other hand, it [the failed proposal for funding] has shown . . . that founding a lab should not depend on such structures because in these structures a top-down strategy and mentality would arise. After that, we had a talk with the two mayors in which we agreed that the only way to legitimize such a place would be to realize it in a participative way.*
>
> (Member of social enterprise, personal communication, March 9, 2016)

In the beginning, the initiative was organized as an association. The initiators were members in this association, and they supported the technology labs voluntarily without having the intention of founding a social enterprise. Only when they realized that the increasing number of tasks required more professional structures did they begin to search for a different legal entity. This process resulted in the foundation of a cooperative in February 2014. Today, the cooperative exists in addition to the local associations, which run the rural open technology labs with the help of volunteers. The local associations constitute a network that meets at least once a year. The cooperative provides its expertise and support to the local associations while benefitting from their contacts, reputation, and inspirations. Thus, even though the social enterprise has its roots in a small group of initiators rather than a community initiative, it has clearly emerged from a collective process and is rooted in civil society.

Social enterprises are driven by their social responsibility for the community or society as a whole and not just by the interests of an exclusive group. As discussed earlier, the Austrian social enterprise aims to make rural communities attractive to skilled and talented people in order to improve the knowledge base and the development prospects of rural regions. This objective can be found in various materials. An evaluation report, for example, states:

> *The open technology labs enable people to live in their region with passion, they provide open spaces for dedicated people, and they motivate people to come back to their region, which was a main target when the labs were founded.*
>
> (Evaluation report, 2015, p. 4)

The social enterprise also asks local initiatives that want to join the network of open technology labs to agree to a charter that defines common principles. These principles not only describe what collaborative work and democratic decision-making should look like in the local initiative but also refer to broader social objectives and the respect of human rights. Participating initiatives declare, among other things, that they see themselves as "co-creators of urban and regional development" and that they make their outcomes "available as open-source" for the society (Austrian Social Enterprise, n.d.).

The social mission for rural communities is also reflected in field notes that the authors recorded during participatory observations. On March 14, 2016, one of the founders of the social enterprise gave a speech at a creative industry event in Vienna. The field notes summarize the speech:

> *He talks about the mission to foster change in rural regions. The members of the social enterprise would be persons who returned to the countryside. A problem in rural areas is the lack of public spaces. Against this backdrop, the approach of the social enterprise would be to create open spaces that do not belong to existing systems and do not oblige their users to specific outcomes.*
> (Member of social enterprise, field note, March 14, 2016)

At a business meeting on September 16, 2016, a member of the social enterprise similarly explained the initial motivation for starting the venture. He said the social enterprise aimed at fighting the serious demographic problems that rural regions face by creating innovative spaces and making innovation culture real (member of social enterprise, personal communication, September 16, 2016). Moreover, the objective to foster rural development was conveyed in interviews conducted with members of the social enterprise:

> *We communicate a certain attitude, and this does not hurt. This attitude is to think cooperatively, and to develop things in close collaboration with one another and to everyone's benefit. So, it is not about 'who gets more, who gets less'. It is a deliberate contrast to the culture of competition, and at the same time it creates hope for rural areas.*
> (Member of social enterprise, personal communication,
> March 9, 2016)

The interviewee suggested that their collaborative work model not only improves results within the organization but also within the respective rural region. Regardless of whether the intended regional change is realistic the evidence suggests that the social enterprise shows social responsibility for the broader (rural) society and not only for a limited group.

In social enterprises, social goals have priority over financial goals, which is reflected in a limited distribution of profits. As shown above, the Austrian social enterprise understands itself as an alternative type of economic organization in which collaborative work and societal goals replace traditional economic principles such as competition and personal benefit. As one member said, "*the issue of maximizing profit does not have any priority here. Everyone will have a good income and will even be able to earn well, but the purpose of the enterprise is not to maximize profits*" (Member of social enterprise, personal communication, March 10, 2016). The profit distribution at the social enterprise involves converting profits into paid time off that all members can use as they prefer. As one member explained in a business meeting:

> *The cooperative would not distribute profits. A surplus would only be compensated in the form of time credits. One member, for example, was very successful and earned additional money for the enterprise. As compensation, he will get four months off from work, which he is going to use for a round-the-world-trip.*
>
> (Member of social enterprise, personal communication, September 16, 2016)

The conversion of profits into paid time off prevents members from focusing solely on making money. Rather, it allows them to consider the cooperative's principle of working for a good life.

According to the statements and self-descriptions, the Austrian social enterprise is broadly consistent with the three criteria of a social mission. It limits the distribution of profits, operates with the aim of benefiting the community and not specific individuals or groups, and its roots are in a not-for-profit civil society initiative.

The Entrepreneurial Dimension

In addition to the social mission, social enterprises also have an entrepreneurial dimension. Three criteria are indicative of this dimension: (1) producing and selling products and services, (2) taking entrepreneurial risks, and (3) employing paid workers. The following section describes whether the Austrian social enterprise fulfills these criteria.

Even though the Austrian social enterprise receives public funds, it does more than implement projects and programs on the behalf of public bodies. It also develops and distributes its own products and services and seeks for funding and revenues to implement them. The income generated by the social enterprise stems from public funds that are obtained for self-developed services, and from selling products and services to customers. With respect to rural open technology labs, the social enterprise offers professional support for the establishment of new labs. For this consultancy and supervision work, it has received financial support from various funding schemes such as "Innovative Upper Austria" (Evaluation report, 2015, p. 27). In addition, it generates income from the sale of several products and services to private customers, particularly in the fields of "regional development, cooperative consultancy, advertisement and marketing, [and] film production" (Evaluation report, 2015, p. 27). It provides, for example, a holiday care program in the field of technology and natural science for the children of employees of an engineering company in Upper Austria. By doing so, it bridges the holidays of nursery schools, arouses children's interest in technology and science, and generates income from a private company.

The social enterprise's product and service portfolio is very diverse. This is because the members of the social enterprise operate as individual entrepreneurs under the umbrella of the cooperative but have different competences and expertise. The Austrian social enterprise performs entrepreneurial activities, implements delegated tasks, and executes tasks based on project work.

Another characteristic of entrepreneurial activity is the risk of failure. While entrepreneurial activities promise high gains, they can also result in a loss of time and money. An indicator for economic risk is the independent production and sale of goods and the lack of a secure source of financing. If the existence and income of an organization depend on market revenues or the successful acquisition of public funds, the risk of failure is inherent. This risk was observed in the Austrian social enterprise. During participatory observation, one of its members repeatedly complained about the unstable revenue situation and the uncertain prospects (Member of social enterprise, field note, October 11, 2016). All members of the cooperative are exposed to economic risk because each one of them is responsible for generating revenues that cover their respective salary and additional overhead costs. While risk buffers can bridge temporary shortages, permanent economic underperformance would endanger one's membership in the social enterprise. The exposure to economic risk is also illustrated by the enterprise's search for a legal entity that would allow it to better deal with risk. As one member explained:

> We had a big project with a volume of approximately €300,000 and many partners. Implementing the project on a voluntary basis appeared to be very difficult, because it involved a high level of risk and an association is not an entrepreneurial organization. For the board members of the association this was a disaster in terms of liability . . . We realized that we would need a different legal form that allows for entrepreneurial activities.
>
> (Member of social enterprise, personal communication, March 10, 2016)

The legal status of a cooperative seemed advantageous because the liability of each member would be limited to his or her contribution. However, even if the legal liability of each member is comparatively low, the members still face significant economic risk because they must generate enough revenues to cover their salaries and overhead costs.

Regarding the third criterion of the entrepreneurial dimension, social entrepreneurs can rarely base their activities exclusively on voluntary work; they require at least a minimum amount of paid work. The Austrian social enterprise is no exception. While the local associations rely on voluntary work, the members of the cooperative are employed by the cooperative and receive a monthly salary. Unlike other cooperatives, however, the members combine independent work with regular income (*"we test a model of being dependent-independent,"* Member of social enterprise, personal communication, March 9, 2016) and decide individually their levels of remuneration (Member of social enterprise, field note, March 14, 2016) by considering their needs for a good life and the revenues they are able to generate. Nevertheless, in an observed team meeting, members expressed worries about the inequality of salaries. The factor between the lowest and the highest salary is 2.7, which implies that the most successful member of the cooperative receives a salary that is 2.7 times higher than the least successful member (Field note, March 14, 2016). The members experience this disparity as a problem for the organization, and in a self-assessment regarding social impact, they rated the criterion of "fair distribution of salaries" with 30 out of 100 points, with 100 points reflecting a fair distribution and 0 points reflecting an unfair distribution (Field note, March 14, 2016).[1]

According to the self-descriptions of the Austrian social entrepreneurs, the social enterprise clearly fulfills the criteria that are indicative for the entrepreneurial dimension. It continuously develops and sells products and services, it faces the risk of failure, and it operates mostly using paid employees.

Participatory Governance

Social enterprises are also characterized by an inclusive governance structure. Three criteria are indicative of an inclusive governance: (1) a high degree of autonomy, (2) decision-making that is independent from capital ownership, and (3) stakeholders involved in decision-making. In what follows, we describe the Austrian social enterprise based on these three criteria.

The members of the social enterprise attach great importance to operating autonomously and being independent from other institutions. It was crucial for the foundation of the cooperative to create independent working structures and to allow members to realize their own visions of new work arrangements (Bergmann, 2014) (Member of social enterprise, personal communication, March 9, 2016). The aim to be independent is reflected in several characteristics of the enterprise. Shares in the cooperative are held only by individuals. Members—except for shareholders—are local associations but are not powerful external organizations. Likewise, the cooperative has an advisory board that consists of individual experts but not of representatives of powerful institutions that exert influence on the organization. The social enterprise generates income by providing goods and services to public organizations and private customers and is thus not dependent on funding institutions or a particular customer. The high relevance of autonomy and independence is also reflected in the enterprise's approach to the open technology labs. According to a social enterprise member, the idea of open technology labs resulted from the lack of open spaces in many rural communities. Access to vacant rooms is often hampered either because the owner does not support the initiative or because the use of the rooms creates an obligation that must be offset by granting a favor as well at other occasions (the member spoke of an "*accommodation bank,*" Member of social enterprise, personal communication, March 10, 2016). The open technology labs therefore intend "*to create open spaces that do not belong to existing systems and do not oblige their users to specific outcomes*" (Member of social enterprise, personal communication, October 13, 2016). The member added that "open spaces can be understood as a citizen's democratic right" (Member of social enterprise, personal communication, September 16, 2016). By claiming to establish rural open labs beyond "*existing systems*" (e.g. apart from the political or economic system), the social enterprise emphasizes that it seeks an independent position in rural communities.[2] It attaches importance to the self-determination of open labs, as it puts emphasis on its own organizational autonomy.

The main decision-making body of the Austrian social enterprise is the "coordinating circle." This name refers to sociocracy—an inclusive, harmonious, less hierarchical governance approach that has been applied by the social enterprise (Boeke, 1945; Endenburg, 1998 [1981]). As one interviewee explained:

> Sociocracy is an alternative approach, as is reflected by the term. 'Socio' refers to relations: it is about joint actions . . . 'Cracy' comes from governance, and this is how 'sociocracy' is to be understood – it means 'joint governance'.
>
> (Member of social enterprise, personal communication, March 10, 2016)

A principle of the sociocratic model is that the management is organized in circles. In the Austrian case, the 14 self-employed members of the cooperative all participate in the coordinating circle and have the right to vote. Thus, none of the self-employed members are excluded from making decisions relevant to the whole organization. Regarding the legal form and voting rights, one member said:

> The cooperative has one big strength—'one head, one vote.' Regardless of the number of shares someone holds in the cooperative, each member has only one vote.
>
> (Member of social enterprise, personal communication, March 10, 2016)

Although being a member requires the person to hold at least one share (worth about €100), the number of shares has no influence on the weight of the member's vote. Thus, decision-making is independent from capital ownership.

The third criterion for participatory governance is the participatory nature of social enterprises. This implies that fundamental decisions are not made by managers over the heads of others but that decisions involve both internal and external stakeholders (Richter, 2018). As discussed above, the Austrian social enterprise includes all employed members in decision-making. Thus, the members have voting rights and are actively involved in the process. The sociocratic approach stipulates that decisions are taken unanimously, which requires all members to agree before a decision is made. If any member has doubts, the coordinating circle cannot reach an agreement. Unlike majority decisions, unanimous decisions prevent a member from being outvoted. As one member explained:

> *Compared with majority decisions, this [form of decision-making] has another quality. In majority decisions that end six to five, for example, you have five persons who lose, and six persons who feel victorious. This is very democratic – it's a majority vote, right? However, it also leads to the feeling of being outvoted and a loser.*
>
> (Member of social enterprise, personal communication, March 10, 2016)

Unanimous decisions lead to intense discussions about a topic. Before a decision is made, each member of the coordinating circle is asked to state his or her opinion and to justify it. This is done two or three times so that the members can find the best arguments. In a field note, the authors wrote: "*It is remarkable how thoroughly and seriously the members reflect on the topic*" (Field note, October 10, 2016).

In addition to the decision-making process, the flat hierarchy shows that the members of the cooperative are on equal footing. One interviewee, who at that time was the speaker for the on-going election period, compared his position with that of his former role of CEO in a commercial enterprise:

> *This [position as CEO] was challenging at that time but it is even more challenging in a sociocratic organization where you work on equal footing. You neither have the power to delegate nor any of the traditional management tools to ask people to execute a specific task. These tools are not available. Actually, we are a group of fairly independent people. I would say that it is not possible to have a hierarchy that is flatter than the one we have.*
>
> (Member of social enterprise, personal communication, March 10, 2016)

Both the flat hierarchy and the active involvement in the decision-making process show a high degree of participation. However, participation is restricted to the members of the cooperative. Except for an informal expert advisory board, the cooperative does not have any boards or committees through which representatives from communities, authorities, or customers could be involved in the decision-making process. Thus, external stakeholders play a very limited role in the Austrian case company.

In the light of self-descriptions and own observations, we can conclude that the Austrian social enterprise fulfills many of the criteria in the participatory governance dimension. It shows a high degree of autonomy from other organizations, their decision-making is fully independent from capital ownership, and the sociocratic governance approach allows all employed members to engage in the decision-making process. However, the participatory nature of the enterprise does not extend to external stakeholders, such as local communities, authorities, and customers.

Changing Mentality: How a Polish Social Enterprise Activates and Encourages People in a Post-Transitional Rural Context

The Polish social enterprise operates in a rural region that was among the poorest at the beginning of the post-socialist transformation in Poland. This poverty was accompanied by a low level of entrepreneurial activity and low civic engagement. Since its foundation, the Polish social enterprise has fought these structural deficits as well as a mentality of inactivity and indifference, which characterizes parts of the rural communities. Steering the mentality of the people towards self-responsibility and engagement is a dominant narrative in the Polish case (which leads us to give the Polish social enterprise the pseudonym "mind changers"). This section provides a comprehensive understanding of the challenges in rural North-East Poland and the way the Polish mind changers counteract these problems. Furthermore, we shed light on the social mission, the entrepreneurial spirit, and the involvement of stakeholders in the governance of the social enterprise.

Challenges in Rural Poland

Rural regions are very important for Poland. They are home to 35 percent of the population (the EU average is 19.1 percent) and account for 54 percent of the territory (clearly exceeding the EU average of 44.1 percent; EC, 2017). The importance of rural regions is also reflected by the comparatively high relevance of the agricultural sector. 10 percent of Poland's overall workforce is employed in agriculture, which is the third largest share of employees working in agriculture after that of Romania and Greece (EC, 2017). However, the relevance of the primary sector also gives rise to concerns. In parts of the country where agriculture was organized in big state farms during communist times the post-1989 political change and economic transition led to the dismissal of around half of the workforce and resulted in high unemployment rates. In these state farms, productivity was low. At the same time, the state farms provided their workers and families all-round services from housing to medical care (although on a basic level). This led to an attitude of dependency and the phenomenon of the "state farm families". Polish scholars characterize state farm families by "learned helplessness, acceptance of relative poverty, low educational and professional aspirations for children, etc" (Rosner & Stanny, 2017, p. 89). We will later discuss the undesired legacies of the former state farms.

Challenges do not only occur in those parts of the country with large, formerly state-owned farms, but also in parts with mainly small, family-run farms. As alternative job opportunities are rare, people continue to farm their land even though the income derived from it does not allow them to live above the poverty line. According to an OECD report:

"In 2015, about 1 in 9 rural inhabitants lived in extreme poverty, compared to less than 1 of every 20 persons living in urban areas. The share of people living in extreme poverty has increased in recent years and more so in rural areas than in urban ones."

(OECD, 2018, p. 23)

Researchers agree that the dominance of small, family-run farms in Eastern and Southern Poland is the reason for low economic performance and development constraints. This is because small farms often go hand in hand with overstaffing, hidden unemployment, very low productivity, and little innovative power (EC, 2017; Rosner & Stanny, 2017). Not surprisingly, the Polish agricultural sector is the most work-intensive agricultural sector in the EU (OECD, 2018). The dominance of small farms hampers the diversification of the economy, which is important for the sustainable development of rural Poland. Despite these challenges, rural Poland's economic performance is better than one would expect in light of these analyses. Between 2000 and 2014, rural Poland experienced a GDP growth of about 61 percent, which is one of the highest growth rates among rural regions in OECD countries (OECD, 2018). It is also true, however, that this increase is distributed unevenly among rural areas.

According to Rosner and Stanny (2017), two major spatial dynamics characterize rural development in Poland. First, there is a center-periphery bias against rural areas in proximity to big cities, which perform better socio-economically than those located in the periphery. Remote rural regions are particularly hit by out-migration and the brain drain of well-educated people who think entrepreneurially. Remote places have a below-average share of young women and children and an above-average share of elderly people, leading to constant depopulation (Rosner & Stanny, 2017). Second, there is a development bias against rural regions in the western and the eastern parts of the country. While rural areas in the west of Poland perform well in terms of socio-economic development, rural areas in the east lag behind and show a more mono-functional, agriculturally dominated structure (Rosner & Stanny, 2017). This development bias is rooted in the partition of Poland and has even deepened since its transformation in 1989. Until the end of World War I, Poland was divided into a Prussian part (the north-western part of the country), a Russian part (the central and eastern part of the country), and an Austrian part (the southern part of the country). Each of these parts took a specific development path. The Prussian part, for example, was characterized by larger agricultural areas and a comparably high level of education; in the Russian part, peasants emancipated themselves from feudalistic dependence comparably late, and the area was dominated by small family farms; the Austrian part had a dense network of towns and villages as well as intensive agriculture. These different starting conditions still influence the development opportunities today, which is reflected, amongst others, by a more diversified economy in western Poland and a slower deagrarization in eastern Poland (Rosner & Stanny, 2017).

The social enterprise is located in a county at the southern edge of the Warmian-Masurian Voivodeship that consists of four municipalities with about 34,000 inhabitants. Apart from the local center (a town with about 14,000 residents) the county is widely shaped by agriculture. In the past, the county was borderland between the Prussian and Russian parts. It is a transition zone between larger farms in the north-west and smaller farming businesses in the east of the county. Until World War II, it was under German rule. After the end of the war and its integration into the Polish national state, it experienced a huge change in population. The German population fled to the west, and new settlers came, particularly from the eastern parts of Poland, which had been reassigned to the Soviet Union (Białuński & Jasiński, 2014). Today, the county faces several challenges as it is still transitioning into a more diversified economy. Although a more diversified business structure has already developed in the local center, the county's economy continues to be dominated by agriculture. The level of prosperity is lower than that of other rural regions in Poland and is reflected by an annual income below the national average and a comparatively high proportion of social welfare recipients (Rosner & Stanny, 2017). Likewise, social responsibility and civic engagement seem to be rather low based on the small number of people donating 1 percent of their income tax to non-profit organizations[3] (Rosner & Stanny, 2017). Nevertheless, the number of NGOs operating in the county is slightly above average, and the turnout of voters in local elections is comparatively high, which both indicate an active civil society. In terms of demography, the county appears to be stable based on the number of inhabitants and age structure. It faces neither a significant population loss nor a noticeably ageing population. Only the number of young women between 25 and 34 years lags behind and might impair the number of births in the near future (Rosner & Stanny, 2017).

When local people talk about their county, the mentality of the people is a commonly addressed issue. They often describe people as being passive, conservative, skeptical toward new developments, and as having an attitude of dependency. Interview statements representative of these sentiments include "*People are very conservative*" (CEO of a local bank, personal communication, February 7, 2017), "*We are afraid of new things*" (Responsible person at the local authority, personal communication, February 15, 2017), and "*People learned to be passive*" (Responsible person at the regional authority, personal communication, February 14, 2017). The lack of personal initiative might be a legacy of communist times when the region had the biggest state farm in the country. An interviewee from the local authority described this idea in detail:

> *I would also like to say that people and the society are determined by what was here before. The biggest state farm was in this county, and therefore most of the people . . . worked in the state farm . . . very simple work, work with animals or on the fields. And the state farm took care of its workers. They were brought to the doctor, etc. The state farm provided everything and that's how it limited the workers' activities.*
>
> (Responsible person at the local authority, personal communication, February 15, 2017)

As mentioned above, the workers on these state farms and their families were called "state farm families" and were characterized by a high level of passiveness and low aspirations. However, this mentality has partly changed in recent years. This change is illustrated by an increase, for example, in the number of people who leave the county to go to university ("*many people left because we have . . . a very good high school, which educates, unfortunately, for the universities*"; Responsible person at the local authority, personal communication, February 15, 2017), and in local civic engagement ("*thanks to some initiatives, people started to take matters into their own hand*"; Responsible person at the local authority, personal communication, February 15, 2017).

Considerable change has also occurred in terms of employment. While in the 1990s the county was badly hit by unemployment ("*the rate of unemployment and social exclusion was even above 50 percent*"; Responsible person at the regional authority, personal communication, February 14, 2017) and gave visitors an impression of apathy and decline ("*when I went to the county . . . it was always depressing because it felt like a dead place*"; Responsible person at the regional authority, personal communication, February 14, 2017), unemployment rates dropped considerably in the last years (*"we have experienced . . . the biggest decrease in unemployment"*; Responsible person at the local authority, personal communication, February 15, 2017). Consequently, phenomena such as pinning unpaid bills to grocery store bulletin boards have almost disappeared. As a regional development expert explained, *"Now it is better, you know, people pay"* (Regional development expert, personal communication, February 4, 2017). Still, poverty and lack of motivation have remained matters of concern and are accompanied by new challenges today. One of the main challenges is that many skilled employees migrated to Western European countries after 1989, which caused shortages in the labor market (*"Today we actually do not find any employees to do the work"*; Executive board member of the social enterprise, personal communication, February 15, 2017). The scarcity of skilled workforces and the out-migration of well-educated young people are growing challenges, but long-standing problems such as unemployment, poverty, and passivity are less severe today.

How the Social Enterprise Fights the Challenges

The Polish social enterprise has developed a holistic approach to counteract structural deficits and to improve the social and economic conditions of the county. First, it intends to foster private initiatives and to diversify the economy by providing loans and guarantees for small businesses. Second, by offering scholarships for talented pupils from disadvantaged families, it aims to overcome hurdles such as insufficient financial means for higher education and low aspirations in such families while ensuring skilled workforces for the region. Third, by operating a theme village in a remote place, it opens a new income source from tourism and contributes to cultural education. Fourth, it integrates people with low job prospects into the labor market by providing funds and trainings for social enterprise start-ups.

These multifaceted activities are driven by the goal to empower local people and to encourage them to take more responsibility for the future of the community. The founder and the current chairman of the social enterprise (addressed as "the president" in Poland) realized that motivating people was an important task when he became the first freely elected mayor of a provincial town after the fall of the iron curtain in 1990. Due to the predominance of state farms, the county lacked alternative job opportunities, skilled workers, civil engagement, and private businesses. The president of the social enterprise described this challenge in an interview:

> *We had a monoculture. There were only state farms and no private initiatives.*
>
> (President of the social enterprise, personal communication, February 20, 2017)

However, after one legislative term, he understood that the possibilities for a mayor to foster change would be limited due to a lack of resources and power associated with the position. In 1994, he left the town hall and established the social enterprise with public and private stakeholders.

The founders chose the legal form of a foundation. In its articles of association, the foundation states that its overall goal is to foster the socio-economic development of the region. While the foundation focused on economic development by providing loans and guarantees for start-ups and small and medium-sized enterprises in its early days, it started to attach greater importance to social goals in the late 1990s. In 1998, for example, it created a scholarship program for talented pupils from poor families; in 2007, the theme village was opened, and it provides work for people with little chance of finding work; and in 2012, it launched an initiative that offers start-up support for small social enterprises. Today, the foundation has about 15 employees.

The mind changers have six different fields of activity. These activities include the provision of loans and guarantees, an English teaching program, a social enterprise support center, a theme village, and a paradise garden. In addition, it also offers a scholarship program, even though this program is formally independent from the social enterprise and organized in a separate legal entity. While some of the activities are executed on behalf of the public administration and a foundation (i.e. the provision of loans and guarantees, the English teaching program, and the social enterprise support center), others have been developed by the foundation itself (i.e. the theme village, the paradise garden, and the scholarship program).

The theme village can be regarded as the most inventive initiative of the Polish mind changers. As such, it is worth a close examination. The theme village is a settlement of historic buildings, traditional workshops, gardens, and event venues. It attracts tourists and serves as a place for education through classes about traditional rural life, ecology, and sciences. The theme village employs disabled persons and other people with little chance of finding work. These employees work in catering, handicraft production, gardening, and landscape preservation. The village is located in a poor rural area and is the only organization in that location that offers work besides agriculture. In recent years, additional office buildings and an incubator for social enterprise start-ups have been added. Future plans include establishing an office for industrial design (the goal of which is to improve the innovative power of local businesses) and extending the catering service (by offering visitors daily organic meals with fresh vegetables from the theme village's garden) (President of the social enterprise, personal communication, February 20, 2017).

In 2006, the founder and current president of the social enterprise presented the idea of the theme village to local authorities, and skepticism prevailed. At that time, theme villages did not exist in Poland, and decision-makers were skeptical about the idea. The founder had to collaborate with local authorities because his desired funding scheme, which offered a highly attractive amount of one million Złoty, required public-private partnerships as a precondition for funding. Even more challenging, the funding scheme demanded the establishment of the initiative in the form of a social enterprise. A representative of the local authority remembers the confusion when the president proposed his idea for collaboration:

> *I remember when [the president] initiated a meeting. I worked in the office then. He told us that there would be a funding competition that supports four powiats [regions] in Poland. The winners would receive one million Złoty. But to get it, the local government had to cooperate locally with an NGO, setting up the initiative and running it in the form of a social enterprise. And I remember when we sat together, we couldn't understand it. The local government and an NGO should start an enterprise? It was unbelievable. But they said that it was a requirement for participating in the competition. I remember that I thought in this meeting: 'I have never built a social enterprise. I don't even know what that is.' Nobody knew anything.*
> (Responsible person at the local authority, personal communication, February 15, 2017)

The mind changers eventually convinced the local authorities to collaborate with them, emphasizing the amount of funding and future job-creation and promising to set up the proposal. The proposal was successful, and from 2007 onwards the theme village took shape. Following the successful establishment of the village, the president and other members of the working group organized a road tour in which they informed interested communities about the project. In Poland, the theme village attracted much attention. Even *"Newsweek Poland"* reported on the village and put the president and his wife on its cover. It became a role model for new theme villages arising throughout the country.

Experts from the environment of the social enterprise acknowledged the theme village for its role-model effect and impact. Representatives of a local bank recognized the country's awareness of the theme village:

> *The theme village is an investment . . . that is very famous now in Poland.*
> (CEO of a local bank, personal communication, February 7, 2017)

Furthermore, the current mayor of the provincial town welcomed the village as a flagship for marketing the municipality:

> *It's a promotion for the gmina. . . . Wherever we are in Poland, attracting investors for our town, we mention the theme village.*
> (Mayor of the provincial town, personal communication, January 24, 2017)

A policy maker from the regional government indicated his appreciation for the reliability and visible results of the village:

> *Generally, the theme village and [the social enterprise] are treated as very important initiatives in the region because they work – they are authentic, tangible.*
>
> (Responsible person at the regional authority, personal communication, February 14, 2017)

An interviewee from the labor office pointed to the role-model effect of the village:

> *It [the theme village] showed other villages here that it is possible, and moreover [it] inspired all the people dealing with crafts in homes.*
>
> (Responsible person at the local authority, personal communication, February 15, 2017)

According to this assessment, it seems the president has realized his objective of convincing people that building up one's own existence in rural places would be possible:

> *I think [the idea came] from the need to give an example to people who live in villages that even living in small villages – without attractions, without lakes, woods – that it is possible to do something that will give work, something that will work economically . . . That even if you live in small places, you are not doomed to it. Or that the only possibility for doing business would be to move to England or Ireland, but that it is possible to create an idea for yourself or for professional and social activity in the place where you live.*
>
> (President of the social enterprise, personal communication, February 20, 2017)

This statement refers to the overall goal of the Polish social enterprise, which is to encourage people to take responsibility and execute personal engagement. The mind changers aim to counteract the passivity and indifference that characterize parts of the rural community. The theme village, along with the provision of micro loans, work integration, scholarships, and English skills seminars, is a cornerstone in the holistic approach to contribute to the sustainable development, social cohesion, and well-being of the rural North-East of Poland.

The Social Mission

Social enterprises are also driven by a social mission. This is true for the Polish mind changers, as we will illustrate drawing on the dimensions of a social mission: (1) being a "collective initiative rooted in the civil society," (2) having the "aim to benefit the community," and (3) aiming at "limited profit making" (Defourny & Nyssens, 2013, pp. 45–46).

The social enterprise is rooted in a public interest initiative of local authorities and private actors who realized in 1994 that a local development agency would be needed to facilitate growth in both the private and the non-profit sectors. The legal form of a foundation aims to ensure that an organization represents the interests of everyone involved. The foundation is controlled by a council of 16 representatives from public, private, and civil society organizations. The council elects the executive board, which consists of the president and two executive officers and which is entrusted with the management of the foundation (President of the social enterprise, field note, April 1, 2017). The president is often described as the mastermind behind the social enterprise and as having a lot of influence and being charismatic and strong-minded. A member of the local authority described the president as "*a great leader*" (Responsible person at the local authority, personal communication, February 15, 2017). The council exercises control and limits the power of the executive board and the president. Projects are developed in a collaborative manner. The scholarship program, for example, emerged from a joint initiative started by the president, his wife, and a group of their friends. The theme village originated from a public-private working group consisting of the president and three other persons. The president referred to the project as "*our common child*" (President of the social enterprise, personal communication, February 20, 2017). The organization is "social" as decisions are prepared or legitimized in collective processes.

Regarding the second characteristic of the social mission, the purpose of the Polish social enterprise has always been the sustainable development of the region. This purpose clearly benefits the whole region and not just an exclusive group of people. An interviewee reflected this goal and related it to the president's former position as mayor:

> *After being the mayor, he started to work for the society he knew from the administrative side, the whole society.*
> (Responsible person at the local authority, personal communication, February 15, 2017)

In his former position as mayor, the president of the social enterprise became familiar with societal issues, which continued to guide his engagement in the social enterprise and prompted him act to the benefit of the society as a whole. In the beginning, the strategy of the social enterprise was to achieve societal goals by supporting small and medium-sized enterprises rather than by using direct social interventions. This strategy changed with the introduction of the scholarship program and the opening of the theme village, which were accompanied by a re-orientation toward the social economy:

> *[The social enterprise] was an organization for businesses – I think only for businesses. It was about business development with grants and loans. And maybe eight to ten years ago, it started to focus on the social economy [laughing] and changed the [organization] and I can say that [the social enterprise] is now the country's leader in the social economy.*
>
> (Representative of another regional development organization, personal communication, February 14, 2017)

This strategic change also led to a change of customers and target groups. Beyond business owners, the social enterprise now also addressed young students and their families, school classes, and people with bad job prospects. However, despite the foundation's social mission, the underlying idea is that everyone is the architect of his or her own fortune. Regardless of how unfavorable a situation may be, if a person is willing to do something, he or she will be able to make a good living. As the president stated:

> *I think what is important and what we do is that we are focused on long-term activities and influence – building, shaping consciousness, taking responsibility for oneself. Not giving up, but asking instead, 'What can I do?'*
>
> (President of the social enterprise, personal communication, February 20, 2017)

Besides enhancing the future prospects of talented pupils from disadvantaged families, the scholarship program also aims at keeping skilled workers in the region:

> *In our town, well-educated people were leaving, and through our program we wanted to support local businesses with well-educated personnel.*
>
> (Member of the social enterprise, personal communication, February 20, 2017)

The scholarship program provides financial support as well as courses and activities for knowledge acquisition, strengthening aspirations, and increasing consciousness for the social environment ("*we want these kids to also engage for their community*"; Member of the social enterprise, personal communication, February 20, 2017). By working with scholarship recipients and school classes in the theme village, the president of the social enterprise and his wife (who is responsible for the scholarship program) also aim to evoke a change of consciousness in the families:

There is the effect of reversed education. This implies that it is not the parents who educate their children, but rather the children who talk about what they learned at home and thereby educate their parents. For example, that engagement is important, that the environment is important etc. I always call it [the] 'effect of reversed education'.
(President of the social enterprise, personal communication, February 20, 2017)

Thus, the social enterprise aims at benefiting the community as a whole, ranging from young, talented pupils to persons of all ages who have difficulties to find work.

As to the third criterion—limited profit making—the social enterprise is a not for profit organization (NPO). Registering as an NPO requires that any surplus income must be reinvested according to the social purpose defined in the articles of association. As one member of the social enterprise explained:

If the NPO generates income from sales, it must pay attention that the income does not exceed the costs of the service . . . otherwise it must invest the surplus in its statutory activities.
(Member of the social enterprise, personal communication, February 16, 2017)

Should these rules not be followed, the exemption from value-added tax and the ability to apply for public funding would be at stake. Thus, the articles of association prevent the distribution of profits to the organization's members. This lack of direct financial incentive also prevents the aim of the organization from shifting toward profit generation.

All in all, there is no doubt that the Polish social enterprise follows a social mission, even though the president was a strong driver for starting the initiative and the strategy for fulfilling social goals is based on the idea that everyone is the architect of his or her own destiny. The overall objective is to support the development of the county as a whole by facilitating civic and professional engagement in order to make the area an attractive place to live, work, invest in, and relax.

The Entrepreneurial Dimension

The social enterprise attaches importance to an entrepreneurial, self-responsible mindset. This is true not only for its attitude toward clients but also for the mind changers themselves. As in the other sections, this discussion concerns the "production and selling of goods and service," "taking entrepreneurial risks," and "the employment of paid workers."

The mind changers provide a wide range of activities including the provision of loans and guarantees, an English teaching program, a social enterprise support center, a theme village, a paradise garden, and a scholarship program (President of the social enterprise, personal communication, April 1, 2017). Among these activities, the first three are mandated services executed on behalf of public authorities and a large foundation. The scholarship program redistributes financial resources but does not provide any products or services. Thus, the production and selling of self-developed goods and services mainly stems from the theme village and the paradise garden. The income from these two activities comprises fees from tourists and school classes for workshops and guided tours, the sale of handicraft products and food in the tavern, fees for events and markets, revenues from consulting, and revenues from companies that use activities in the theme village as part of their corporate social responsibility strategies. According to the president of the social enterprise:

> *The companies come here to revitalize their social sensitivity. So, for instance, the president of a big, well-performing company comes and plants trees or removes weed together with unemployed persons.*
> (President of the social enterprise, personal communication, February 20, 2017)

Sales of goods and services account for 20 percent of the social enterprise's income, whereas funds (which finance the execution of mandated tasks) account for 75 percent and donations account for 5 percent. However, one of the future goals of the social enterprise is to generate more revenues from sales and to gain more independence from funding. Even though the overall share of sales is rather low, the social enterprise engages in the production and selling of goods and services and therefore clearly meets the respective criterion.

The second criterion of taking entrepreneurial risks means, among other things, to seek new opportunities that imply risks instead of sticking to well-known activities. The president of the social enterprise fully represents this entrepreneurial, risk-taking spirit, which is evident from his decision to leave public administration to take a position in the widely unknown and risky area of NPOs 25 years ago. According to a member of the local authorities:

> *[The president] went into a field where everything and nothing was allowed. It always depended on how you looked at it. He made the decision 25 years ago, and not all similar organizations have done well, and not all social enterprises in Poland have been successful. NPOs are completely different from public authorities.*
> (Responsible person at the local authority, personal communication, February 15, 2017)

The president is always searching for new opportunities. The success of the social enterprise, according to the president:

Our success is that we do absolutely non-standard activities.
(President of the social enterprise, personal communication,
February 20, 2017)

One of these non-standard activities is the theme village. After setting it up with EU funds, the village now operates mostly without public funding. The president regards the realization of the theme village as a tremendous success for the social enterprise:

I think the biggest achievement is that the [theme village] operates without any external funding. It doesn't receive any subsidies, it is self-sustainable.
(President of the social enterprise, personal communication,
February 20, 2017)

To run the theme village without external funding also implies that the theme village faces the risk of failure. It could fail, for example, if it does not attract enough visitors.

The company's non-standard activities, such as the theme village and the paradise garden, bear risks but so do the mandated services. Mandated services are put out to tender at regular intervals. If the mind changers were no longer mandated or if funding schemes were terminated, the loss of income could have severe consequences. The worst-case scenario would require the liquidation of the enterprise. Other sources of risk are external factors, such as political decisions, that can endanger non-standard activities as well as the execution of mandated services. A newly implemented allowance for children, for example, turned out to have negative consequences for the social enterprise support center. By running the support center, the social enterprise committed itself to help several unemployed people complete a start-up program and establish their own social enterprises. However, after the child allowance was introduced, the start-up program seemed to lose its attractiveness, as participants began to withdraw from the program:

We had a group of people who wanted to start social cooperatives. When the child allowance '500 Plus' started, they [the participants] figured out that it was not profitable for them to work because they had kids. They would have a higher income from '500 Plus' and so they resigned. The allowance had a very big influence on this decision.
(Staff member of the social enterprise, personal
communication, February 20, 2017)

Although it had positive effects on the household incomes of families, the political decision to introduce an attractive child allowance undermined the aim of motivating people. A member of the executive board put it more dramatically:

The whole economic sense lays in ruins.
(Executive board member of the social enterprise, personal communication, February 20, 2017)

Consequently, the continuation of the start-up program was at risk. Since the social enterprise was evaluated based on the number of created workplaces for unemployed people, the decrease in the number of participants made it difficult for the social enterprise to meet this requirement and increased the probability of losing an important source of income. The risk of losing a considerable source of income implies that the mind changers face entrepreneurial risks because their "financial viability depends on the efforts of their members and workers to secure adequate resources" (Defourny & Nyssens, 2013, p. 45).

Regarding the third criterion, the proper execution of both the mandated and the sales-related tasks requires several well-trained employees. The Polish company employs its staff members as paid employees. The wages are comparatively low and correspond to the minimum wage in Poland. The wages in this part of Poland are generally low. However, at least for some members the low wages are a source of dissatisfaction, which ultimately has motivated staff members to leave the organization (Staff member of the social enterprise, personal communication, February 20, 2017). The president justifies this wage level by pointing out the idealism that a lot of the employees have, often because they themselves have been beneficiaries of the scholarship program:

Look at our scholarship holders who work in the social enterprise . . . for little money: [Female employee 1] works in our organization, not in a big company. [Female employee 2], [female employee 3] and all of them . . . they are all completely different persons who have a different view of the world and different values.
(President of the social enterprise, personal communication, February 20, 2017)

In addition to the paid employees, the social enterprise also relies on voluntary work, which is mainly provided by current scholarship holders at specific events, such as charity balls (Staff member of the social enterprise, personal communication, February 20, 2017).

Paying employees, taking considerable operational risks, and producing and selling goods and services—all designate the mind changers as a social enterprise with distinct entrepreneurial elements. In particular, the search for greater sales income and a reduced dependency from funding schemes clearly shows an entrepreneurial mindset.

Participatory Governance

The third pillar of social enterprises is a participatory governance structure that respects the interests of internal and external stakeholders. To what extent the Polish social enterprise meets this requirement will be explored using three criteria: (1) "high degree of autonomy," (2) "decision making independent from capital ownership," and (3) "involvement of stakeholders in decision making."

The legal status of a foundation characterizes the Polish social enterprise as an independent organization that is not fully autonomous in its decisions. The social enterprise is accountable to its council, which represents 16 different stakeholders from public, private, and civil society organizations (President of the social enterprise, field notes, April 1, 2016). The council controls, consults, and even suggests activities but does not assign specific tasks to the social enterprise. The autonomy of the social enterprise is further limited by the aims and fields of activities defined in its articles of association. However, the articles list a broad range of more than 40 eligible operational fields, which gives the social enterprise a lot of freedom (Polish Social Enterprise, n.d., §38). Even if a field of activities is not listed (as was the case with activities in tourism), the executive board can make a request to the council. In turn, the council can change the articles of association if the new activity is in accordance with the social enterprise's overall objectives. With regard to management tasks, the executive board has considerable room for maneuver. The executive board and its president represent the social enterprise to the outside world, manage its finances, decide the level of wages, are entitled to change the organizational structure, appoint and dismiss employees, and develop strategic action plans (Polish Social Enterprise, n.d., §33). Even the liquidation of the enterprise is partly in the hands of the executive board. Although the final decision would be made by the council, it is the responsibility of the executive board to prepare the liquidation and to terminate all activities (Polish Social Enterprise, n.d., §33). If the formal limitations of the executive board are low, its practical limitations are even lower because of the authority of the president, his expertise, and the trust that others place in him (*"he is trustworthy and generally well-liked"*; Responsible person at the local authority, personal communication, February 15, 2017). All in all, the social enterprise has a high degree of autonomy that is hardly restricted by its articles of association or the supervisory function of the council.

The second criterion—democratic governance—is characterized by an equal decision-making power for all persons involved, irrespective of their financial contributions to the organization. In the Polish social enterprise, the providers of capital as well as the donators are represented in the council. Besides these two types of financial contributors, persons with high ethical and professional authority can also be appointed to the council (Polish Social Enterprise, n.d., §19). Each member of the council has one vote that is independent of that person's amount of financial contribution. Decisions are made with majority vote and require that at least half of the council members are voting (Polish Social Enterprise, n.d., §24). The three members of the executive board have no financial stake in the organization. Thus, decision-making does not depend on financial contributions or capital ownership in the organization.

Participatory governance also concerns the involvement of different stakeholders in decision-making; a stakeholder is "anyone who effects or is affected by [a] company's activities" (Colenbrander et al., 2017, p. 547). Stakeholders are people from within the organization (besides the managers also employees or members) as well as people or institutions from the environment of the organization (such as local communities, authorities, business partners, and customers; Richter, 2018). Regarding the Polish mind changers, the council comprises a wide range of external stakeholders, including representatives from the municipality, the county, and the region, as well as persons from public organizations, NGOs, and private businesses operating on the local, regional, and national level. As council members, they make fundamental decisions, such as decisions regarding the appointment and the wage level of the three executive board members. Moreover, they assess the work and the strategic plans of the executive board against the background of the overall objectives of the organization. The three positions on the executive board are held by a representative of the external stakeholders (currently the manager of a local cooperative), a representative of the staff members (internal stakeholders), and the president. The votes in the executive board are weighted. While the president has 50 percent of the voting power, the two other board members have 25 percent each. Thus, the president has more power but cannot overrule the other two board members. Decisions require agreement from the executive board, which aims at preventing autocratic decision-making. However, the actual decision-making power of the president is considerably higher than the power formally granted to him. The president puts topics on the agenda, generates new ideas, and develops strategic plans, whereas neither the other executive board members nor the employees have any ambitions to produce their own ideas or to exert influence. As an executive board member explained:

> *The president has the fantasy, we simply accept that. Only the sky is the limit. He has an idea, we put it into practice . . . He gives us jobs, he gives us salaries. What else should we want?*
> (Executive board member of the social enterprise, personal communication, January 23, 2017)

Unlike the decision-making process within the social enterprise, the relationship between the president and external stakeholders appears to be more collaborative. In the preparatory meeting for the theme village, for example, ideas from the president but also from other group members were realized. For instance, the members took a stance regarding the legal status of the organization, and they *"managed to persuade the president that it will not be a cooperative"* (Representative of the local business community, personal communication, January 25, 2017). However, the president can be very persuasive and can get his way with external stakeholders. A representative of a local authority described the president's persuasive power as if stakeholders follow him without any opposition:

> *He has always found people that follow him and everyone has fulfilled their role properly.*
> (Responsible person at the local authority, personal communication, February 15, 2017)

The president's power is based on his charisma, far-reaching experience and network, visions, and resoluteness. He can be regarded as a charismatic leader. While the Polish social enterprise formally relies on democratic principles, the actual decision-making practice is characterized by a more authoritarian style at the expense of equal involvement for all stakeholders.

Regarding participatory governance, the Polish mind changers show a mixed picture. On the one hand, they operate very autonomously and independently from capital ownership, thus fulfilling the requirements for a self-determined, inclusive governance. On the other hand, the social enterprise is characterized by the president's strong leadership and the low desires of particularly internal stakeholders to take responsibility. Hence, participatory governance is mainly bound to formal arrangements while the decision-making power is concentrated in the hands of the president.

After the rich description of the four cases from the perspective of an insider, in the next chapter we will switch to an analytical perspective. While we will build the analysis on a common theoretical ground, we will again analyze each of the cases separately.

Notes

1 The self-assessment was based on the "economy for the common good" approach and a so-called "common good matrix," which is a set of indicators that assess enterprises according to the criteria of "human dignity," "solidarity and social justice," "environmental sustainability," and "transparency and co-determination" (www.ecogood.org/en/common-good-balance-sheet/common-good-matrix/, August 1, 2018).

2 The demarcation from commercial and political fields and the aspired independence is further underlined in the charter of the social enterprise, which states: "Our openness is limited where self-interest and ideological interests gain the upper hand" (Austrian Social Enterprise, n.d.).

3 In Poland, taxpayers can indicate a non-profit organization of their choice to receive one percent of their income tax. The "1 percent option" aims at supporting the development of the NGO sector and encouraging citizens to contribute to solving social problems by financing respective organizations (EC, 2016). The use of the 1 percent option is regarded to be an indicator for social responsibility and civic engagement.

References

Austrian Social Enterprise. (2015). Evaluation report (translated by the authors).
Austrian Social Enterprise. (n.d.). Charter (translated by the authors).
Bergmann, F. (1977). *On Being Free.* Notre Dame, IN: University of Notre Dame Press.
Bergmann, F. (2014). *Starting with New Work: Creating a New Culture.* (n.p.): Author.
Bergmann, F. (2017). *Neue Arbeit, Neue Kultur.* Freiburg im Breisgau: Arbor Verlag.
Białuński, G. and Jasiński, G. (2014). *A Brief History of Warmia and Mazury.* Olsztyn: Oficyna Retman.
Boeke, K. (1945). *Sociocracy: Democracy as It Might Be.* Retrieved from http://worldteacher.faithweb.com/sociocracy.htm.
Central Statistics Office. (2016). *Statistical Yearbook of Ireland 2016.* Cork: Central Statistics Office.
Colenbrander, A., Argyrou, A., Lambooy, T. and Blomme, R. J. (2017). Inclusive governance in social enterprises in the Netherlands—a case study. *Annals of Public and Cooperative Economics, 88*(4), 543–566.
Defourny, J. and Nyssens, M. (2013). Social innovation, social economy and social enterprise: What can the European debate tell us? In F. Moulaert, D. MacCallum, A. Mehmood, and A. Hamdouch (Eds.): *The International Handbook on Social Innovation* (40–52). Cheltenham, UK: Edward Elgar.
Endenburg, G. (1998/1981). *Sociocracy: The Organization of Decision-Making.* Delft: Eburon.
European Commission (EC). (2016). *Social Enterprises and Their Eco-Systems: A European Mapping Report*, Updated country report: Poland. Brussels: Directorate-General for Employment, Social Affairs and Inclusion.
European Commission (EC). (2017). *CAP Context Indicators 2014–2020, Update 2017.* Brussels: European Commission (EC).
OECD. (2001). *Local Economic and Employment Development (LEED) Best Practices in Local Development.* Paris: OECD Publishing.
OECD. (2018). *OECD Rural Policy Reviews: Poland 2018.* Paris: OECD Publishing. DOI: 10.1787/9789264289925-en
O'Hara, P. and O'Shaughnessy, M. (2015). *[Midwest] Country Story 1989–2015. The [Irish Social Enterprise] Model of Community Based Local Development.* Limerik: University of Limerik.
Österreichische Raumordnungskonferenz (ÖROK). (2015). *14. Raumordnungsbericht. Analysen und Berichte zur räumlichen Entwicklung Österreichs 2012–2014 [14. Regional Planning Report. Analysis and Reports of the Regional Development in Austria 2012–2014].* Wien: Österreichische Raumordnungskonferenz (ÖROK).
Polish Social Enterprise. (n.d.). *Statute of the Social Enterprise.*

Richter, R. (2018). The Janus face of participatory governance: How inclusive governance benefits and limits the social innovativeness of social enterprises. *Journal of Entrepreneurial and Organizational Diversity*, 7(1), 61–87.

Rosner, A. and Stanny, M. (2017). *Socio-Economic Development of Rural Areas in Poland*. Warsaw: Institute of Rural and Agricultural Development in the Polish Academy of Sciences. Retrieved from http://admin.www.irwirpan.waw.pl/dir_upload/site/files/Lukasz/MROW_en_2017.pdf

2 How Rural Social Enterprises Innovate and Sustain

Potentials and Challenges From the Research Perspective

In this chapter, we first develop a multilevel network model that integrates and extends the frameworks recently put forth by Lang and Fink (2018) and Richter (2017). The second subchapter is devoted to the research methods and data collection. We provide an overview of (1) the methodology and research design, (2) the selection of cases, (3) the applied methods, and (4) data processing and analytical methods. Subsequently, we present the four single case analyses explaining how the social enterprises mobilize the resources and reconfigure them to make a change.

The Analytical Framework

To carve out the specific role of social enterprises as change agents in structurally weak rural regions, we set out to develop a multilevel network model. In this model, we integrate different literature streams and condense their key insights to conceptualize the role of enterprises in the multilevel network arena of rural contexts. We specifically draw on a social capital approach (Putnam et al., 1994) that provides an interesting analytical perspective from which to study the embeddedness of social enterprises in the rural context (Granovetter, 1985; Johnstone & Lionais, 2004; Welter, 2011; Lang & Roessl, 2011; Kibler et al., 2015). Even though an established definition of social capital does not exist, scholars agree that on a generic level, the notion of social capital broadly refers to resources embedded in networks that can be mobilized through social interactions that lead to potential benefits for both individual and collective actors (Brunie, 2009). However, it is important to know that privileged access to resources, besides having an enabling effect, can also have negative effects, such as "nepotism, corruption, and suppression" (Szreter & Woolcock, 2004, p. 655).

Previous studies suggest that rural communities are places with supposedly high levels of social capital and traditions of collective problem solving, which make them the ideal context for social enterprises (Jack & Anderson, 2002; Zografos, 2007; Farmer et al., 2008; Munoz et al., 2015). However, the actual forms and levels of social capital might differ among specific rural places (Breitenecker & Harms, 2010). In this framework, *place* refers to a sociological understanding of location that highlights community, social networks, and the cultural identities of individuals and collective actors (Harvey, 1996; Hudson, 2001). Generally, the measurement of social capital is not without problems. These problems relate to the challenge of conceptualizing components and outcomes of social capital and assigning them to either the collective or individual level (Portes, 1998). Consequently, little research explores how social enterprises deal with the complex interplay of different forms of social capital when developing their business models.

So far, social networks and related resource exchanges involving rural social enterprises have mostly been discussed as horizontal connections— an approach that implicitly assumes that actors have equal social status and power in terms of the ability to mobilize resources (Putnam et al., 1994; Ferlander, 2007). We propose that to fully understand the role of the rural social enterprises, it is necessary to also consider the resource exchanges in vertical networks, that is "across power differentials" (Szreter & Woolcock, 2004, p. 655). By accounting for resource exchanges in horizontal and vertical networks simultaneously, the interplay between structure and agency can be better understood (Giddens, 1984; Steinerowski & Steinerowska-Streb, 2012). We argue that in contrast to other disciplines, the vertical form of social capital has not yet received appropriate attention in the entrepreneurship literature. Building on recent multilevel conceptualizations in geography and planning (Lang & Novy, 2014; Agger & Jensen, 2015; Braunholtz-Speight, 2015), we theorize that rural social enterprises represent intermediate actors in the network hierarchy who can establish links between communities and holders of critical resources on different levels of the institutional environment. Thus, we focus our framework on three levels of the network hierarchy: regime, intermediary, and community.

The *community level* represents the bottom level in the network hierarchy. In our conceptual framework, a community refers to a social group whose members share a specific interest that often happens to be place-based. Examples of communities are groups of individuals who voluntarily engage in a cultural initiative or have a joint concern for elderly care or job creation. Additional examples are farmers who join a cooperative to develop new crops and parents who engage in an initiative for a new playground in the village center. *Bonding social capital* is an attribute of homogeneous networks of members who share the same interest. Such bonding ties differ in strength. Bonding social capital can provide instrumental support for its members. At the same time, however, networks based on bonding ties tend to be inward-looking due to the existence of social norms (Granovetter, 1973; Ferlander, 2007; Poortinga, 2012). This may constrain behavior and the flow of information. We assume that there is only a limited pool of resources available in any given community, which limits the possibility that the community members will reach their common goals. Therefore, they might reach out to people outside their community who can provide them with access to new information and resources.

The top level in the network hierarchy is the *regime level* (Geels, 2002, 2004). The hierarchical positioning of regime-level actors compared to community level actors comes down to differences in "explicit, formal, or institutionalised power or authority" (Szreter & Woolcock, 2004, p. 655). This translates into the possession of resources by regime-level actors that are critical for community purposes. Regime-level actors comprise, for example, supra-national organizations such as the OECD, national governments, universities, trade unions, international associations such as Ashoka, and larger corporations. The respective composition of regime-level actors, of course, is contextually dependent upon country. Regimes are usually slow to change, which leads to path dependency and vendor lock-in, but they can be dislodged and ultimately replaced through disruptive innovation practices from the cumulative impact of several rural social entrepreneurs and their ventures (Lang & Fink, 2018).

Between the regime level and the community level there is the *intermediary level*. Actors at this level can mobilize resources on the other two levels. They are also able to broker resource exchange vertically between community- and regime-level actors. The intermediary level accommodates actors such as social enterprises, municipalities, and regional development agencies. However, we argue that it is the simultaneous horizontal and vertical networking activity of social enterprises that makes them particularly relevant for innovation and development in rural settings.

Empirical evidence shows that social enterprises often learn about specific community needs through regular networking activities in rural areas in which they are directly approached by community members (Fink et al., 2017). Social enterprises eventually establish the link downwards to the respective community and develop a business model that addresses its specific interests. Although the existing bonding social capital of the community can be mobilized for this purpose, their business idea might require the rural social enterprises to reach out to other communities too. This can be useful to tap complementary resources such as volunteer support and donations (Hatak et al., 2016) but also to combine the interests of different communities, such as entrepreneurship education for students and seniors or entrepreneurship education and IT training. On a conceptual level, social enterprises thus stimulate *bridging social capital*, which is based on horizontal connections (of different strengths) between people who have diverse interests and perhaps also diverse sociodemographic backgrounds and social identities. Like bonding capital, the network members ultimately benefit from bridging capital because they potentially gain access to instrumental support (Granovetter, 1973; Ferlander, 2007; Poortinga, 2012). However, by bringing together groups that have not had previous relationships with each other, social entrepreneurs are especially dependent on the community members being open to new approaches (Brennan et al., 2009).

Furthermore, social enterprises are also intermediary actors in building *linking social capital*, which is the vertical form of social capital that spans across the different levels of the network hierarchy. Like horizontal bridging capital, linking capital also "cuts across different groups" (Ferlander, 2007, p. 119), but it refers to relationships of different strengths between actors who interact across power differentials (Szreter & Woolcock, 2004). Social enterprises enable linking capital between the community and regime levels. As change agents in rural settings, they rely on powerful institutional resources, and thus regularly develop network contacts with regime-level actors (Hulgard & Spear, 2006; Lehner, 2011). Furthermore, institutions on the regime level shape social enterprises' ecosystems and are therefore highly relevant for the daily practices of rural social enterprises. Due to their potential access to and mobilization of regime-level resources, social enterprises can leverage the positive effects of bridging and bonding capital embedded in the networks on the community level. Regime-level resources that are critical for communities can include funding, land and infrastructure access, accountability, consultancy, and technical support. Such resources need to be mobilized on the regime level to effectively address an issue that drives members of a community, such as the need for a community hall or a playground.

In line with Osborne et al. (2016), we argue that only a combined perspective of bonding, bridging, and linking social capital can deliver a comprehensive picture of the multilevel network configurations involved in rural social entrepreneurship that helps explain the specific role of social enterprises as being drivers of innovation and change. Linking social capital triggers the simultaneous emergence of bridging and bonding social capital, but it also limits the autonomy of the community-level actors. Vertical linkages can be a way of facilitating the establishment of bonding and bridging capital because it involves powerful actors from higher levels of the institutional hierarchy. On the one hand, linking capital helps connect community members with shared interests and establish stable organizational structures for the social enterprise. A group of people who, for example, are concerned with helping young jobseekers find employment might establish a small business that operates a job club with the support of government funding. These organizational structures often do not emerge without external guidance and resources from higher-level actors. At the same time, relationships between community members with disparate interests cannot easily be established without the facilitation of social enterprises and the resources of regime-level actors. On the other hand, accepting support from the more powerful regime level actors implies a loss of autonomy for the community because it becomes dependent on the resources of the regime level. This situation implies that the regime-level actors can both empower and disempower communities at any time in the process, endangering the sustainable development of the initiative. Considering these arguments, social entrepreneurs can stabilize vertical links between the community level and the regime level.

According to our framework, the specific role of rural social enterprises stems from their horizontal and vertical networking, which enables them to be instrumental to the objectives of actors on both the regime and the community level. Rural social enterprises leverage community-level resources through their vertical access up to the regime level. At the same time, they leverage regime-level resources through their vertical access down to community-level actors. However, social enterprises are only successful in mobilizing resources on both levels if they can teach resource holders on the regime level to trust their promises, even if keeping these promises is contingent upon the community-level actors' trust in them and vice-versa. To be trusted, social enterprises need to be perceived as legitimate actors. In our analytical model, social legitimacy refers to the perceived degree to which actors from different levels of the network hierarchy socially approve and desire the development of social enterprises in a specific place (Kibler et al., 2014, 2015; Bitektine & Haack, 2015). Social enterprises are confronted with network actors' diverse expectations and thus differing degrees of social legitimacy (Giuliani, 2003; Kibler et al., 2014).

Previous research suggests that social legitimacy within the network is related to the degree and nature of the social entrepreneur's attachment to the place, that is, how much the social entrepreneur cares about the community within which the venturing activity is embedded (Lang et al., 2014). Like Kibler et al. (2015), we distinguish between emotional and instrumental place attachment. *Emotional place attachment* refers to the rural social entrepreneur's feelings about and affective bond with a place. *Instrumental place attachment* refers to the rural social entrepreneur's closeness to a place based on an evaluation of how the place enables the venture to achieve its aims and to realize its desired activities. To gain social legitimacy and thus to mobilize network resources, social entrepreneurs need to highlight both emotional and instrumental attachment in their business model and thus provide a value proposition of the venture to the actors on all levels of the network hierarchy. Signaling place attachment to different communities provides social entrepreneurs with access to embedded resources because community members perceive the social entrepreneur as a legitimate actor (Kibler & Kautonen, 2016).

However, the community members need to be open to the activities of social enterprises in order to positively read the signals and to provide the necessary resources (Thuesen & Rasmussen, 2015). The ability to mobilize horizontal bonding and bridging social capital on the community level helps social enterprises directly and plausibly articulate place attachment to regime-level actors. When they credibly position themselves as advocates of the local rural community, rural social enterprises acquire legitimacy from the regime level and encourage its actors to feed resources downwards to the horizontal networks on the intermediate and community levels. By focusing their business model of (social) innovation on the community level, rural social enterprises become attractive network partners for powerful stakeholders on the regime level. These stakeholders are driven by the goal of contributing their resources to have a positive impact on a more general level, such as social and economic development, by creating jobs or strengthening social cohesion.

Thus, to be successful change agents, social enterprises need business models that communicate the right mix of emotional and instrumental place attachment to each network partner in order to mobilize different types of social capital throughout the network hierarchy. The actual innovativeness of social enterprises depends on their ability to strategically re-combine and leverage place-based resources in the business model. As Schumpeterian entrepreneurs, whose key function is the innovative re-configuration of existing resources in a business model, rural social enterprises address both the interests of the local rural community and the interests of regime-level actors. Through the participative process of developing and implementing the innovation with the network partners, the social enterprises also induce social innovation (Bock, 2012, 2016), because the activities and their effects have the potential to change relationships and perceptions within the community and to counteract social challenges.

By cutting across the levels of the network hierarchy, social enterprises solve the dilemma of a simultaneous action problem (Granovetter, 1973; Obstfeld, 2005) and idea problem (Burt, 2004; Obstfeld, 2005). They tap the resource power of regime-level actors to address the idea problem on the community level—the difficulty of developing novel solutions that address the interests of the communities due to the similarity and redundancy of information and knowledge in cohesive groups (Granovetter, 1973)—and their lack of power. Simultaneously, social enterprises tap the action power of communities to address the action problem of regime-level actors, which is the difficulty of regime-level actors to implement ideas and strategies due to a lack of familiarity with the places and limited access to groups that can implement ideas on-site (Richter, 2017). Both regime-level actors and interest groups form a relationship based on mutual dependence: the regime-level actors require communities for the implementation of ideas and for assuring their own legitimacy, while communities require regime-level actors because the latter control resources (ideas, funds, power) that are crucial for them. Figure 2.1 displays the analytical framework that provides the backbone of the analysis of the four cases. The mutual dependence of both regime-level actors and interest groups is symbolized by the bold top-down and bottom-up arrows.

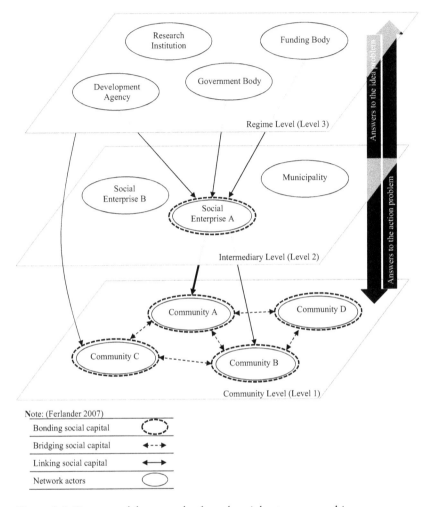

Figure 2.1 Conceptual framework of rural social entrepreneurship

Research Methods and Data

Empirical research is fundamental to this work. It paves the way for new knowledge about how rural social enterprises develop novel solutions, how they facilitate social innovation and change, and how they act as intermediaries between different institutional levels and spatial scales. When we started the data collection, there was no generally accepted theory of rural social enterprises. Thus, we needed a research design that allows for an explorative approach and for the collection of diverse and rich data, including information about practices and beliefs, intentions and representations, norms and values, and statutes and laws. This data was collected through participant observation, research conversations (narratives, semi-structured interviews, and expert interviews), and document analysis. Against this backdrop, we decided to implement *comparative qualitative case studies* (Eisenhardt, 1989) of rural social enterprises in four European countries: Austria, Ireland, Greece, and Poland. Along the lines of the research process and its main methodological decisions, this section will provide an overview of (1) the methodology and research design, (2) the selection of cases, (3) applied methods, and (4) data processing and analytical methods.

Methodology

This work follows the paradigms of qualitative empirical research. The decision for a qualitative research design is a consequence, first, of the search for factual knowledge about a subject with a growing body of knowledge but little theoretical agreement among scholars (e.g. Mair & Marti, 2006; Martin & Osberg, 2007; Bacq & Janssen, 2011; Doherty et al., 2014). Collecting explicit knowledge helps to explore the field and to reconstruct the functioning of the organizations and their institutional framework conditions. It serves to clarify "what" questions. In this context, data collection is an open, barely standardized, process-oriented undertaking. Second, qualitative methods are beneficial for answering "how" questions and for understanding the subjective meaning of others (Przyborski & Wohlrab-Sahr, 2010). Qualitative research requires empirical material that can be used to disclose patterns of meanings and beliefs, and norms and values. This interpretative work requires data that has been generated in forms of dialogical communication such as semi-structured qualitative interviews (Flick et al., 2008). Apart from these forms of explicit and implicit knowledge, information about actual practices is of great interest, such as how social entrepreneurs interact with other network partners. An appropriate way to gain insight into these practices is participatory observation. Compared to reported practices (such as those captured through interviews), participatory observations provide more direct and unbiased access to practices because direct observations are less vulnerable to incorrect memory recall and social desirability bias. They enable researchers to observe practices in authentic situations and to overcome barriers that often exist between researchers and actors in the investigated field. This is particularly true if participatory observations are part of ethnographic fieldwork. By executing long-term explorations on-site in formerly unknown fields and cultural environments, researchers can gain a more comprehensive understanding of the investigated phenomenon than would be possible with more selective and distant methods. Moreover, ethnographic fieldwork grants researchers more familiarity with the field, which makes it more likely to arrange interviews with relevant interview partners and to access documents otherwise rarely available. For these reasons we have *combined the qualitative approach with ethnographic fieldwork*. We triangulate the insights with findings from the analysis of documents. The analyzed documents were internal to the organizations (e.g. minutes of board meetings and governmental evaluation reports) as well as published (e.g. annual reports, legal decisions, and marketing materials).

Applying different methods—qualitative interviews, participatory observations, and document analyses—refers to the *mixed-methods design* of the present research. Using different methods means collecting data of different ontological status and from varying empirical premises. This improves both the empirical knowledge base and the validity of the data. The triangulation of different types of data helps researchers to fully understand a phenomenon. This became evident, for example, in the investigation of the opportunities and limits of social service markets for rural social enterprises. The analyses of documents such as laws, public funding schemes, and tender documents provide first insights into the market of social services in which many rural social enterprises operate (e.g. in the field of labor market integration). Adding information from the qualitative interviews with social entrepreneurs clarifies whether and in which way the social enterprise operates in its respective field (e.g. whether it offers courses for enhancing the employability of unemployed people). Participatory observations of team meetings give insights into occurring problems (e.g. the fact that public allowances hardly cover the expenses necessary for the implementation of work integration courses). This example demonstrates that the applied mixed-methods approach provides complementary information. Only the triangulation of data from document analyses, qualitative interviews, and participatory observations enables the researcher to fully understand the role of social service markets for rural social enterprises.

An important methodological decision was the comparative investigation of four case studies rather than focusing on a single case. Implementing cross-case comparisons has several advantages (Sayer, 1992; Yin, 2009). We expect that exploring different cases enhances the knowledge base of the phenomenon and makes it ascertainable in more detail. While on the national level, comparisons prevent methodological nationalism (Wimmer & Glick-Schiller, 2002), on the level of the phenomenon, comparisons of different cases prevent rushed generalizations based on only one observation. Cross-case analyses serve to identify commonalities and differences between cases. Common characteristics of different cases are a prerequisite to abstract from the single case and to develop assumptions about the phenomenon as a type. If all investigated rural social enterprises, for example, had the involvement of volunteers who support the enterprise with non-paid work in common, it could be assumed that rural social enterprises generally tend to make use of volunteer work.

If, on the contrary, a case had little in common with other cases in a specific aspect, this might indicate that specific framework conditions have paved the way to the observed peculiarity. Thus, reconstructing the meaning of a specific case against the background of other cases in its concrete institutional and territorial context and historical trajectory may be an insightful undertaking (Yin, 2009). Moreover, the analyses of four cases can provide first indications of relationship patterns between different characteristics. If two characteristics always appear together but not together with other characteristics, this points to a possible relation which could be further explored for causal effects between the two characteristics (Eisenhardt & Graebner, 2007). As such, cross-case analyses can serve as a causal analysis methodology that "produces limited generalizations concerning the causes of theoretically defined categories of empirical phenomena . . . common to a set of cases" (Ragin, 1989, p. 35).

The qualitative ethnographic investigation of rural social enterprises in four European countries has been made possible by financial means of the EU. This research project has received funding from the Horizon 2020 Marie Skłodowska-Curie RISE program, which finances the long-term, cross-sectoral exchange of researchers and practitioners. For the researchers of the involved research institutes—Leibniz Institute for Research on Society and Space in Germany and the Institute of Innovation Management at Johannes Kepler University Linz in Austria—the funding scheme provided ideal conditions for the execution of the fieldwork. The fieldwork began in each of the four cases with a two-week exploratory stay. This stay enabled the researchers to become familiar with the environment, to establish initial contacts with relevant actors, and to develop a data collection strategy and research tools. Several months later, a six-week research stay followed in each of the places. This was the main phase for doing ethnographic fieldwork, conducting interviews, and collecting relevant documents. All in all, the research project was carried out between February 2016 and March 2018.

Case Selection

Each case comprises a social enterprise and the surrounding rural region. Four criteria guided the case selection. First, we identified social enterprises according to the definitions of Dees (1998/2001) and Defourny and Nyssens (2013), according to which social enterprises are organizations that combine independent entrepreneurial action with strong social goals and principles of participatory governance. Moreover, the selected social enterprises should regard and present themselves as social enterprises and not merely as commercial companies or charity organizations. We selected only social enterprises whose operational base was situated in a rural region. For the identification of rural regions, we applied the regional typology of the EU, according to which a predominantly rural area is characterized by a low population density and the absence of an urban center (European Commission, 2013). Second, we ensured that the selected enterprises and rural regions were located in different parts of the EU to prevent national and geographical bias and to ensure that the sample represents social enterprise approaches and framework conditions from different parts of the continent. The focus on Europe, however, helps to ensure a basic comparability between the cases. Among other things, European social enterprises share a certain political awareness evoked by the social business policy of the EU (European Commission, 2011, 2015). Third, we selected rural regions that face structural deficits relative to the national average, such as high out-migration and low in-migration, above-average unemployment and poverty rates, and a low level of educational degrees and qualifications. These structural deficits should, fourth, be addressed by the enterprises. We thus looked for social enterprises whose social mission is, at least partly, to counteract the social challenges that result from structural deficits in their respective rural regions. In our case studies, the social enterprises counteract the lack of talented people and open space in rural communities (Austria), the low provision of public services and low degrees of qualifications (Ireland), the precarious economic and social conditions of small family farms (Greece), and limited civic and economic engagement and long-term unemployment (Poland).

The basis for cross-case comparisons is to keep the four criteria described above constant. If some characteristics are kept constant and other aspects vary systematically, assumptions about patterns of relations can be developed (Tilly, 1984). Following our requirements, the introduced four rural social enterprises agreed to join the research project. They are in Mid-West Ireland, North-East Poland, Upper Austria, and Central Greece, thus representing rural regions in different parts of Europe (see Figure 2.2).

Applied Methods

The applied mixed-methods design encompasses three main methods of data collection: participatory observations, qualitative interviews, and collecting relevant documents. Subsequently, we will justify the value of each of the methods for this research and show how the methods have been implemented.

In our research, participatory observations serve as the main method in the ethnographic approach. They are a fundamental empirical source with which to understand the functioning of the social enterprise in its cultural-institutional context and with which to reconstruct the subjective meanings of the people in the field. For this purpose, participatory observations require the physical presence of researchers in the field for a medium or longer period and the involvement of the researchers in

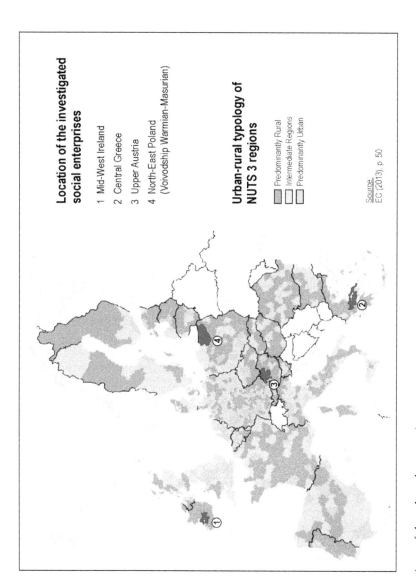

Figure 2.2 Locations of the selected case regions

the activities of the observed people. This co-presence helps to familiarize researchers with the observed phenomenon in its "natural" environment to overcome barriers between researchers and subjects, and to win the confidence of subjects in order to gain direct and unbiased access to information.

In our case, the opportunity to use a desk in the main office of the social enterprises and to work in the office side-by-side with staff members over a period of eight weeks has been essential for conducting participatory observations. Our presence in the social enterprises' office enabled us to learn the daily work processes, to take part in team meetings, and to have informal conversations with staff members. Apart from internal observations, we could join meetings with external stakeholders, which helped us better understand the role of the social enterprise in its cultural and institutional environment. In the case of the Austrian social enterprise, participatory observations expanded to work shadowing, as the researchers accompanied a central person of the social enterprise to meetings with various partners and stakeholders for several days. This provided valuable insights into the development of new ideas, the maintenance of networks, and the strategies of legitimization and self-representation. The observations were constantly and immediately documented in field notes, which used a template that distinguishes between general and context information (e.g. place and time of the observation), as well as empirical, methodological, and theoretical notes (Przyborski & Wohlrab-Sahr, 2010). The latter served to reflect theoretically on the observations and to develop first concepts and categories. As such, the field notes also fulfilled the function of a memo as constantly developing theoretical notes are a requirement when grounded theory methodology is properly applied (Strauss & Corbin, 1990). However, it is worth noting that we clearly distinguished the writing of empirical notes from the production of methodological and theoretical notes. While the former is a neutral description of the observations, methodological notes require a reflective perspective on the researcher's own role in the field. Theoretical notes require that the findings are detached from the actual case and that more general descriptions and explanations are developed.

While participatory observations have been employed to collect data about observable practices and discursive information, qualitative interviews have served to gather additional information about aspects that are not directly observable, including knowledge, meanings, beliefs, values, "hidden" practices, and institutional conditions. We have developed the interview guideline to gather both narrative descriptions as well as factual knowledge. The interviews started with the narrative part (Schuetze, 1977; Lieblich et al., 1998) by asking the interviewees about their personal relation with the region ("Which personal bonds do you have to [this region]?") and the respective social enterprise ("How did you get to know [this social enterprise]?"). These open, semi-biographical questions aimed at inspiring the interviewees to narrate. In this way, we triggered the forces of narrations that help to reveal a person's position and selected beliefs, values, and subjective meanings conveyed independently from the researchers' own systems of relevance. After these initial questions, the guideline provided selected topical sections, each consisting of an open initial question and several detailed inquiries. The topical sections informed the interviewer about the topics that should be raised in the interview but did not prescribe a fixed sequence of questions. Likewise, the detailed questions served as reminders in cases in which the interviewees did not raise the topic themselves. This flexibility should ensure that the interview kept the character of a natural conversation and that the interviewees acted according to their own systems of relevance as much as possible.

The sampling strategy followed partly role-related, partly theoretical considerations. Before the fieldwork, the involved researchers agreed upon types of interviewees that would be promising in view of the analytical framework and the objective to gain a comprehensive understanding of the case. The researchers were guided by their experiences from a similar data collection conducted in central and eastern European rural municipalities a decade ago (Fink et al., 2013). These types of interviewees included people from within the organization (the CEO, employees, board members) and from the organizations' environment. The latter comprised interviewees from the community level (consumers and local decision-makers), the intermediary level (other social enterprises), and the regime level (policy makers, rural development experts). The sampling strategy within this framework was theoretical. The selection of interviewees was a recursive process of conducting an interview, reflecting on theoretical conceptions, identifying needs for deepened and enhanced empirical insights, selecting another interviewee who promised to provide the required insights, conducting the interview, reflecting, etc. This process came to an end when the theoretical conceptions had been consolidated, that is, when theoretical saturation had been achieved (Strauss & Corbin, 1990). Even though unexpected practical hurdles forced the researchers to adjust the sample (e.g. if requested persons refused to give interviews), they were able to implement the described sampling strategy and to conduct between 11 and 16 qualitative interviews for each case (see Table 2.1).

Prior to each interview, we informed the interviewees about the purpose of the research and about how we would process and store the interview data (including anonymization). We obtained their written consent to the process and to the potential publication of aspects of the information they supplied.

In addition to participatory observations and qualitative interviews, documents were used as a third empirical source of data for the investigation. They provide additional information about organizational structures and institutional framework conditions and serve to validate and consolidate the results. The researchers collected three types of documents. First, they gathered documents that were created by the social

Table 2.1 Overview of the four case studies and the collected empirical data

Case study	Location	No. of expert interviews	Pages of field notes	No. of analyzed documents
1	Mid-West Ireland	12	33	8
2	Central Greece	11	16	4
3	Upper Austria	11	32	9
4	North-East Poland	16	30	6
	Total:	50	111	27

enterprises themselves, including statutes, charters, strategy papers, and company reports. These documents helped to reconstruct strategies of legitimization and self-representation as well as organizational governance structures. Second, the researchers collected policy papers about development strategies and the role of social enterprises in the provision of social services. The analyses of these documents helped explain the statutory and institutional opportunities and limitations of rural social enterprises in their regional and national environments. Third, the researchers collected study reports and other external analyses of the investigated social enterprises and their contexts. Amongst others, the mapping studies of the European Commission about the ecosystems of social enterprises in the EU and its member states turned out to be very valuable for the consolidation of the results (European Commission, 2014a, 2014b, 2016a, 2016b, 2016c; Anastasiadis et al., 2018).

Table 2.1 provides an overview of the empirical data collected with the methods described above. In total, we collected and analyzed 50 qualitative interviews, 111 pages of field notes, and 27 documents across the four case studies.

Data Processing and Analysis

The goal of the analysis was twofold. First, the analysis aimed at understanding rural social enterprises as a specific type of organization in relation to their cultural and structural framework conditions in rural regions and beyond. Second, it aimed at developing theoretical assumptions about how social enterprises are involved and interact in rural communities and networks and how they, by doing so, generate and implement innovative solutions for challenges in rural regions. To meet these goals, we applied interpretative and reconstructive analytical methods, which follow the principles of grounded theory (Strauss & Corbin, 1990; Corbin & Strauss, 2015), as well as comparative methods (Tilly, 1984; Ragin, 1989; Ahram, 2011).

Further analysis requires that the empirical data be processed and prepared. For our research, the qualitative interviews had to be anonymized with regard to the interviewed persons and transcribed (and partly translated from Polish and Greek into English). After this, we included the three sources of empirical data—interview transcripts, field notes and documents—in a MAXQDA file. The software package MAXQDA was then used to systematically analyze the material as follows. First, we coded the interviews line by line and further developed the concepts and categories. Four main categories were identified and further refined: "functioning of the social enterprise," "cultural and structural conditions in rural and national contexts," "involvement of social enterprises in communities and networks," and "emergence of social innovations." Second, we coded the material selectively with regard to the developed categories. At this stage, the three sources of empirical data were integrated and triangulated, thus counterchecking and consolidating the developed categories. While steps one and two were implemented separately for each of the four cases, the third step of the analysis served to compare the cases. The comparison of categories across the cases enabled us to identify commonalities and differences and to develop typifications and assumptions about patterns of relations.

Now that the analytical framework and the methods are in place, we can move to the analysis of the four cases from the perspective of the researchers. For each case, we will first analyze how the social enterprise mobilizes resources on the different levels of the network hierarchy through legitimacy gained by credibly communicated instrumental and emotional place attachment. Specifically, we show how the social enterprise leverages the power differentials between regime, intermediary, and community level in the business model to simultaneously address the idea and action problem and thus provide a convincing value proposition to all involved. Second, we analyze in what respect and how the social enterprises creatively recombine the resources mobilized within the network structure in a Schumpeterian way. Here we focus on the aspects of innovativeness, pro-activeness, and riskiness of the activities of the social enterprise. We further investigate in what respect and how far the social enterprises make a change in the place through the innovation itself and through the involvement of the collaborators from the network in the participatory process of development and implementation of the innovation. We conclude each case analysis with a concise summary of why the social enterprise has been (un)successful in addressing challenges faced by the respective local community.

Filling the Voids: Dependency on Funding Schemes and Political Decisions

Mobilizing Resources in a Multilevel Innovation Network

The regional development company was formed as a reaction to a decade of extremely high unemployment and high levels of emigration in the 1980s and the devastating impact those factors had on the viability of rural communities in Ireland. Those communities were challenged by a shortage of human capacity, infrastructure, and economic opportunities. Traditionally, local public authorities have little input into delivering core services to communities in rural Ireland. As a heritage of British centralism, political representation and administration have been concentrated in cities like Limerick, Cork, and Galway. Rural communities are remotely governed by authorities located in these urban centers. Rural development companies like the social enterprise emerged to fill the gap that public authorities left in the rural hinterland. Their business models focus on meeting core public responsibilities such as delivering regional, national, and EU funding programs aimed at social, economic, and environmental development, enhancing employability among the population, supporting micro-sized and small businesses to establish and promote the Mid-West Ireland as a tourist destination.

In addressing these needs, the Irish social enterprise takes a participative approach. It strengthens the capacity for self-help and enhances social cohesion across communities by facilitating community-led local development activities. The regional development company successfully supports participative bottom-up community initiatives proposed by communities without forcing its own ideas on the communities. Once communities recognize a common need and suggest ways in which it can be addressed, the regional development company offers its expertise in mediating community activation and mentoring application processes for suitable funding schemes. However, the approach is that the impetus has to remain with the communities in order to keep community members engaged, encourage them to take ownership of the process, and make rural communities more inclusive. To advance regional development in Mid-West Ireland, the regional development company manages a range of EU and National programs and projects including the Rural Development Programme (LEADER), Local Community Development Programme (LCDP), the Rural Social Scheme (RSS), the Tús Scheme, Local Training Initiatives (LTIs), the Jobs Club, the Equality For Women Measure and the Towards Occupation Programme.

The starting point for the activity of the regional development company is a community that shares a specific interest. Members of such a community contribute their individual resources to the network of likeminded communities. These resources comprise e.g. skills and competences, voluntary work, and often also funds. Together they are shared between the members and represent the bonding social capital of the community. The regional development company connects to the community and enhances the bonding social capital by implementing a participatory process of carving out explicitly formulated interests the community strives to jointly address. For example, some years ago a group of inhabitants in a village near Limerick formed a community and started tackling the need to create jobs, enhance the quality of life and to create a location in which the locals are able to socialize indoors and outdoors. The village was strongly hit by the closure of a major factory for consumer electronics, which resulted in an unemployment rate of well over 30 percent with the typical consequences for social life in the place. The village's civic center CEO remembers that *"there was nothing in here to meet. Village life simply did not take place"* (CEO of civic center, personal communication, December 8, 2016). She also recalls the lack of some basic leisure infrastructure in town: *"There have not been any playgrounds and parks"* (CEO of civic center, personal communication, December 8, 2016). The community activation activities run by the regional development company included a survey, a series of moderated workshops and discussion fora with the community members. As a result of these activities the community articulated, among others, the need for a civic center and a park in the middle of the village. These facilities should be a place to meet and socialize and offer a venue for a variety of activities for locals of different age and with different backgrounds.

Previously, another community developed a joint interest in reactivating the town center as an attractive place to live, do business, and spend time. However, during the first decade their activities had limited impact and an initiative—the Friends of the Village—formed, which led to a reorganization of the activities with a focus on jobs, recreation, and social space. Also, in the same village, the Rural Community Network formed around the goal of enhancing the quality of life and reducing the social isolation of the elderly. These initiatives were pursued by different communities. The regional development company, however, realized the potential of bringing the initiative together. One member of the regional development company summarizes the overlap in the specific interests of the three communities in the village as *"It's about innovating the redevelopment of small towns. For housing and for business . . . That would make it really attractive for people"* (Regional development officer at the social enterprise, personal communication, December 14, 2016) and the CEO concludes the crucial role of bringing together different communities with overlapping interests:

> *What's missing is the cross-connectedness . . . In one community you get all the organisations lined up doing what they are doing but no connection. In the other one there is a connection. That works well. The other one remains broken.*
>
> (CEO of social enterprise, personal communication, December 15, 2016)

By establishing links between the different local communities, the regional development company activated bridging social capital in the village. The maintenance of civic center and park as well as the café shop located in the civic center created jobs. The center is a flexible venue for social and cultural events and meetings and the locals have a beautiful place to meet and spend time together.

Because the regional development company has a geographical focus that goes well beyond this village, it could also link the local communities with similar initiatives in other parts of the region. For example, the community concerned with the establishment of a civic center was linked with a community that had developed a family resource center in another village located some 20 kilometers west of the civic center. Such links to other communities with similar concerns in different stages of the development process or in different locations can activate valuable resources such as expertise and experience. At the same time, successfully addressing the needs of a community in one location might also address the needs of other communities with similar interests nearby. Such synergies enable the provision of an even more differentiated offer to the regional population, because local offers can focus on specific interests. In this way the offer in the other village can especially focus families, because the civic center covers other aspects of the social life of the regional populations.

So far, we have described the networking activity of the regional development company on the horizontal level in terms of strengthening links between members of the same community (bonding social capital) and establishing links between members of different communities (bridging social capital). Because the innovative character of rural social enterprises stems from their ability to reconfigure existing resources on different network levels, we will now shift our focus towards the vertical links in the network hierarchy. This activity of social enterprises comes down to positioning themselves as intermediary actors who can establish downward linkages to the local community to tap bonding and bridging social capital for their business model. The Irish regional development company gets in contact with communities either because they actively approach the social enterprise or because members of the social enterprise hear about the initiative of the community and regard this initiative as promising. In case the regional development company management believes they are able to contribute to the realization of the community's initiative they liaise with the community members and initiate the participatory process described above. In the course of this participatory process the social enterprise establishes a strong vertical link with the community. At the same time, rural social entrepreneurs need to link upwards to regime-level actors to energize their business model. Such cross-level linking requires the rural social entrepreneur to offer clear value propositions to both the community and regime-level actors. For the value propositions to be credible, rural social entrepreneurs need to be perceived by the regime-level actors as legitimate advocates of the interests and needs of the actors on the community level and vice versa.

This legitimacy can stem from the rural social entrepreneurs' emotional and instrumental attachment to the local community.

The regional development company gains legitimacy from the emotional place attachment of the CEO and of a large share of the management team. Their emotional place attachment is based on their local embeddedness as well as on the fact that the founder has been a successful manager and business developer in other localities in the region "*I live about five miles from here . . . originally I came from a different region, but I've been married and living in this region since 1979*" (Founder of social enterprise, personal communication, December 12, 2016). Also, the current CEO demonstrates strong emotional place attachment by stressing his embeddedness in the region "*I have been living here with my family and friends and in my job I have contributed my best to enhance the quality of life for the locals*" (CEO of social enterprise, personal communication, December 15, 2016). This credibly communicated emotional place attachment makes the regional development company a legitimate advocate for the interests of the community, both vis-à-vis the members of the community and regime level actors such as the central government, international firms operating in the region, research institutions like universities, the offices of funding schemes of the European Union such as LEADER and supranational organizations concerned with economic development such as the OECD.

In contrast to gaining legitimacy through emotional place attachment, the regional development company addresses communities in Mid-West Ireland with concrete instrumental value propositions. For instance, when the civic center was developed in the village the community lacked expertise e.g. in managing a project of this size, as well as in architecture and regarding relevant legal regulations. Here the regional development company steps in with its value proposition by offering mentoring and training to community members. In return they gain legitimacy among the community members, which provides access to the ideas and network resources of the community. The CEO describes the legitimacy gained through instrumental place attachment referring to the project in Kellybost:

> *When you saw a need and an opportunity, and you put a strategy together, the next thing was to do things that created a bit more awareness, bring people together about it . . . We as an organisation built up the whole training side and demonstrate the kind of training and qualifications that there should be.*
>
> (CEO of social enterprise, personal communication, December 15, 2016)

Of course, conducting mentoring is in the interest of the social enterprise because it helps to effectively mobilize the bonding social capital that is instrumental to the business model as an intermediary actor in the network hierarchy, as the following statement by the CEO shows:

> *People are talking about the resources they have, but they don't know what to do with them . . . A couple of people have a very strong social consciousness and maybe not as much of a business focus. There is that challenge in identifying the people for boards so that you get the mix right . . . One of the things that helps is mentoring . . . And the other thing is training programmes.*
> (CEO of social enterprise, personal communication, April 28, 2016)

The regional development company underpins its credible value proposition to one community by establishing links to other local communities with complementary resources. Thus, the social entrepreneur offers a clear value proposition in order to mobilize bridging capital in the place. The founder states: "*We worked fairly hard in supporting all the groups in [the village] to come together, to talk to one another, to become part of one umbrella group*" (Founder of social enterprise, personal communication, December 12, 2016). The example of recruiting volunteers across different communities shows how the regional development company addresses the bridging challenge in order to mobilize resources and scale projects on the community level:

> *If we're to grow the services, we're either going to have to get more volunteers or we're going to have to charge . . . You put on a public event to create wider awareness because it might not only be the ones that talked to you; there could be others.*
> (Development officer at social enterprise, personal communication, December 14, 2016)

Another aspect of the value propositions to community members refers to the social enterprise's ability to facilitate links to regime-level actors and mobilize their resources for the initiative of the community (see Figure 2.3). The founder of the regional development company describes this aspect for the project phase when the state-of-the-art user concept for the civic center in the village was to be developed as: "*usually our role would be mentoring and then linking them to the right research centres and universities*" (Founder of social enterprise, personal communication, December 12, 2016). Value propositions in terms of upward linking to higher level actors also refer to guiding communities through institutional change that threaten the success of ongoing community projects, as described by the founder of the regional development company: "*In the most recent changes the municipalities were created. There is not yet a mindset of people connecting to their municipality. You know, if you're* talking to people on the street here and you ask them what the municipality, they live in does, that's gonna be: 'Ha? What's that?'" (Founder of social enterprise, personal communication, December 12, 2016). Finally, linking activities offered by the social enterprise include promising communities access to considerable funding that can ultimately address their needs. For the development of the civic center in the village the CEO highlights the crucial role of resources mobilized through such vertical linkages:

> *All our support work and the feasibility studies and all the plans have all been supported by LEADER. But the big capital money would come from another programme nationally. It's all about the right timing and space to support that group to get the money.*
> (CEO of social enterprise, personal communication, December 15, 2016)

However, moving upwards to the regime level, social entrepreneurs actually have to convince regime-level actors of their legitimacy in order to get access to those resources they already promised to the community members. The regional development company directly and personally linked community members and regime-level actors to mobilize resources as the CEO describes:

> *A top executive of [an international dairy company] is from the region and we could link him to the initiative in [the village]. He has been instrumental to the project . . . not only because of the financial support, but also because of the expertise and contacts he provided to the community.*
> (CEO of social enterprise, personal communication, December 15, 2016)

To win the support of regime-level actors, it helps when the rural social entrepreneur is legitimized by his emotional and instrumental place attachment and the fact that he has been successful in other ventures, such as the CEO of the regional development company with the establishment of a mountain bike trail as a successful tourist attraction. Place attachment makes regime-level actors perceive social enterprises credible advocates for the interests of the communities they work with. Previous success in development projects in the region demonstrates the ability to implement innovation and change in the specific institutional context. Both signals to regime-level actors that they can use the social enterprise as an effective agent of their political agendas.

This is the main social entrepreneurs' value proposition towards regime level actors. The social enterprise promises the national government and the Local Community Development Council (LCDC) that the funds provided will be used to coordinate the activities of the communities to fit the local development plan aimed at meeting the EU policy goals of job creation and economic development. A representative of the Local Community Development Council explains:

> We give [two regional development companies active in Mid-West Ireland] 2.9 million euro to put it into community development that is following the guidelines of our regional development plan.
> (Chairman of the Local Community Development Council, personal communication, December 13, 2016)

Successful upward linking and access to such regime-level resources requires an in-depth understanding of strategic spatial planning in the country and particularly of how to satisfy the policy goals laid out on different administrative levels.

> That's a top-down spatial plan. When you move down, there are regional plans that look at all kinds of infrastructural development that should happen. And then down you have county development plans. Each of them has to take cognizance of the one above and there are consultation processes in them all. What [the regional development company] would try to do is feed into the other ones and influence what was going on in the others.
> (Founder of social enterprise, personal communication, December 12, 2016)

The social enterprises also link the communities to regime-level actors beyond the national borders (see Figure 2.3). The founder of the Irish social enterprise recalls:

> In the very early days, we were involved in setting up a trans-European rural network . . . This was pre-LEAD . . . We tried to set up rural organisations across Europe . . . that was enormous learning because I was seeing and hearing what was going on in other places . . . We linked with local authorities in Austria and Germany to come in and to work with us and develop multiannual development planning.
> (Founder of social enterprise, personal communication, December 12, 2016)

The insights from the international partners informed the regional development company in their work with the local communities.

Reconfiguring Resources to Make a Change: (Social) Innovation

The business model of the regional development company is based on the delivery of services to communities that help them to address their needs

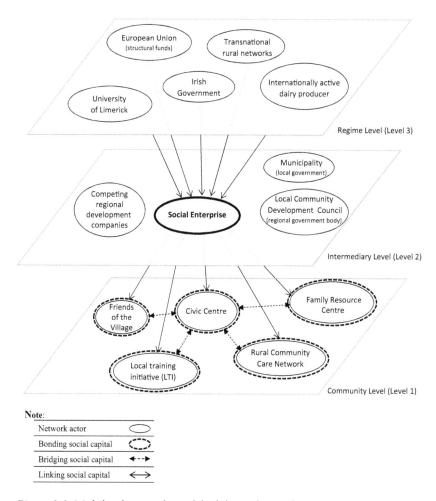

Figure 2.3 Multilevel network model of the Irish social enterprise

and at the same time help regime-level actors to achieve their broader targets like economic development, job creation, and social inclusion. Their broader targets are for example specified in the national development plans and broken down to the regional development plans. They are also reflected in national law. Apart from the government other actors on the regime level also define the rules of the game relevant for regional development. Research institutions such as the University of Limerick publish case studies and assessments of different approaches to regional development in Ireland. Such evaluations impact on public opinion and the policy makers, and thus guide the design of the framework conditions for regional development of rural Ireland. Also, the management of large firms which are rooted in the region, but active on an international scale bring in new practices from other contexts and, as a major employer in the region, frame economic and social development. In the village the involvement of the chief executive of an internationally active dairy producer energized the development of the civic center, but at the same time the involvement of the regime-level actor directly in a community-level initiative has set limits to the creativity of the community, because of the anticipated dominance of the opinion leader's voice. Thus, crossing the border between the levels of the institutional hierarchy implies the risk for the local community of losing control over their initiative. Thus, it is important to take explicit ownership of the activities in the place at all times. In the case of the civic center this was accomplished by a balanced composition of the board steering the project. With funds from schemes delivered by the European Union fed into the network the funding criteria and rules on how to spend the funds become relevant. As a consequence, the policy goals on the European level energize, but at the same time, set boundaries to any regional development in Mid-West Ireland.

In the participatory process moderated by the regional development company the bonding and bridging social capital is mobilized and matched with resources accessed through the vertical linkages with actors on higher levels of the institutional hierarchy. The participatory process not only supports that community members take ownership of the project and its outcome, but it also ensures that the community proactively develops solutions that fit the specific context and demand structure in place. In this way the participative approach pursued by the regional development company avoids standardized solutions that ignore the local setting and that need to be implemented top down.

Thus, the reconfiguration of resources that already exist in the network happens in two ways: First, resources from different communities are brought together and enable the single community to realize new activities that would not have been possible without access to the complementary resources. As an effect new activity emerges on the community level. Second, the regional development company leverages the resources mobilized through bonding and bridging activities with resources accessed on the regime level through vertical linkages. These powerful resources enable the regional development company to significantly scale and/or enhance activities on the community level. Thus, the vertical networking of the regional development company enables the actors on the community level to provide valuable activities.

The value of the activity on the community level is, on the one hand, reflected by a change in place that improves the lives of the locals, because it satisfies a need that has not been addressed before or that has not been addressed in this quality so far. This change unfolds among those active in the community during the participative process of developing the strategy and implementing the new solution addressing the need. As soon as the new solution has been implemented the change also reaches other locals who have not been involved in the project but enjoy the benefits of its outcome. The civic center in the village first has to change the place by carving out the explicit formulation of what the community really needs and by the establishment of new relationships that bringing together members of different communities. Providing an indoor and outdoor space to socialize in and a venue for joint activity, the social life in the place has changed by, for example, strengthening social cohesion among locals and improving the quality of life more generally.

On the other hand, the vertical link induces change on the regime level, because the regional development company lobbies the initiatives emerging on the community level among regime level actors who, to a large extent, design the institutional framework conditions that represent the boundaries for rural development in the area.

Each successful development project such as the civic centre further underpins the legitimacy of the regional development company. However, one failure can put the legitimacy of the social enterprise at risk. This risk can be realized in two aspects. It can either undermine the credibility of the emotional place attachment. This, for example, could have happened in the village if the regional development company had favored the project for the development of the Family Resource Centre in this village at the expense of the development process for the civic centre. While the involvement of social enterprises in more than one community development project is a prerequisite for enabling bridging social capital and thus for realizing what has been offered in the value proposition, parallel activities in a region are highly sensitive because of the threat of jealousy between the local communities. For the social enterprise the risk is not only linked to actual unfair distribution of resources among the communities, but even the perception of a lack of loyalty on the side of the social enterprise towards the community would dramatically diminish its legitimacy.

The second aspect is that one failure can erode the credibility of social entrepreneurs' instrumental place attachment. Not having been able to deliver according to the promises made in the value proposition towards the community and the regime actors will dramatically reduce the credibility of future promises. Thus, it is of utmost importance for the sustained success of a social enterprise such as the regional development company to ensure that process and results of each community development project are perceived as new and valuable to both the communities and the regime-level actors.

Summary of Why the Social Enterprise (Un)successfully Addresses the Challenge

The Irish regional development company has been very successful in addressing the needs of the local communities. They take the intermediary role of a social enterprise and link both the local communities with the regime-level actors and the local communities with each other where there is a fit in the initiatives pursued. Within this horizontal and vertical network the Irish regional development company can mobilize and innovatively reconfigure critical resources that enable solutions to the challenges of the local communities that would not have been delivered without the social entrepreneur's activity. However, in working with the local communities they take an intensive participatory approach, but do not become members of the community. Because they keep the necessary distance to the community and maintain their role as fair moderators they can work and link different communities in the same region without provoking loyalty conflicts. It is important to point out that the Irish regional development company steps in when a community group has already emerged around a certain initiative or an idea for an initiative. Often these initiatives are induced by a pressing need or challenge that the (parts of the) local population faces. Thus, the regional development company moderates and fosters local initiatives, but it does not initiate them. This is possible because the challenges addressed by the communities supported by the regional development company represent gaps in the provision of services typically associated with European welfare states and thus, they are easy to spot and visible to a sufficient number of individuals in the civil society who become active. From an action perspective the Irish social enterprise has an impact on the place because it supports and empowers community members to act. These actions lead to innovation in terms of the delivery of offers that are new and valuable for the locals.

The Pain of the Really Check: Entrepreneurship Meets Cooperative Farming

Mobilizing Resources in a Multilevel Innovation Network

The stevia cooperative, a social enterprise with four employees and 82 members, was established in 2012 in a medium-sized city in Central Greece. The cooperative produces 70 tons of dried stevia leaves per year in a predominantly rural region. Traditionally, the cultivation of tobacco provided a considerable share of the income of small family farms in the region. The recent limitations on the tobacco industry imposed by the Greek government and supported by the European Union threatened the survival of those family farms. At the same time, recession and massive unemployment in the aftermath of the 2008 financial crisis have posed a severe challenge to the economic and social stability of the region. Unemployment and recession have intensified the importance of fostering self-employment and creating opportunities for generating sustainable income for small family-run farms. However, due to its austerity policy the Greek state has limited leeway to initiate such development.

To address the challenges of unemployment and economic downturn in the region the stevia cooperative has drawn former tobacco farmers' attention to an innovative crop: the stevia plant. Stevia is a low calorie, diabetic-friendly sugar substitute. The stevia plant thrives in conditions similar to those required for growing the tobacco plant. Traditionally, farmers in the region tend to be risk-averse and conservative regarding innovation. However, successful EU-funded experiments on growing stevia plants under the supervision of agronomists from a regional university and the entrepreneurial spirit of a social entrepreneur who is rooted in the region kick-started a new business that resulted in the foundation of the social enterprise. This social enterprise is devoted to the development of a business model that brings together family-run farms from the region to grow stevia plants. The dried leaves of these plants are then shipped to a partner abroad who extracts the stevia substance. The substance is then transported back to Greece, where the stevia cooperative packs and markets it for the European market. While farmers used to focus on the raw product in the past, the stevia cooperative has initiated a vertical integration of the value chain. Its business model aims at attributing a bigger share of the overall value created to small farmers. Today, the stevia cooperative is among the few stevia producers in Europe.

The main factor that fostered the formation of the community of local farmers as the nucleus of the stevia cooperative was their shared interest in sustainable farming and the need to substitute tobacco by a new crop that better fits the current trends in European societies. A technical sciences and engineering graduate and investment banker from the region was hired as CEO of the stevia cooperative to induce entrepreneurial spirit into the group of local farmers. The CEO was brought in by the former leader of the association of tobacco cooperatives, who is an influential opinion leader in the region. His influence is not only rooted in his extensive experience and expertise in farming and his in-depth understanding of the cooperative movement in Greece, but it also has a spiritual dimension that is in line with the strong role of the orthodox church in rural Greece. Together, these two factors give him an authoritarian role, which he uses for his engagement in community development and sustainable farming projects such as the stevia cooperative. The opinion leader and the CEO share the understanding that rural social entrepreneurship requires a good balance between tradition and innovation. Each of them represents one of these poles and the integration of both in the organizational structure of the stevia cooperative ensures that this balance is kept. A board member of the stevia cooperative states:

[They] are very important in the region [and are] very well respected. [The opinion leader] stands for the great tradition of [the region], but lacks modern management practices. [The CEO] is a management

and entrepreneurship expert, but lacks seniority. Together they are very strong. They can make change happen.

(Board member of cooperative, personal communication, April 1, 2017)

The CEO seized the advantage tied to the strong social bonds between the local farmers and now members of the stevia cooperative to form a cohesive group. While the social bonds between the local farmers were traditionally strong in the social realm, it required a lot of work to translate them into joint action in the economic realm. Numerous individual conversations and group meetings were needed for the CEO to get across the necessity to join forces as a community in order to gain enough strength to successfully develop a new agricultural product that is competitive on the European markets. Finally, a sufficient number of local farmers could be convinced that they were facing the same challenges and should thus fight to overcome these challenges together. To do so, the CEO used his entrepreneurial perspective and coined the main disadvantages of the region—i.e. unemployment and economic downturn—as challenges that can be turned into an entrepreneurial opportunity by developing a proper business model. Fostering bonding social capital in the community of local farmers through the explicit formulation of a joint identity and an entrepreneurial vision helped to enhance the commitment of the members of the cooperative. During the first years, the members of the stevia cooperative invested private funds over and above their share in the cooperative and their workforce in the development of stevia plantations without getting paid for the leaves delivered to the cooperative. Only as the sales of the final product marketed by the stevia cooperative grew did the farmers receive payments for the first years of production. This commitment reflects the strong bonding social capital among the members of the cooperative. One of the board members describes the bonding social capital underlying the social enterprise as follows:

We are a family and should help each other. In the cooperative, we have common interests and should act as one. We all want to make our living with farming.

(Board member of cooperative, personal communication, April 1, 2017)

While the ties between the members of the stevia cooperative are strong (bonding social capital), the horizontal links with other communities (bridging social capital) are limited (see Figure 2.4). The stevia cooperative only marginally taps into the resource pools of other communities to gain access to complementary resources. There is some exchange with a regional cooperative concerned with clean energy production regarding circular production models in farming, which might lead to a future collaboration. In addition, there are horizontal links with the regional agri-food association, which foster mutual support and knowledge exchange in marketing. Apart from these horizontal links that emerged between the stevia cooperative and other local communities, the CEO of the social enterprise taps two additional resources of other regional communities to underpin its business model. First, the identity of the stevia cooperative builds on the heritage of the tobacco cooperatives that have been the dominant actors in organizing the social and economic life of the local farmers for a long time. A local representative of the chamber of commerce describes the situation when the tobacco production disappeared as follows: "*After the end of tobacco production there was the danger that farms would close, farmers would leave the region, and everything would be abandoned*" (Director of the regional chamber of commerce, personal communication, March 29, 2017). The stevia cooperative has managed to address this danger and is now perceived as legitimate successor of the tobacco cooperatives. Second, the social norm of solidarity that has traditionally been fostered by the Orthodox Church is a key element of the identity of the stevia cooperative. Here, the spiritual authority of the opinion leader helped to translate the norm of solidarity from the religious context into the business context. The CEO could build on these two resources and integrate them into the participative business model of the stevia cooperative.

To mobilize resources from higher levels of the regional network hierarchy as well, social entrepreneurs also establish vertical links to regime-level actors. By doing so, they take the role of intermediaries who broker resources between actors at the community and the regime level. For being accepted as intermediary, social entrepreneurs have to offer credible value propositions to both community and regime-level actors. Whether a value proposition is perceived as credible by these actors depends on the legitimacy social entrepreneurs enjoy, which in turn depends on the emotional and instrumental attachment they have to the local community.

Reconfiguring Resources to Make a Change: (Social) Innovation

The CEO of the stevia cooperative has gained legitimacy among the members of the cooperative through his and his family members' roots in the region and the fact that he has had a successful career as investment banker and business developer in Europe and Asia. He is well aware of the importance of the emotional dimension of his embeddedness in the place for enabling his intermediary role as social entrepreneur, as the following statement illustrates: "*They have known me since I was a little boy, saw me growing up and they followed my international career. This familiarity opens doors*" (CEO of cooperative, personal communication, April 1, 2017). His emotional place attachment is also underpinned by a strong endorsement from the spiritual opinion leader. The subsequent quote of a member of the stevia cooperative confirms the emotional dimension of the CEO's place attachment, and at the same time stresses the instrumental dimension: "*He is one of us, but he is an expert who can deal with the big players. We need his expertise, but cannot work with somebody who does not understand us*" (Member of the cooperative, personal communication, March 14, 2017). Thus, in addition to emotional place attachment the CEO also addresses the community of local farmers with instrumental aspects of his value proposition. Especially, his expertise in start-up management, such as financing and organizing new ventures, and his entrepreneurial mindset are of direct use for the community. Also, his legal expertise and accounting knowledge have been helpful to establish legitimacy among the community members. These signals of competence communicate to the local farmers that the CEO is useful and supports their common interests. They have also helped the farmers to realize that it is more likely to achieve their goals with having these skills on board.

Emotional place attachment makes the CEO a credible member of the cooperative who is accepted in the community as one of them. The CEO's instrumental place attachment, which is illustrated by his offer to work for the cooperative and bring in complementary resources, makes the members of the community accept him as their advocate vis-à-vis actors on higher levels of the network hierarchy. These actors include representatives of the regional and national government, organizations such as the chamber of commerce, and international business partners such as the company that extracts pure stevia from the leaves. Thus, the CEO has a double role: on the community level, he is a member of the cooperative, who induces entrepreneurial spirit into the community to foster their proactive innovativeness and their willingness to accept risk. He has, for example, been successful in increasing the members' willingness to invest money as well as time in the cooperative and to use new crops and new cultivation techniques. At the same time, however, it has been a major challenge for the CEO to convince the members that taking risk is a cornerstone of entrepreneurial venturing. Nevertheless, his activities on the community level fostered the development of bonding and bridging social capital and, thus, enhanced his access to the resources of the community.

On the intermediary level, the CEO acts as middleman who establishes links between the community and regime-level actors (see Figure 2.4). The CEO, for instance, uses his personal contacts to the national government and EU institutions to organize and finance the participation of the stevia cooperative in national and international fairs. These fairs provide the cooperative the broad visibility necessary to establish in European markets. The CEO also makes sure that the social enterprise participates in international research projects and conferences to gain state-of-the-art know-how and to increase its profile. Interestingly, he does not do this single-handedly, but often takes members of the stevia cooperative to international events, research project reviews, and meetings with national and EU decision makers, as demonstrated by the following statement from a board member of the stevia cooperative: "*One of us often joins [the CEO] on his business trips. It is important that they get to know us and that we get to know them. Decisions are easier if you know the faces behind the projects*" (Executive board member, personal communication, April 1, 2017). This successful vertical linking of the stevia cooperative with regime-level actors gradually underpins the credibility of the CEO's initial value proposition to the community members. In turn, it further enhances his access to the resources embedded on the community level.

This privileged access to community resources provides the basis for the CEO's credible value proposition towards regime-level actors. His legitimacy on both the community level and the regime level is thus crucial for making the social enterprise's business model work. To gain legitimacy on both levels, the CEO promises the community members access to regime-level resources to gain access to community resources and at the same time he promises access to community resources to regime-level actors to gain access to regime-level resources. As long as no stable vertical network relations have been established between the community and the regime level, these promises are a risky move. However, without taking this risk the CEO would not be able to implement the business model of the stevia cooperative. However, in the case of the CEO of the stevia cooperative the personal risk is limited because the social enterprise is only one of the start-ups included in the CEO's portfolio. Thus, more than a traditional social entrepreneur, he takes the role of a business angel who takes a share in the business in exchange for his time and effort invested in scaling the new venture along a high-risk/high-gain growth path.

Similar to the community level, also on the regime level the CEO's place attachment plays a crucial role to gain legitimacy as an advocate of the community. The Deputy Governor of the region describes the CEO as "*a born entrepreneur. He is energetic and committed. He has been successful abroad, so he will also succeed here*" (Deputy governor, personal communication, March 7, 2017). Based on this legitimacy, the CEO can credibly communicate his value proposition to the actors on the regime level. As CEO of the stevia cooperative he makes promises to the regional and national government as well as to supporting international organizations that the resources provided will be used efficiently and effectively to establish an entrepreneurial mindset, enhance economic activity, and ultimately create jobs in the region to foster structural change. The CEO of the stevia cooperative has been very successful in developing vertical links to regime-level actors, as demonstrated by the following statement by a Greek governmental official: "*[He] is a role model and a change maker. People need to be activated. They need to understand that*

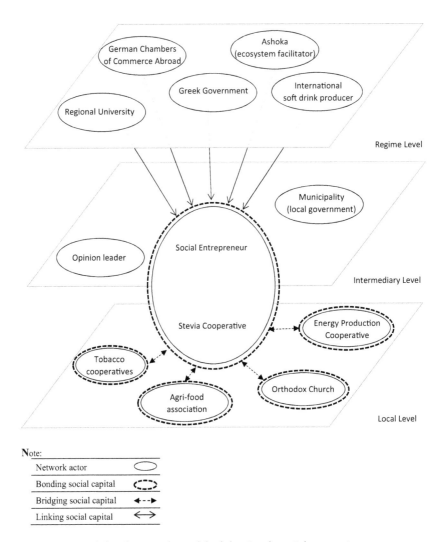

Figure 2.4 Multilevel network model of the Greek social enterprise

entrepreneurship is good for us. [He] will show them!" (Representative of regional government, personal communication, May 12, 2017)

   While regime-level actors are highly convinced of the CEO's abilities, the CEO doubts that the regime-level actors' intentions to induce change in the region will transform into actual change on the community level. In his view, politicians can at best reduce the barriers to economic development and innovation in the region. When it comes to initiating and fostering sustainable change of economic and social conditions in the region the CEO strongly believes that businesses have the power to act as change agents. This mindset has manifested in his intensive efforts to establish vertical links between the stevia cooperative and international companies. These efforts have resulted in a big standing order from a rapidly growing soft drinks company that uses the stevia produced by the cooperative as a sweetener for its product. This deal can be seen as the biggest success in the development of the stevia cooperative so far, as it dramatically boosts the volume of sales and secures a stable inflow of cash that can be reinvested in firm growth.

However, the scaling strategy pursued by the CEO is in conflict with the risk aversion of the farmers who, as members of the cooperative, ultimately decide on the investment strategy. To date, the CEO has failed to convince the members of the cooperative to take the risk and leverage their financial resources with a loan from a bank or a state business agency, as this would enable them to acquire modern machinery. Even though the machines would pay off within two years of production, the members' bad experiences with bank loans in the aftermath of the 2008 financial crisis has the effect that the members refuse to apply for debt capital. This deadlock is a major source of frustration for both the CEO and the members of the cooperative. The CEO cannot follow his entrepreneurial ambitions that call for fast growth. The members of the cooperative feel pressured by the CEO to take a risk that they do not want to bear. However, more rapid growth might be necessary to keep up with competitors. While the stevia cooperative could claim to be the only commercial producer of this novel crop in Greece at the time the cooperative was founded, the number of competitors has grown over the years. Even though the stevia cooperative still benefits from first mover advantages, especially regarding its public image, its members will have to accept that the chance to generate returns is tied to accepting risk in order to make their cooperative financially sustainable. Interestingly, the members have taken relatively high risks when they committed to the stevia cooperative. This is because they invested their time and efforts in developing the stevia plantations but did not receive any return for the dried leaves sold. Although these investments did not require high financial commitments, they were very risky as the success of the business model was far from certain.

Reconfiguring Resources to Make a Change: (Social) Innovation

The stevia cooperative brings together an entrepreneur, i.e. the CEO, and a community, i.e. the farmers. Both parties have a rich portfolio of resources. The CEO has in-depth expertise and rich experience in the business world. He has also developed a pronounced entrepreneurial mindset that enables him to perceive challenges as opportunities for innovative business models. The farmers are experts in cultivating crops and build their community on a rich history of cooperation and mutual trust. These two resource pools are complementary in nature, but the underlying drivers are fundamentally different because of the differences between the CEO's and the farmers' basic assumptions how the world works. While the CEO has a dynamic view on economic and social change that implies that constant action is needed in order to keep the current competitive position and make a business sustainable, the farmers have a more static and repetitive understanding of time. Under this traditional understanding change is a cycle that is rooted in the seasons. This implies that for a business to be sustainable each actor needs to follow his or her routines.

In the stevia cooperative these two understandings create tensions between the CEO, who wants to promote growth by raising external capital, and the members of the cooperative, who only want the business to grow if the growth is financed out of the cash flow. The organizational structure of the cooperative does not allow the CEO to overrule the members' vote. Thus, the potential to innovatively combine the production expertise of the local farmers with the entrepreneurial spirit and international ambition of the CEO is partly eroded. Due to this deadlock the business model of the stevia cooperative appears to be stuck in the middle. The innovative recombination of resources available in the network structure has enabled the stevia cooperative to succeed in the phase of product development. However, the unresolved tensions between change and stability prevent the cooperative from realizing economies of scale in production and entering international markets. The situation is further complicated by the fact that the farmers refuse investments targeted at enhancing the efficiency of the production process. This additionally limits the cooperative's cash flow and, as a consequence, its ability to scale the business in the markets.

The CEO is aware of this issue and has developed a strategy that allows the organization to become ambidextrous, i.e. to integrate the conflicting objectives of change and stability. His approach follows the lines of the well-established strategy in management theory that separates the two forces in different parts of the organization. While the cooperative taps traditions and routines in order to jointly grow stevia plants, the CEO has unfolded activities on the intermediary level that are only loosely linked to the cooperative. These activities comprise plans to set up facilities in the place to extract pure stevia from the leaves. These facilities would be operated by a separate firm and funded by private investments as well as loans and subsidies. This funding structure would allow the separate firm to grow rapidly in terms of both the volume of pure stevia produced and the geographic reach of the target market. In this scenario, the stevia cooperative would be one of the suppliers of stevia leaves for the extraction facility. The members of the stevia cooperative, however, would only have a share in the separate firm if they decided to take the risk and invest. The share would enable them to participate in the growth.

More importantly, it would ensure that the idea that drove the foundation of the stevia cooperation in the first place would be maintained—the vertical integration of the value chain, which aims at directing a bigger share of the profits towards the farmers. Thus, the strategy of separating the production part from the processing and marketing part of the organization is risky, because a key aspect of the social dimension of the venture might get lost. At the same time, a fast-growing processing and marketing firm would create more jobs and foster economic development in the region.

The stevia cooperative has been a driver of change. The idea to grow stevia plants was new for the region. According to the members of the stevia cooperation they were even the first to grow stevia in Greece. The move into stevia production was triggered partly by the downturn in the tobacco markets and partly by the rising interest in super foods, which also led to a search for sugar substitutes. Here, the diverse resource pools available in the stevia cooperative unfolded their synergetic potential. The threat of decreasing farming incomes due to the regulative restrictions on tobacco and the evident need for change because of the recession following the 2008 financial crisis enabled the opinion leader and the CEO to convince a sufficiently large group of farmers to join the entrepreneurial venture. While the organizational structure of agricultural cooperatives has a long tradition in the region, the combination of participatory governance and a strong entrepreneurial leader with a non-farming background as CEO was an innovation. This organizational innovation allows that the research and development efforts pursued in cooperation with various partners are translated into a competitive product innovation. Specifically, the expertise in growing stevia under the specific conditions in Greece was developed in close collaboration with two Greek universities and a local cooperative concerned with sustainable energy production. In addition, the stevia cooperative still works with technology-intensive small and medium-sized firms to constantly improve cultivation and its final products. The superior quality of stevia produced by the Greek cooperative is appreciated by a growing number of customers that range from individual households in the region and national wholesalers to international food producers.

Summing up, the stevia cooperative has been able to successfully innovate on different levels and to different extents. First, there was an innovative reconfiguration of resources available in the network structure. This is particularly true for the resource pools of the farmers and the CEO that have been employed innovatively to establish the organizational structure of the cooperative. Second, the joint research and development process led to a significantly better plantation process for stevia leaves. Third, the product—a sugar substitute—was an innovation in the regional market that is valuable also far beyond the cycle of people directly involved in the stevia cooperative.

These innovation activities have also made a change in the place. They have directly secured the income of a substantial number of small family farms and have thus contributed to the local economic and social stability. In addition, the successful venture has indirectly changed the mindset of the locals, because it is a proof of concept for entrepreneurial activity that builds on the farming tradition in the region. Especially, the experience of empowerment by joining forces in a situation of crisis has enhanced the proactiveness of the locals to take their future in their own hands.

Although the members of the stevia cooperative are more reluctant to incorporate the principals of entrepreneurship than the CEO and the political decision makers would have hoped, they are definitely more open to new ideas and modern management practices now than before joining the stevia cooperative. Thus, the stevia cooperative has made some change not only to the economic and social living conditions, but also to the mindsets of its members. In turn, the members act as multipliers who spread the word on the potentials of alternative crops, modern growing techniques, and entrepreneurship in the region.

Summary of Why the Social Enterprise (Un)successfully Addresses the Challenge

The stevia cooperative has successfully established the plantation of a new crop—the stevia plant—in the place and made significant progress in the marketing of the final product in the national market. With the establishment of the new venture producing and marketing stevia they realized an innovation in the place that generates a stream of income for the farmers participating in the cooperative. With stevia former tobacco farmers can stay in the business. However, as the competition among stevia producers intensifies with more and more national and international competitors entering the market, the Greek stevia cooperative will have to prove the sustainability of the business model.

For this, the organization will likely have to adapt its structure that currently spans across two levels of the institutional network hierarchy. The cooperative is located at the community level, while the social entrepreneur—who is a member and acts as the CEO of the cooperative— takes the role of the intermediary, who links the community level actors with actors of the regime level. At the same time the CEO also motivates and activates the members of the cooperative. This is necessary, because the stevia production does not directly address the local community's main challenges of unemployment and out-migration, but rather secures existing jobs and only creates employment opportunities for high-skilled individuals in the long term as the business grows in European and international markets.

With the social mission to be reached in the distant future, the need to address the challenge of unemployment and outmigration does not motivate the community members to contribute to the cooperative by itself and the credibility of the social mission of the venture among the members of the cooperative requires constant and intensive communication. Thus, the CEO takes a double role of being one of the members of the cooperative and a mediator of the vertical network links with regime-level actors. However, this stretch of the social enterprise causes intensive tensions and frustration for the CEO, who reacts with a strategy of personal detachment. Rather than being the entrepreneur in the venture, he is a business angel invested in the venture. He designs the business strategy, consults, trains, and opens his network to the founder team. Like a business angel he intervenes in the operative business wherever necessary to protect the investment and to foster growth.

From an action perspective the Greek social enterprise has an impact in the place because its learning-by-doing approach of new business creation fosters entrepreneurship among the local population, which in the long run will be instrumental to fighting the local community's main challenges unemployment and outmigration. The CEO acts as a mentor and role model for locals to unfold entrepreneurial activities, which eventually result in the delivery of offers that are new and valuable for the locals.

Skillful but Vulnerable: How the Austrian Social Enterprise Mobilizes Complementary Resources from Bottom to Top

Mobilizing Resources in a Multilevel Innovation Network

Rural Austria has a comparably strong economy. It is home to successful manufacturing and world-leading engineering companies. The rural service sector benefits from the strong tourism industry in the Alps. In rural Austria, a social and economic transformation currently takes place. Unlike in other countries, the question is not what comes after agriculture but how to implement the socio-technical change from manufacturing and service industries to the knowledge and digital economy. Implementing this change requires that rural communities offer talented people an attractive environment in which to live and work and to bring young locals in contact with digital technologies. However, surveys show that rural regions constantly lose young and skilled people, who move to bigger cities to study and to start their professional career, and that only a few of them decide to return. Against the backdrop of this so-called brain drain, the Austrian social enterprise has developed the idea of establishing open technology labs in rural communities. Open technology labs are self-organized places that are equipped with technical devices and can be used for free. They welcome everyone who wants to experiment, meet creative people and exchange knowledge. Especially for creative people, the possibility to meet like-minded persons is a criterion for their decision to return to a rural community after their education. By establishing rural open technology labs, the Austrian social enterprise aims at attracting talented people to counteract brain drain and to contribute to the sustainable development of rural communities. Activities in the field of technology education further support this aim (Austrian Social Enterprise, n.d.).

The idea to establish open technology labs in rural communities was new at that time because until then these labs only existed in bigger cities. The Austrian brain gainers were among the first who transferred this idea to rural regions and adjusted it according to the specific needs there. It is important to note that the brain gainers promote this idea, but leave it to local communities to actually establish open technology labs. This means that they provide knowledge about how to set up a new open technology lab and help local communities to make contact with supportive institutions. At the same time, however, they neither build local infrastructures nor run these labs themselves. By focusing on the diffusion of the idea they do not control the process in the local communities. The Austrian brain gainers understand this approach as a means to create social value rather than to solely reap the benefits themselves and to defend the intellectual property rights. This approach is in accordance with the logic of empowerment and open source that characterizes social enterprises (Santos, 2012). To create social added value the approach is advantageous because the diffusion of the idea is not limited by the capacities of the social enterprise and thus has the potential to gain more social impact. Local communities take responsibility for adjusting and implementing the idea, which makes the initiatives more sustainable.

Two key actors are required to realize the diffusion and implementation of rural open technology labs: the social enterprise and the local communities, who act as support teams. The social enterprise has developed the rural open lab approach. Today, it promotes the approach and supports the establishment of new labs with know-how and contacts. Even though the first stimulus is provided by the social enterprise, the realization would not be possible without a local support team, who is inspired by the idea. The social enterprise believes that this team should comprise a minimum of five persons to successfully establish and host a rural open technology lab. The team is not put together by the social enterprise but formed by like-minded people who share the belief that having an open technology lab in their village is highly desirable and beneficial for the community. This suggests that they are a rather homogenous group of people with similar values and a shared interest. As such they are a community initiative with bonding social capital (Gittel & Videl, 1998; Putnam, 2000) (in Figure 2.5 this is symbolized by a dashed line around the open lab support team).

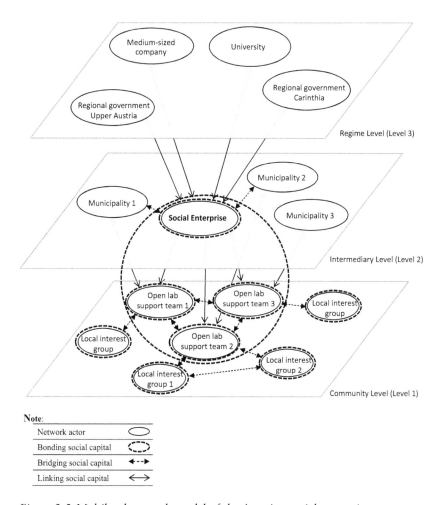

Figure 2.5 Multilevel network model of the Austrian social enterprise

The support team does not have to sign a formal contract with the brain gainers, but has to acknowledge the social enterprise's charter—a list of guiding principles that define the values the team should adhere to and how to run the rural open technology lab. The charter characterizes the open lab support team as a community that is resourceful and interested in socio-political matters (Austrian Social Enterprise, n.d.). It defines the rural open technology labs as self-organized, independent institutions that offer space for creative and meaningful activities and play a role in the development of the respective region. Furthermore, the charter lists guiding values such as *"openness and diversity," "participation, transparency, and trust"* as well as striving for *"social change and humanism"* (Austrian Social Enterprise, n.d.). Even though the social enterprise asks all local communities to sign the charter, it does not control compliance or sanction infringements (Member of social enterprise, field note, March 15, 2016). The document rather serves as a measure of self-selection, which shall ensure that local support teams share the vision of the brain gainers. A social enterprise member adds that the charter serves as a *"linking element or quality criterion and expresses the attitude that is underneath these open spaces [open labs]"* (Member of social enterprise, personal communication, March 9, 2016). By calling the charter a *"linking element"* the statement emphasizes the charter's function to vertically connect the local support teams with the social enterprise. Moreover, the charter aims to ensure shared interests and values, which exceeds a mere functional relation. This suggests that the social enterprise and the open lab support teams are also connected with bonding ties. Figure 2.5 illustrates the additional boundary links by a bold dashed circle encompassing the social enterprise on the intermediary level and the local support teams on the community level.

Beside these bonding ties vertical ties link groups across different levels of power, namely the social enterprise on the intermediary level and the local support teams on the community level. Resources are exchanged across these levels. The social enterprise has developed the idea of open technology labs and contributes reputation, know-how, and important contacts to the establishment of these labs. However, the resource flow is not one-sided; the social enterprise benefits from the local support teams as well. The local support teams establish and run the rural open labs and thereby add to the reputation of the brain gainers. They also provide access to engaged people in the villages and towns, which strengthens the social enterprise's role as an advocate of creative people in the countryside. Moreover, the social enterprise benefits from the contacts to creative people with interesting ideas, which can be a valuable resource for later projects. All in all, both the social enterprise and the open lab support teams benefit from the vertical social capital that results from vertical network contacts.

Another important principle of the charter is that the *"locations and organizations are linked to each other and are in constant exchange so as to learn from one another and to follow shared interests"* (Austrian Social Enterprise, n.d.). Although the actual exchange between local support teams depends on geographical proximity and personal bonds between the teams and their members, it is important to note that the social enterprise fosters exchange by inviting the local support teams to annual meetings and putting emphasis on creating and maintaining a strong network between them. In doing so, the brain gainers stimulate bridging ties between the local teams (illustrated by dashed lines between local support teams in Figure 2.5). Unlike bonding ties, bridging ties link communities from different locations or with different interests. Bridging ties enable out-of-the-box thinking and help the involved communities to benefit from the others' competences. A rural open technology lab, for example, has particular competences in video production while another open lab has competences in 3D printing. Both benefit from the cooperation: while the 3D printing experts have been able to create a video that promotes 3D printing with the help of the video experts, the video experts have learned to create 3D-printed components for their equipment with the help of the 3D experts. However, bridging ties do not only exist between local support teams but also between other local interest groups in proximity to an open technology lab. These local communities share a specific interest (e.g. gaming, yoga, cooking, radio production) and use the open technology lab as a place to meet and exchange. As long as the objectives of the respective interest groups do not violate the charter, all local communities are welcome to use the open technology lab. However, the labs are more than just event locations because the local support teams actively host the various interest groups and stimulate exchange between them so that additional bridging ties emerge. Both in the case of local support teams and interest groups these bridging ties will develop into bridging social capital. The different communities benefit from additional competences and different perspectives, which can lead to the emergence of something new.

Moreover, the social enterprise requires the local support team to obtain support from the local authorities. To establish the open technology lab the municipality is asked to provide adequate rooms with basic infrastructure such as heating and internet access for free. In return, the municipality does not only benefit from an increased attractiveness of the village for creative people but also from making use of otherwise abandoned public buildings. Rural municipalities in remote regions in particular often own a number of vacant or underused buildings and therefore welcome engaged groups that want to make use of them.[1] The provision of the infrastructure requires that the municipal council agrees in a democratic vote. Insisting on the commitment of local authorities and councils is a clever idea of the Austrian brain gainers because it adds to the legitimacy of the initiative, reduces the costs of running the open technology labs and thus enhances their sustainability. For the social enterprise, the commitment from the municipality is an additional guarantee that the remotely operating support teams are well organized and reliable. It is important to note that this requirement helps to link the local support team to the respective municipality. In many cases, the social enterprise actively helps the local team to establish the contact and convince the local authorities (in Figure 2.5 symbolized by the twofold contacts of the social enterprise with the municipality on the intermediary level and the local support team on the community level). Members of the social enterprise, for example, repeatedly travelled to Northern Italy to negotiate with local authorities together with the local support team and thereby paved the way for opening the first rural open technology lab in Italy (Members of the social enterprise outreach team, field note, September 14, 2016). In other cases, the local support team establishes the contact to the municipality itself but nevertheless benefits from being a member of the social enterprise's network due to the legitimacy gained (illustrated in Figure 2.5 by the direct vertical link between the municipality and the local support team). In either way, the social enterprise helps to establish vertical links in the network hierarchy, which provide the local support team and the municipality with linking social capital. The former benefits from the provision of the infrastructure for free, the latter from the use of otherwise vacant public premises and the growing attractiveness of the rural community.

For the social enterprise, vertical links with open technology lab support teams are a source of legitimacy when it comes to cooperation with regime-level actors. As a consequence, the social enterprise constantly highlights its dense network of local support teams in meetings with representatives of regional governments, companies and universities (Field notes, March 7, March 11, September 16, and October 4, 2016). The vertical links turned out to be of particular importance in negotiations on the further development of a so-called "Network of Innovation Culture" in two Austrian provinces. As a social enterprise, the brain gainers cannot offer free support throughout the innovation process but must find a way to generate income based on the acquired expertise and contacts. They managed to be mandated by the regional government with the further development of a network of rural open labs serving as an infrastructure for innovation culture. To demonstrate this cooperation, the social enterprise held a press conference together with a member of the regional government, in which the politician stated:

> *Our state faces challenges that can only be solved together with the people. From the government's perspective, the social enterprise provides an approach that has demonstrated for years how people can be involved in shaping the future.*
>
> (Press information, January 19, 2016, translated by the authors)

The mentioned participatory approach is based on the many vertical and bonding ties the social enterprise maintains with the local support teams as well as the bonding and bridging ties among and between the local support teams themselves. The vertical links with local communities turned out to be fundamental for the establishment of vertical links with regime-level actors. Due to its vertical links with both regime-level actors and community initiatives the social enterprise can take the position of an intermediary. It bridges the gap between both groups and provides solutions for the action problem of regime-level actors (the regional government depends on the community-level actors' power to act) and the idea and resource problem of community initiatives. In its role as intermediary, the social enterprise is in the position to mobilize financial resources from regime-level actors, which, ultimately, also benefit local communities.

Figure 2.5 shows the multilevel network model that depicts the Austrian social enterprise and the involved actors and described links. It is important to note that only those actors who are considered in the model play a role in the establishment of rural open technology labs. Thus, the model only shows a selection of the many network contacts the Austrian social enterprise has. This is also true for the local support teams and interest groups. Due to the sheer number of more than 20 open lab support teams and more than 50 local interest groups established at the time of the study, a detailed illustration of all of them in the network model is not feasible. Therefore, we have decided to show the point in time when the social enterprise had just established three open technology labs. The first three labs were an important milestone. They served to test and adjust the approach and acted as door opener for the diffusion of the idea.

Legitimacy Through Emotional and Instrumental Place Attachment

The social enterprise does not only acquire legitimacy and access to resources through network contacts and vertical, bridging and bonding ties, but also through emotional and instrumental place attachment. The more convincing the social entrepreneur's emotional bonds with the region and the people, the more likely he/she is regarded as legitimate advocate of the region and the more likely he/she has access to resources from both the community and regime-level actors. The Austrian brain gainers are very skilled at expressing their place attachment in order to benefit the social enterprise. Interestingly, the two founders and still members of the social enterprise address different types of place attachment: while one of them rather shows emotional place attachment, the other expresses his bonds with the region rather in an instrumental way. Let us first take a closer look at the founder with more emotional bonds. Emotional place attachment is indicated by the founder's bonds with his rural environment. In particular, most of his activities and network contacts (among them many regional decision makers) exist in his hometown and the surrounding areas, but not so much in other regions or countries. Besides his position in the social enterprise, he is engaged in a large number of clubs and initiatives. Although his place attachment was rather loose in earlier times, this changed when he returned to his home region after he had lived in other places for years:

> *I have to say that I had already had left the town and intended to never come back . . . I was always disappointed about the place*

*because here was not much to do, no perspectives. However, all of
a sudden new perspectives and opportunities appeared. We got new
places and heard out-of-town visitors saying 'it's amazing what's
going on in your town'.*

(Member of social enterprise, personal communication,
March 10, 2016)

The embeddedness and emotional place attachment of the founder have
enabled him to gain the trust of both regional decision makers and locals.
This is important because regional decision makers control the access to
free infrastructure for the open technology labs and the locals run the
open technology lab on a voluntary base.

The other founder has his roots in the same region but his network
clearly exceeds the regional context. He maintains many contacts to
people in Vienna, the capital of Austria, and travels regularly to Berlin and other places in Europe. Nevertheless, in regional meetings and
media reports he often points to his origin in a village in Upper Austria.
He use this biographical reference in a strategic manner to demonstrate
his familiarity with the region, to gain trust from decision makers, to
appear as an advocate of the region and, finally, to promote his services. An example for the rather instrumental use of place attachment
is a newspaper article that is based on an interview with the social
entrepreneur:

*'Sometimes rural life is a shock.' This was the feeling of [the social
entrepreneur] when he returned to his home village after having lived
in cities for 11 years. In fact, one would not expect creative people,
innovation spirit and high-tech in the village, located not far away
from [the provincial town]. 'After returning I asked myself: What
do people need in the countryside? What lacks?' [the social entre-
preneur] states. This was the starting point for the social and professional education worker to develop the idea of rural open technology
labs in 2008.*

(Article in an Austrian Newspaper, September 20, 2013)

This story illustrates the social entrepreneur's concern for the development of the rural region and shows that it is not only a personal interest
that motivated him to develop the rural open technology lab approach.
Showing instrumental place attachment is beneficial for the founder's
role as an advocate of the rural region, because it might make it more
likely to receive funding, especially from regime-level actors. In contrast,
showing emotional place attachment improves access to resources from
the community (e.g. volunteer work) and intermediary level (e.g. provision of infrastructure for free). Thus, the two founders complement each
other and thereby manage to gain legitimacy.

Reconfiguring Resources to Make a Change:
(Social) Innovation

The Austrian social enterprise is innovative for at least three reasons. First, rural open technology labs themselves were a novelty in the place. The Austrian brain gainers were among the first who transferred the idea from cities to the countryside. In doing so, they counter the prejudice that rural regions preserve the well-known rather than inspire exploration of the new and unknown. The rural open technology labs are an example of where established ideas and concepts are transferred to other contexts. Another example of the capability of recontextualizing ideas is the repair café approach that first appeared in the Netherlands in 2009 and was transferred by the brain gainers to Austria and integrated into the open technology labs (Richter, 2017).

Second, the social enterprise creates places where people can be creative and innovative. It invites people to experiment and to share ideas and knowledge so that something new can emerge. To make this happen the social enterprise puts much emphasis on the fact that the open technology labs are not bound to the logic of making profit nor on other logics. That's why the brain gainers call them "white spaces". It is expected that a "community education process" is set in motion that makes people share their knowledge and skills.

Third, how resources are reconfigured to establish and run rural open technology labs is innovative for rural settings. The members of the local support team are crucial for the labs because they contribute volunteer work and thereby ensure their operation. The volunteer work, which is obtained through vertical links between the community level and the intermediary level, is also a door opener for obtaining another resource: the free provision of suitable space equipped with a basic infrastructure. The social enterprise leverages the bonding and bridging ties at the community level to convince municipalities at the intermediary level to co-support the establishment of rural open technology labs. However, the social enterprise does not only obtain the infrastructure from municipalities but also legitimization, as the provision of the infrastructure requires a democratic vote in the municipal council. Finally, the social enterprise leverages the resources acquired at the community and intermediary level to obtain structural funding from the regional governments of Upper Austria and Carinthia. The funding covers the training of local support teams, fostering the exchange between support teams, and scaling the rural open lab approach. It is the structural funding that eventually provides the social enterprise to also generate an income from its efforts around the rural open technology labs. This points to the difference between the Austrian social enterprise and organizations that are mere public service providers. It proactively develops products and services and then looks for resources to realize them instead of simply implementing public funding schemes. All in all, the Austrian social enterprise skillfully acquires resources from the three hierarchical network levels and reconfigures them to implement the rural open technology lab approach.

However, the question remains whether the social enterprise has actually managed to foster change. The social enterprise's aim is to fight brain drain and to foster innovation in rural regions. Our empirical evidence suggests that these aims are not illusory. Regarding the aim to attract creative people to return to the region, a member of a local support team, for example, recalls that it was the open technology lab that enabled her to find like-minded people after having returned to her home village: "*I made contacts with people and organizations in the village thanks to the open technology lab*" (Member of the open lab support team, personal communication, September 5, 2016). Another interview partner reports that even though he moved to Vienna to study, he keeps in touch with people from his home village. This is also due to his involvement in the open technology lab, particularly in the "*community maintenance interest group*" that still meets in the lab (Member of a local interest group, personal communication, September 14, 2016). These examples point in the right direction. However, migration trajectories depend on many factors, of which the existence of an open technology lab is only one pull factor.

Regarding the aim to foster innovation the different rural open technology labs perform very differently. While some open labs suffer from little engagement, low user frequency, and a lack of ideas, others attract very active users, who carry out many activities. One of the observed open technology labs has triggered a community education process. In this lab, the users actively share their knowledge, offer courses and initiate events. They for example teach each other how to repair broken devices. Others are invited to a so called "death café," where people reflect on death. Such community education processes can be regarded as social innovation because they represent new forms of social exchange in the place. It also counteracts the problem that knowledge and skills of elderly people often get lost, and it generates desirable outcomes such as an improvement of social cohesion even across different social and age groups. Other innovative outcomes are spin-offs in the fields of healthy nutrition and 3D printer construction. In both cases the rural open technology labs operated as incubators for non-profit organizations as well as business start-ups.

Not least, innovative solutions can also affect regime level actors. In the Austrian case the regional government has decided to subsidize the development and maintenance of a network of rural open technology labs. As elaborated on above, the regional government particularly values that the social enterprise's approach enhances the innovation culture in rural places. This points to an enhanced awareness of policy makers for the need to foster knowledge production and creativity especially in rural regions.

Summary of Why the SE (Un)successfully Addresses the Challenge

The Austrian social enterprise follows the social mission to make rural Austria an attractive place for creative persons in order to counteract the brain drain of young and skilled people. To achieve this goal the brain gainers have developed the open technology lab approach and support rural communities in establishing these labs. The rural open technology labs serve engaged people to meet, experiment, and share knowledge and skills. We find empirical evidence that rural open labs indeed are appealing for creative people and heighten the place attachment and the likelihood that creative and skilled people return to rural communities. We also observe that in some open technology labs community education processes emerge. Rural open technology labs are an innovative approach and a fertile ground for social innovations because they are relatively new to the places, they change social practices (people share knowledge which otherwise often get lost), and produce socially desirable outcomes.

The successful establishment of rural open technology labs is possible because the social enterprise initiates a bottom-up process in which bonding and bridging links emerge and help to mobilize resources on different levels in the network hierarchy. The combination of resources from the community level (creative ideas, volunteer work), intermediary level (free provision of infrastructure and legitimacy through a democratic vote), and the regime level (provision of public funds) stabilize the open technology labs and make it a facilitator for community education processes. At the same time the dependence from complementary resources bears the risk that open labs become inactive or close in the case that one of these resources should not be available anymore.

Top Down to Success: Establishing an Innovative Approach in an Unfavorable Environment

Mobilizing Resources in a Multilevel Innovation Network

Until 1989, north-east Poland was home to big state farms. The farms provided work as well as housing, medical care, local supplies, and other services to a significant share of the region's inhabitants. Thus, everyone knew that all-encompassing institutions, such as the state and the farms, ensured that everything was taken care of. After the collapse of the socialist system, policy makers realized that the region was badly prepared for the transition into capitalism. The level of qualifications was low, civic engagement was underdeveloped, and an attitude of dependency prevailed. Landowners and business people, who often take responsibility in rural development, did not exist or started to appear only gradually. Although the situation in the region has changed a lot since then, undesired legacies of socialist times and the time of transition can still be found. Interview partners, for example, often described the mentality of the people as being indifferent, passive, and skeptical towards new developments. A lot of people are poor and have low aspirations to change their situation. The economy has improved but still lacks innovative power. The Polish social enterprise has developed a holistic approach to fight these challenges and to change the people's mentality. Among the diverse activities of the social enterprise, the so-called theme village has attracted our attention because it addresses several challenges described above and it is an innovative product developed by the social enterprise. The theme village is a settlement of historical buildings, traditional workshops, and gardens that provides insights into the traditional rural way of life and offers concerts, markets and other events to school classes, tourists, and locals. The theme village integrates disabled persons and other people with low job prospects into work and generates income from tourism in a region that is still dominated by agriculture.

The beginning of the theme village goes back to the European Union's EQUAL community initiative, which had the aim of fostering work integration and social cohesion. After Poland joined the EU in 2004, it implemented this initiative and thereby introduced the concept of social enterprises. The initiative required applicants to realize a social inclusion project based on a partnership between a social enterprise and a public authority to receive funding (European Commission, 2016b). The president of the social enterprise saw the call for tenders and suggested the local government apply for a joint project to establish a theme village. The idea stemmed from the president's trips to Austria, Germany, and Ireland, where he visited theme villages, which had developed into successful tourist destinations and places to preserve the cultural heritage. At that time, theme villages were unknown in Poland, and the tender offered the opportunity to be the first to implement this idea there. The local government was skeptical. However, due to the promised funding of 1 million Złoty and the social enterprise's promise to carry out the main work in the proposal phase the local government eventually agreed to join the project. A representative from the local authority remembers: *"The mayor said to me: 'Listen, we will join but don't expect much help from us'"* (Personal communication, February 15, 2017). A preparatory group was set up to develop the proposal, including the president (as representative of the social enterprise), the director of the local labor agency (as representative of the local authority), the director of the local business club, the manager of a local bank, and two unemployed persons as the main beneficiaries of the project (President of the social enterprise, personal communication, February 20, 2017). The project received funding, and from 2007 onwards the theme village took shape. Since then, the theme village provides persons with low job prospects and disabilities work, for example as potters, gardeners, cooks or waitresses.

An important cornerstone of the project was the selection of an appropriate location for the planned theme village. The preparatory group invited villages in the region to apply. At that time, these villages suffered from a lack of businesses and jobs in other fields than agriculture. An interviewee from the local authorities explains:

> *It was a time when nobody established a business or invested in these places. We had no jobs for the people here, and the problem with transport was really big . . . It was an issue for people to commute 30 kilometres to the next provincial town.*
> (Responsible person at the local government, personal communication, February 15, 2017)

Consequently, the villages were excited about the opportunity to establish a theme village and to get jobs nearby. In the words of a representative from the local authority: "*Everyone dreams about work in the place where they live*" (Responsible person at the local government, personal communication, February 15, 2017). The villages offered land and empty buildings to attract the project. In accordance with the objectives of the social inclusion program, the preparatory group selected the village where the project could have the biggest social impact and where local residents were most determined to get the project. The preparatory team eventually selected a small village in the middle of fields and woods with no job offers besides agriculture but with "*a community that really wanted to take the opportunity, to learn something new and to change the situation for the better*" (President of the social enterprise, personal communication, February 20, 2017).

For the theme village the support of the locals was crucial because a good coexistence is essential in small places. Today, locals work at the theme village, they visit markets and concerts there, and they send their children to childcare particularly during school vacations. Taking into account their supportive role, the local community is considered to be a first actor on the community level of the network model. Because of the shared interest in establishing a theme village and the social proximity between the community members, the people of the local community are linked to each other with bonding ties (see Figure 2.6).

Another relevant group on the community level includes formerly unemployed persons who found a job in the theme village. All of them faced challenges finding work due to low qualifications, reduced mobility, or mental disabilities, which put them at risk of social exclusion. A member of the preparatory group emphasizes their success with training the

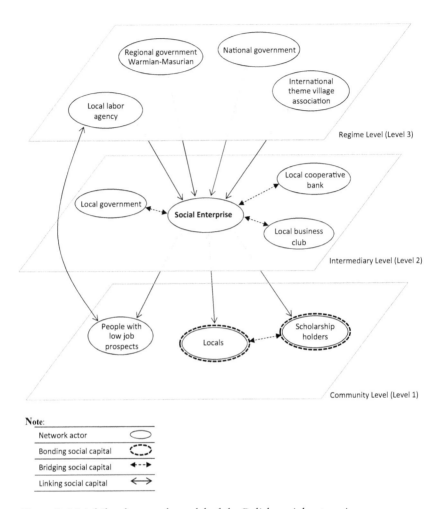

Figure 2.6 Multilevel network model of the Polish social enterprise

group of formerly unemployed persons in endangered professions and skills such as pottery, embroidering, sewing, forging or cooking old Prussian dishes. At the beginning, the people had to be convinced

> *that there will be a job and that they will earn money if they develop these skills. Everything had to be trained. I think that our honesty made them trust us, so that they said: 'Yes, we want to learn.'*
> (Responsible person at the local authority, personal communication, February 15, 2017)

While some of these formerly unemployed people are permanently employed at the theme village others work there on a temporary basis.

A third group of formerly unemployed participate in work integration courses, which are executed by the social enterprise in its role as a social enterprise support center. On behalf of national work integration programs these courses aim to train formerly unemployed people to set up and run their own social enterprises. A building in the theme village houses a business incubator, which can be used by the participants of the work integration courses for developing their social business plan and learning from the theme village. The group of formerly unemployed people thus shares a specific interest and therefore forms a relevant community. This community is integrated at the community level of the network diagram. However, as the community is neither stable nor self-organized, we assume that there are no or only limited bonding ties between the community members.

Students who hold a scholarship from the social enterprise form another community in the network diagram. The scholarship program[2] enables talented pupils from disadvantaged families to further develop their skills and competences by receiving a tertiary education, which would not have been possible without the scholarship. An important element of the scholarship program is that the students learn to not only receive support, but also to give something back to society. This means that the social enterprise expects them to do volunteer work, for example by collecting money for children's summer camps. A member of the social enterprise explains:

> At a charity ball, the scholarship holders collect money for the summer holidays of kids from the surrounding villages. This is the role of the scholarship holders. In May, June, July, August, September and October, the theme village houses these events. The scholarship holders are volunteers, in the garden and on every market. They are here and help to organize this.
> (Personal communication, February 20, 2017)

Without the volunteer work of the scholarship holders the social enterprise would not be able to offer activities free of charge or for a small fee. The affordability of these activities is, however, decisive for reaching poor families in the area. All scholarship holders share an interest in receiving higher education and can therefore be regarded as community at the community level of the network diagram. As all scholarship holders complete a training program in which social values play a significant role, we assume that they are linked with bonding ties.

By requiring scholarship holders to care for, and to play and work with children from the region the social enterprise fosters bridging ties between locals and scholarship holders. The students learn to take social responsibility and to share their skills and knowledge with the children. At the same time, the locals benefit from these activities as well, as their children experience the importance of education and commitment to social and environmental issues. The president of the social enterprise highlighted these effects, which he calls "reversed education", in an interview:

> *We see that the participation of young people in different activities of our organization makes that these young people educate their grandparents and parents afterwards, particularly those with a state farm past and the related mentality. . . . So, it is not only the parents who educate their children but in reverse young people transfer at home what is important. That engagement is important, that ecology is important, etc.*
> (President of the social enterprise, personal communication, February 20, 2017)

On the community level of the network diagram, we do not find any other bridging links besides those between the scholarship holders and the locals. However, we find vertical links between each of the communities and the social enterprise (see Figure 2.6). A reason for the low number of bridging links on the community level might be that the Polish social enterprise shows characteristics of paternalistic governance with the president as patriarchal leader. The patriarch tends to pull the strings that prevents an exchange between the individual communities, such as formerly unemployed persons and scholarship holders. Nevertheless, both the communities and the social enterprise benefit from the vertical links due to the additional resources that can be accessed. While the communities can access the social enterprise's resources such as jobs, scholarships, childcare, and activities offered during school holidays, the social enterprise can access the communities' resources such as volunteer work and skilled labor. In addition, the social enterprise also gains legitimacy due to its efforts to support children and students from poor families in disadvantaged areas. This legitimacy is of particular importance for the social enterprise's links with regime-level actors because the social enterprise's positive impact on marginalized groups makes it more likely that it can mobilize resources from these actors.

Regarding the theme village project, the social enterprise is not the only actor on the intermediary level of the network diagram. The project involves additional actors besides the community-level actors and regime-level actors. These actors include the social enterprise's partners in the preparatory group, i.e. the local government, represented by the head of the local labor agency, a local cooperative bank, and the local business club. Interestingly, these partners represent the main societal fields, which are the state (local government), the market (local bank and business club), and the civil society (social enterprise). As these partners worked together across fields to realize the theme village, we assume that they established bridging links. The resulting bridging social capital is not only relevant in this particular project, but also in other occasions, such as placing qualified workforces in companies. For example, if scholarship holders decide to return to the region after finishing their studies and ask the social enterprise to help them find a job, the social enterprise uses its contacts with the business community, the labor office, and the bank to support the respective person. At the same time, local companies repeatedly expressed their interest in hiring former scholarship holders (Member of the social enterprise, personal communication, February 20, 2017).

In addition to the partners on the intermediary level, the president of the social enterprise maintains close contacts with various actors on the regime level, such as members of national government and parliament. In the president's words: *"I have a lot of friends who are ministers, who have been minister"* (President of the social enterprise, personal communication, February 20, 2017). These contacts date back to his work in a national parliament working group on guarantee funds and to his role as former head of the Polish Guarantee Fund Association. These positions provided him significant insights into national and European funding programs and raised his awareness for the EQUAL program and the opportunities that this program offered for a sustainable development project in his region. The implementation of the program to establish the theme village required intensive consultations with the Ministry of Family, Labor, and Social Policy, which managed the EQUAL program at the national level. Thus, there is a vertical link between the social enterprise (on the intermediary level) and the national government (on the regime level). Besides financial resources to establish the theme village, the development of the theme village approach also required ideational resources. Journeys to existing theme villages in other European countries provided inspiration and the necessary know-how. During these journeys, the president established contacts with the international theme village association in Germany, which led to the foundation of a national theme village interest group in Poland ("Polskie Wioski Tematyczne"). The social enterprise benefits from the vertical link to the international theme village association, partly because the exchange with other theme villages provides new ideas and inspirations and because these international contacts add to the social enterprise's reputation as the mastermind of theme villages in Poland and as an internationally acknowledged organization. For the international theme village association, in turn, the social enterprise serves as a bridgehead to the almost 50 theme villages that exist in Poland today (Lokalna Grupa Dzialania, 2016).

Another vertical link that is crucial for maintaining and further developing the theme village is the one between the social enterprise and the local labor agency. The local labor agency provides subsidies for integrating persons with disabilities into work, and supports the village by sending long-term unemployed people for internships.[3] These subsidies reduce the labor costs for tasks that require employees with low qualifications, such as landscaping. Moreover, vertical links exist with the regional government, in particular the department of social policy. This department manages the national social economy scheme for the voivodship and mandates the social enterprise to execute the social business work integration program. A part of this program is conducted via a social business incubator, which is located in the theme village. Thus, the vertical link to the regional government enables the social enterprise to access financial resources for the theme village and to use synergies between the supported social business start-ups and the theme village, which serves as a role model for the start-ups.

Figure 2.6 summarizes the network of the Polish social enterprise as it has been described so far. Again, only those actors and relations are visualized that are relevant for the presented theme village. The social enterprise has vertical links with both the community level and the regime level. Except for the link between the local labor agency and formerly unemployed persons, all vertical links pass the social enterprise. The social enterprise is in the advantageous position to broker resources while it makes less effort to foster the direct exchange between the different stakeholders.

Legitimacy Through Emotional and Instrumental Place Attachment

When we asked the president of the social enterprise in an interview about his motivation to build the theme village he answered:

I think it is a result of digging in the history of [the provincial town]. For many years, I have bought old postcards and historical souvenirs from the town from the times before war. It is a combination of interests together with the ambition to find out what we can achieve with a social enterprise.
(President of the social enterprise, personal communication, February 20, 2017)

The president's reference to the history of the town as a main motivation for establishing the theme village indicates his emotional place attachment. The emotional relationship he has with the region becomes even more evident when walking through the theme village. Several buildings are decorated with old photographs of the town and the traditional workshops are a reminiscence of the history of the place. "*The town,*" the president adds, "*was a center of the ceramic production in former East Prussia . . . The traditions in pottery are very strong. Thus, the thematic focus of the theme village was dictated by these traditions*" (Personal communication, February 20, 2017). The manifold references to the history and the traditions of the region are surprising, as the region was under German rule until the end of World War II. When it became part of the Polish national state, it experienced a high level of migration, which could lead to a loss of the region's traditions. The more interesting it is to see how much the president is digging in the regional traditions. It is obvious that this interest is an expression of emotional bonds with the place.

In addition to the president's emotional place attachment, the social enterprise also uses instrumental place attachment to gain legitimacy. This shows, for example, when the president introduces the social enterprise to people who are not familiar with the company. The outline typically starts with a description of the challenging situation the region faced at the beginning of the post-socialist transformation. It then illustrates the significant changes that the region has experienced and explains how the social enterprise has facilitated these changes. In particular, the role of the social enterprise was to change the mind of the people and to help build a dense network of small and medium-sized enterprises. The story shows the social enterprise's efforts to improve the region's social and economic situation and highlights its success in doing so. Thus, the narration refers to the place attachment in an instrumental way even though instrumental place attachment is rooted in an emotional place attachment of the social entrepreneur.

The significant role of the social enterprise and its president in the social and economic change of the region is also acknowledged by the regional government. A representative of the Department of Social Policy remembers that the region gave a depressing impression in the 1990s. She attributes an important role in the recovery of the region to the social enterprise and acknowledges that the theme village was a role model for other social enterprises and social inclusion initiatives. She concludes: "*As a result, the social enterprise has been mandated with operating the social business support center*" (Responsible person at the regional government, personal communication, February 14, 2017). By linking the social business support center with the achievements of the social enterprise in the region, the regional government acknowledges the significant role the social enterprise plays in the region and thus confirms the social enterprise's narration. The mind changers' instrumental references to place attachment seem to have fulfilled their role—to legitimize the social enterprise as an advocate of the rural region.

We assume that demonstrating place attachment legitimizes the social enterprise towards regime-level actors. Interestingly, place attachment seems to be less relevant in the communication with community-level actors. A reason might be that the investigated region has a comparatively hierarchical sociopolitical system, which requires the social enterprise to demonstrate its legitimacy towards more powerful actors at higher levels of the network model but not necessarily towards less powerful actors at lower levels.

Reconfiguring Resources to Make a Change:
(Social) Innovation

The most innovative project of the Polish mind changers is the theme village. While various services of the company are delivered on behalf of public authorities and private foundations, the theme village has been developed by the social enterprise itself and is therefore different from activities typically offered in the region, as the president states: "*Our success is that we do absolutely non-standard activities . . . such as the theme village. I would say it is our experimental training ground*" (Personal communication, February 20, 2017). The social enterprise was among the first to build a theme village in Poland. They already existed in other European countries. The president has recontextualized the idea by transferring it to Poland and adjusting it to the requirements of the funding program and the cultural legacy of the region. Both members of the social enterprise and its stakeholders emphasize the innovative nature of the village. The mayor of the provincial town states outright: "*For example, the theme village is an innovation*" (Personal communication, January 24, 2017). Interviewees from the local bank, instead, do not find the theme village as such "*really innovative*" but the combination of traditions and new forms of cultural education:

> The theme village is mostly about this old traditions and culture and teaching about history and, you know, education about the region. And to connect this with something new, like new ideas about how to inform people about this and how to show the region, so it's like tradition and innovation in one thing.
> (CEO of a local bank, personal communication, February 7, 2017)

It is not easy to offer activities like the ones offered in the theme village in a region that is comparably poor and in the field of education where customers are rather price sensitive. Only the skillful combination of resources—mobilized from the three societal fields state, market, and civil society—enables the social enterprise to make the village a successful project. First, the social enterprise is supported by the state through subsidies for work integration of disabled persons and other persons who face difficulties finding work. It also receives public grants from the social business start-up program, which covers the costs for running the business incubator in the theme village. Second, it generates market income through fees for guided tours and workshops (such as team building and social responsibility workshops for companies), entrance fees for concerts, the sale of souvenirs and of food in the tavern, and consultancy fees. Third, it is supported by the civil society through volunteer work (for example by scholarship holders who organize holiday events and childcare for children from the region). As running the theme village based on these diverse resources is a constant challenge, the Polish mind changers regard it as one of their biggest achievements that the theme village is an independent, financially stable project (President of the social enterprise, personal communication, February 20, 2017).

The Polish social enterprise mobilizes resources through a top-down rather than a bottom-up process. The basis for the successful establishment of the project is the president's contacts to regime-level actors and his experience with public funding structures. Directly after Poland's accession to the European Union he was among the first who recognized the opportunities of the new EU funding schemes. Having addressed these newly emerging schemes in close consultation with the national and regional program managers he had the authority to convince the local authority and the business community to join the preparatory team and develop a project proposal. Thus, the vertical ties to regime-level actors leveraged the establishment and strengthening of bridging ties to intermediary-level actors. The legitimacy of the actors who joined the preparatory team made it possible to convince community-level actors to join, particularly the locals from the village where plans were in place to establish the theme village. Thus, it is the social enterprise's vertical ties to more powerful regime-level actors that give the social enterprise legitimacy towards less powerful actors on the community level. Reasons for this observation might be predominant authoritarian attitudes or the low esteem given to civic engagement in Poland as recent reports have revealed (Institute of Public Affairs, 2018; Pazderski, 2018).

Criteria for a social innovation are: (1) a new solution spreads beyond the narrow environment in which it emerged, (2) it is adapted by other people, and (3) it changes the thinking and practices of people (Howaldt & Schwarz, 2010; Christmann, 2011). In the present case, the diffusion of the idea to establish a theme village can be observed easily. The president of the social enterprise, who organized a tour to promote the theme village, played an important role in scaling up the idea. The president remembers:

> *It was a time when [the CEO of the bank] and I travelled through Poland. We were at various places and met people from organizations, from the business, from administration, and we explained how important local cooperation is. Afterwards, similar initiatives emerged in many places.*
>
> (President of the social enterprise, personal communication,
> February 20, 2017)

Promoting the theme village approach in the whole country shows that the social enterprise treated the approach as open source. The impact of the project and its promotion is reflected in the fact that in 2016, only

10 years later, 49 theme villages existed in Poland (Lokalna Grupa Dzialania, 2016).

All our interview partners in Poland regarded the theme village as a very successful project. The common view was that the biggest impact of the theme village derives from it being a role model. The statement of a decision maker from the regional government stands for other comments that describe this role model effect:

> *I think after EQUAL [the EU EQUAL program] people started to talk about the theme village, there was a real boom. We also helped. We invited people from all over Poland, representatives of similar organizations as mine, to meet in the theme village, to show how it looks like. It was a couple of years ago, but when I meet people from back then, they always ask 'what's going on in the theme village?' I answer 'come and see, there are so many more things today'. So this was a sort of education for our colleagues.*
> (Responsible person at the regional government, personal communication, February 14, 2017)

The diffusion of the approach in Poland and the new combination of already existing elements—theme villages as tourist attractions, for cultural education, and for social inclusion through work integration—suggest that the theme village approach is a social innovation. The president of the social enterprise also regards the theme village as a measure to change the mindset of the people and to increase their civic engagement. He believes that the village shows that it is possible to realize a business in remote rural regions and that it pays to engage rather than to complain about unfavorable framework conditions (President of the social enterprise, personal communication, February 20, 2017). The representative of the local authority confirms at another occasion that civic engagement in the community begins to grow and that the theme village inspired people to set up their own businesses, for example to produce *pierogi*, a traditional Polish sort of dumplings:

> *The theme village . . . inspired all the people dealing with crafts at home. Sewing, embroidering, pottery. Because they often meet in the theme village . . . I cannot count how many bars with pierogi opened after the theme village was established.*
> (Responsible person at the local authority, personal communication, February 15, 2017)

However, other interviewees do not see a big change in the level of activity and the mindset of the people, because parents would pass passivity and low aspirations on to their children, particularly in remote rural places (CEO of a local bank, personal communication, February 7, 2017; Regional development expert, personal communication, February 4, 2017).

Finally, the Polish company shows that social enterprises can also change the mindset of regime-level actors. Representatives from the local and regional government characterize the president as a pioneer, who repeatedly put pressure on public authorities to deal with new developments and take action. An interviewee from the local government remembers the reluctance the president encountered from the municipality when he and the preparatory group looked for a suitable location for the theme village. One option was an empty school building and its premises but the municipality refused, because social enterprises were new, and the municipality had doubts about the sustainability of the project. However, over time, the ideas of the social enterprise caused the municipality to reconsider. If social businesses asked to use vacant public premises today, the municipality would be more open: *"Today, there are completely different times. Requests are treated in a more supportive way, and municipalities more likely want to get rid of buildings"* (Responsible person at the local authority, personal communication, February 15, 2017).

Summary of Why the SE (Un)successfully Addresses the Challenge

Founded as a regional development company that fights the structural deficits in the rural north-east of Poland, the EU EQUAL program gave rise to a second career as a social enterprise with both a strong social mission (changing people's mindsets to make the region a better place) as well as entrepreneurial interests (establishing a successful tourist attraction). Although it is unrealistic to expect that a single enterprise can change an entire region, the Polish mind changers have had considerable impact in the region and beyond. This was possible due to their ability to identify and seize new trends and opportunities, and to diffuse them across the country. They paved the way for a growing social economy in the region and for the rediscovery of handicraft traditions.

How the social enterprise gives rise to social innovation can be seen in its theme village, which was the first of its kind in Poland and stimulated the establishment of dozens of others across the country. The theme village is an example of developing an innovative solution through recontextualizing existing elements, and for the skillful reconfiguration of resources from the three main societal fields: state, market, and civil society. Mobilizing these resources is possible because of the social enterprise's role as an intermediary that has vertical links with regime-level and community-level actors, and bridging ties with actors on the intermediary level. Interestingly, the mobilization of resources is a top-down rather than a bottom-up process. Maintaining vertical links with regime-level actors provides legitimacy and leverages the mobilization of resources on the intermediary and the community level. The access to community-level actors and their needs is rather a consequence than a precondition for setting up the project.

Key Takeaways From the Single Case Analysis

The aim of this chapter was to reveal how rural social enterprises succeed with counteracting challenges in rural Europe and how they reconfigure resources to achieve this goal in an innovative way. For this purpose, we have reconstructed the hierarchical networks of social enterprises and analyzed how resources are obtained from bonding, bridging, and vertical social capital embedded in the network contacts. We find that the investigated rural social enterprises act as intermediaries who broker resources between the regime and the community level. This way they solve the action problem of regime actors as well as the idea and resource problem of communities. Rural social enterprises owe this position the legitimacy that is attributed to them thanks to their place attachment and their ability to combine upwards contacts and regime actors with access to rural communities.

We have identified three strategies for how social enterprises establish horizontal and vertical links in hierarchical innovation networks. First, we observe a bottom up strategy, which is characterized by the establishment of initial links to communities who search for solutions to their needs. Acting as advocates of these groups and leverage bonding and bridging social capital enables social enterprises to mobilize resources on higher hierarchical levels. The Austrian and the Irish social enterprise correspond to the bottom up strategy. Second, we observe a top down strategy in which successfully established links to regime level actors provide the social enterprise authority to establish contacts with organizations and communities on lower hierarchical levels. The Polish social enterprise resembles this strategy. Third, the Greek social enterprise is characterized by both a bottom up and top down strategy. The two-sided organizational structure enables the Greek cooperative to address regime actors and simultaneously to establish links with actors on the community level.

The social enterprise networks offer simultaneous access to resources on different hierarchical levels. This is important because rural social enterprises realize their approach by combining resources mobilized at different levels such as public funds and subsidies, political support and free use of infrastructure, volunteer work and social and cultural capital. Moreover, the mobilized resources often originate from different horizontal domains such as the state (e.g. political support), the market (revenues from sales), and the civil society (volunteer work). This finding suggests that social enterprises must have the capability to mobilize and combine different sorts of resources to successfully address a social challenge.

Making use of only one type of resource (e.g. revenues from sales) often does not compensate the costs because the costumers and beneficiaries of social entrepreneurial services and products often are not in a position to pay the full or even part of the price for the service (e.g. participants of work integration courses). However, the dependence on different types of resources also has critical implications. It makes social enterprises more vulnerable because if access to only one resource terminates the provision of the whole service or even the survival of the enterprise can be at stake.

Social enterprises promise to develop innovative solutions for challenges and to facilitate social change. Indeed, our investigation suggests that social enterprises have the capability to generate novel solutions and fight social problems. We find that they innovate in two different ways: *product/service innovation* and *process innovation*. In the first case it is the social enterprise that develops an offer that addresses the specific needs of the target group. In the second case the social enterprise develops a new way of delivering services and products to the target group. The two types of innovation pursued by social enterprises seem to be scalable to a different extent. Because the small size of the target group of the products and services delivered by social enterprises is the reason for neither state nor corporates to move, social enterprises address this specific need in the first place and scaling the business would call for a larger market, growth strategies for social enterprises based on service and product innovations seem to be unlikely. Thus, the small market provides the entrepreneurial opportunity for social enterprises, but it at the same time restricts their growth potential through scaling their output. However, in case there is a similar pattern of need in different locations, innovative products and services can also be scaled. The Polish case organization for example has scaled the product/service of a theme village that was new and valuable for rural settings in Poland across the whole country. Interestingly, the theme villages have not been developed by the case organization, but by local social enterprises. These local social enterprises benefitted from the case organization's proof of concept and also gained direct support through shared expertise. It is important to note that the diffusion of the Polish product/service innovation has not weakened the market position of the inventor through intensified competition. On the contrary, the rising number of successful imitators has strengthened the legitimacy of social enterprises in Poland and thus contributed also to the success of our Polish case enterprise.

At the same time new and valuable ways of delivering products and services can be transferred from the context in which the social enterprise has originally developed them to other contexts. An innovative process of participatory community development that was developed for establishing a playground in a remote village can be transferred to other product/service innovation projects or to other geographical contexts. Our Irish case organization has scaled their innovative process of product/service delivery across diverse issues of regional development in a rural setting reaching from the development of health care networks to job training and education programs. The Austrian case organization has transferred their innovative process of setting up and running open technology labs across rural regions in Austria and three neighboring countries.

Notes

1 A regional development expert, for example, complained about underutilized school buildings in rural Lower Austria and regarded the co-utilization of school buildings by open technology labs as a good possibility for tackling the problem (Regional development expert at the government of Lower Austria, field note, March 11, 2016).
2 The scholarship program is executed by an organization that has been out-sourced by the social enterprise years ago. Actually, the scholarship organization and the social enterprise work very close together not least because the head of the scholarship organization is the wife of the president. Both organizations share resources such as premises and volunteer work.
3 A representative of the labor agency emphasizes that persons who do internships are only initially paid by the labor agency. If their work is satisfactory, they receive their salary from the social enterprise (Responsible person at the local authority, personal communication, February 15, 2017).

References

Agger, A. and Jensen, J. O. (2015). Area-based initiatives—and their work in bonding, bridging and linking social capital. *European Planning Studies*, 23, 2045–2061. DOI: 10.1080/09654313.2014.998172

Ahram, Ariel I. (2011). The theory and method of comparative area studies. *Qualitative Research*, 11(1), 69–90.

Anastasiadis, M., Gspurnig, W. and Lang, R. (2018). *A Map of Social Enterprises and Their Eco-Systems in Europe. Country Report: Austria*. Brussels: European Commission.

Austrian Newspaper. (2013). Article (translated by the authors).

Austrian Social Enterprise. (n.d.). Charter (translated by the authors).

Bacq, S. and Janssen, F. (2011). The multiple faces of social entrepreneurship: A review of definitional issues based on geographical and thematic criteria. *Entrepreneurship & Regional Development*, 23(5–6), 373–403.

Bitektine, A. and Haack, P. (2015). The "macro" and the "micro" of legitimacy: Toward a multilevel theory of the legitimacy process. *Academy of Management Review*, 40, 49–75. DOI: 10.5465/amr.2013.0318

Bock, B. B. (2012). Social innovation and sustainability: How to disentangle the buzzword and its application in the field of agriculture and rural development. *Studies in Agricultural Economics*, 114, 57–63.

Bock, B. B. (2016). Rural marginalisation and the role of social innovation: A turn towards nexogenous development and rural reconnection. *Sociologia Ruralis*, 56(4), 552–573.

Braunholtz-Speight, T. (2015). Scottish community land initiatives: Going beyond the locality to enable local empowerment. *People, Place and Policy*, 9, 123–138. DOI: 10.3351/ppp.0009.0002.0004

Breitenecker, R. J. and Harms, R. (2010). Dealing with spatial heterogeneity in entrepreneurship research. *Organizational Research Methods, 13,* 176–191. DOI: 10.1177/1094428109338871

Brennan, M. A., Flint, C. G. and Luloff, A. E. (2009). Bringing together local culture and rural development: Findings from Ireland, Pennsylvania and Alaska. *Sociologia Ruralis, 49,* 97–112. DOI: 10.1111/j.1467-9523.2008.00471.x

Brunie, A. (2009). Meaningful distinctions within a concept: Relational, collective, and generalized social capital. *Social Science Research, 38,* 251–265. DOI: 10.1016/j.ssresearch.2009.01.005

Burt, R. (2004). Structural holes and good ideas. *American Journal of Sociology, 110*(2), 349–399.

Christmann, G. B. (2011). Soziale innovationen, social entrepreneurs und raumbezüge [Social innovations, social entrepreneurs, and spatial references]. In Petra Jähnke, et al. (Eds.): *Social Entrepreneurship: Perspektiven für die Raumentwicklung* (193–210). Wiesbaden: VS Verlag.

Corbin, J. and Strauss, A. (2015). *Basics of Qualitative Research: Techniques and Procedures for Developing Grounded Theory.* Thousand Oaks, CA: Sage.

Dees, J. G. (2001/1998). *The Meaning of "Social Entrepreneurship."* Retrieved from https://centers.fuqua.duke.edu/case/wp-content/uploads/sites/7/2015/03/Article_Dees_MeaningofSocialEntrepreneurship_2001.pdf

Defourny, J. and Nyssens, M. (2013). Social innovation, social economy and social enterprise: What can the European debate tell us? In F. Moulaert, D. MacCallum, A. Mehmood, and A. Hamdouch (Eds.): *The International Handbook on Social Innovation* (40–52). Cheltenham, UK: Edward Elgar.

Doherty, B., Haugh, H. and Lyon, F. (2014). Social enterprises as hybrid organizations: A review and research agenda. *International Journal of Management Reviews, 16*(4), 417–436.

Eisenhardt, K. M. (1989). Building theories from case study research. *Academy of Management Review, 14,* 532–550. DOI: 10.5465/AMR.1989.4308385

Eisenhardt, K. M. and Graebner, M. E. (2007). Theory building from cases: Opportunities and challenges. *Academy of Management Journal, 50*(1), 25–32.

European Commission (EC). (2011). *Social Business Initiative: Creating a Favourable Climate for Social Enterprises, Key Stakeholders in the Social Economy and Innovation.* Brussels: European Commission.

European Commission (EC). (2013). *Rural Development in the European Union: Statistical and Economic Information Report 2013.* European Commission, Directorate-General for Agriculture and Rural development.

European Commission (EC). (2014a). *A Map of Social Enterprises and Their Eco-Systems in Europe: Country Report Austria.* Brussels: European Union.

European Commission (EC). (2014b). *A Map of Social Enterprises and Their Eco-Systems in Europe: Country Report Greece.* Brussels: European Union.

European Commission (EC). (2015). *A Map of Social Enterprises and Their Eco-Systems in Europe: Synthesis Report.* Brussels: European Commission, Directorate-General for Employment, Social Affairs and Inclusion.

European Commission (EC). (2016a). *Social Enterprises and Their Eco-Systems: A European Mapping Report. Updated Country Report: Ireland.* Brussels: Directorate-General for Employment, Social Affairs and Inclusion.

European Commission (EC). (2016b). *Social Enterprises and Their Eco-Systems: A European Mapping Report. Updated Country Report: Poland.* Brussels: Directorate-General for Employment, Social Affairs and Inclusion.

European Commission (EC). (2016c). *Social Enterprises and Their Eco-Systems: Developments in Europe.* Brussels: Directorate-General for Employment, Social Affairs and Inclusion.

Farmer, J., Steinerowski, A. and Jack, S. (2008). Starting social enterprises in remote and rural Scotland: Best or worst of circumstances? *International Journal of Entrepreneurship and Small Business*, 6, 450–464. DOI: 10.1504/IJESB.2008.019138

Ferlander, S. (2007). The importance of different forms of social capital for health. *Acta Sociologica, 50*, 115–128. DOI: 10.1177/0001699307077654

Fink, M., Lang, R. and Richter, R. (2017). Social entrepreneurship in marginalised rural Europe: Towards evidence-based policy for enhanced social innovation. *Regions Magazine, 306*(1), 6–10. DOI: 10.1080/13673882.2017.11878963

Fink, M., Loidl, S. and Lang, R. (2013). *Community Based Entrepreneurship and Rural Development.* London: Routledge.

Flick, U., von Kardorff, E. and Steinke, I. (2008). *Was ist qualitative Forschung? Einleitung und Überblick [What is qualitative research? An introduction and overview].* In U. Flick, et al. (Eds.): *Qualitative Forschung: Ein Handbuch [Qualitative Research: A Handbook]* (13–29). Reinbek bei Hamburg: Rowohlt.

Geels, F. W. (2002). Technological transitions as evolutionary reconfiguration processes: A multi-level perspective and a case study. *Research Policy, 31*, 1257–1274. DOI: 10.1016/S0048-7333(02)00062-8

Geels, F. W. (2004). From sectoral systems of innovation to socio-technical systems: Insights about dynamics and change from sociology and institutional theory. *Research Policy, 33*, 897–920. DOI: 10.1016/j.respol.2004.01.015

Giddens, A. (1984). *The Constitution of Society.* Cambridge: Polity Press.

Gittel, Ross and Videl, Avis. (1998). *Community Organizing: Building Social Capital as a Development Strategy.* Thousand Oaks, CA: Sage.

Giuliani, M. V. (2003). Theory of attachment and place attachment. In M. Bonnes, T. Lee, and M. Bonainto (Eds.): *Psychological Theories for Environmental Issues.* Aldershot: Ashgate.

Granovetter, M. S. (1973). The strength of weak ties. *American Journal of Sociology, 78*, 1360–1380. DOI: 10.1086/225469

Granovetter, M. S. (1985). Economic action and social structure: The problem of embeddedness. *American Journal of Sociology, 91*(3), 481–510.

Harvey, D. (1996). *Justice, Nature and the Geography of Difference.* Oxford: Blackwell.

Hatak, I., Lang, R. and Roessl, D. (2016). Trust, social capital, and the coordination of relationships between the members of cooperatives: A comparison between member-focused cooperatives and third-party-focused cooperatives. *Voluntas, 27*, 1218–1241. DOI: 10.1007/s11266-015-9663-2

Howaldt, Jürgen and Schwarz, Michael. (2010). *Soziale Innovationen—Konzepte, Forschungsfelder und—perspektiven [Social Innovations—Approaches, Research Areas and Perspecties].* In J. Howald and H. Jacobsen (Eds.): *Soziale Innovation: Auf dem Weg zu einem postindustriellen Innovationsparadigma* (87–108). Wiesbaden: VS Verlag.

Hudson, R. (2001). *Producing Places.* London: Guildford Press.

Hulgard, L. and Spear, R. (2006). Social entrepreneurship and the mobilization of social capital in European social enterprises. In M. Nyssens (Ed.): *Social*

Enterprise at the Crossroads of Market, Public Policies and Civil Society. Abingdon: Routledge.

Institute of Public Affairs. (2018). *Citizenship Empowerment: Potential for Civic Participation in the Visegrad countries, 2017 & 2018.* Warszaw: Institute of Public Affairs. Retrieved from www.isp.org.pl/en/publications/citizenship-empower ment-potential-for-civic-participation-in-the-visegrad-countries-2017-amp-2018

Jack, S. L. and Anderson, A. R. (2002). The effects of embeddedness on the entrepreneurial process. *Journal of Business Venturing, 17,* 467–488. DOI: 10.1016/ S0883-9026(01)00076-3

Johnstone, H. and Lionais, D. (2004). Depleted communities and community business entrepreneurship: Revaluing space though place. *Enterpreneurship and Regional Development, 16,* 217–233. https://doi.org/10.1080/08985620 42000197117.

Kibler, E., Fink, M., Lang, R. and Muñoz, P. (2015). Place attachment and social legitimacy: Revisiting the sustainable entrepreneurship journey. *Journal of Business Venturing Insights, 3,* 24–29. DOI: 10.1016/j.jbvi.2015.04.001.

Kibler, E. and Kautonen, T. (2016). The moral legitimacy of entrepreneurs: An analysis of early-stage entrepreneurship across 26 countries. *International Small Business Journal, 34,* 34–50. DOI: 10.1177/0266242614541844

Kibler, E., Kautonen, T. and Fink, M. (2014). Regional social legitimacy of entrepreneurship: Implications for entrepreneurial intention and start-up behavior. *Regional Studies, 48,* 995–1015. DOI: 10.1080/00343404.2013.851373

Lang, R. and Fink, M. (2018). Rural social entrepreneurship: The role of social capital within and across institutional levels. *Journal of Rural Studies.* DOI: 10.1016/j.jrurstud.2018.03.012.

Lang, R., Fink, M. and Kibler, E. (2014). Understanding place-based entrepreneurship in rural central Europe—a comparative institutional analysis. *International Small Business Journal, 32,* 204–227. DOI: 10.1177/0266242613488614

Lang, R. and Novy, A. (2014). Cooperative housing and social cohesion: The role of linking social capital. *European Planning Studies, 22,* 1744–1764. DOI: 10.1080/09654313.2013.800025

Lang, R. and Roessl, D. (2011). Contextualizing the governance of community co-operatives: Evidence from Austria and Germany. *Voluntas, 22,* 706–730. https://doi.org/10.1007/s11266-011-9210-8.

Lehner, O. M. (2011). The phenomenon of social enterprise in Austria: A triangulated descriptive study. *Journal of Social Entrepreneurship, 2,* 53–78. DOI: 10.1080/19420676.2011.555775

Lieblich, A., Tuval-Mashiach, R. and Zilber, T. (1998). *Narrative Research: Reading, Analysis, and Interpretation.* Thousand Oaks, CA: Sage.

Lokalna Grupa Dzialania "Warmínski Zakatek" (2016). *Polskie Wioski Tematyczne.*

Mair, J. and Marti, I. (2006). Social entrepreneurship research: A source of explanation, prediction, and delight. *Journal of World Business, 41*(1), 36–44.

Martin, R. L. and Osberg, S. (2007). Social entrepreneurship: The case for definition. *Stanford Social Innovation Review, 5*(2), 28–39.

Munoz, S-A., Steiner, A. and Farmer, J. (2015). Processes of community-led social enterprise development: Learning from the rural context. *Community Development Journal, 50,* 478–493. DOI: 10.1093/cdj/bsu055

Obstfeld, D. (2005). Social networks, the tertius iungens orientation, and involvement in innovation. *Administrative Science Quarterly, 50*(1), 100–130.

Osborne, C., Baldwin, C. and Thomsen, D. (2016). Contributions of social capital to best practice urban planning outcomes. *Urban Policy and Research*, 34, 212–224. DOI: 10.1080/08111146.2015.1062361

Pazderski, Filip. (2018). *Analyse: Demokratische Skeptiker oder politisierte Aktivisten? Über die Zivilgesellschaft und die Beziehung zur Demokratie in Polen und den Visegrád-Ländern*, Bundeszentrale für politische Bildung [Analysis: Skeptical towards democracy or political activism? About the civil society and the relation with democracy in Poland and the *Visegrád contries*], Berlin. Retrieved from www.bpb.de/internationales/europa/polen/268605/analyse-demokratische-skeptiker-oder-politisierte-aktivisten-ueber-die-zivilgesellschaft-und-die-beziehung-zur-demokratie-in-polen-und-den-visegrad-laendern

Poortinga, W. (2012). Community resilience and health: The role of bonding, bridging, and linking aspects of social capital. *Health & Place*, 18, 286–295. DOI: 10.1016/j.healthplace.2011.09.017

Portes, A. (1998). Social capital: Its origins and applications in modern sociology. *Annual Review of Sociology*, 24, 1–24. DOI: 10.1146/annurev.soc.24.1.1

Przyborski, A. and Wohlrab-Sahr, M. (2010). *Qualitative Sozialforschung: Ein Arbeitsbuch [Qualitative Social Research. A Workbook]*. München: Oldenbourg.

Putnam, R. D. (2000). *Bowling Alone: The Collapse and Revival of American Community*. New York: Simon Schuster.

Putnam, R. D., Leonardi, R. and Nanetti, R. Y. (1994). *Making Democracy Work: Civic Traditions in Modern Italy*. Princeton, NJ: Princeton University Press.

Ragin, C. C. (1989). *The Comparative Method: Moving Beyond Qualitative and Quantitative Strategies*. Berkeley: University of California Press.

Richter, R. (2017). Rural social enterprises as embedded intermediaries: The innovative power of connecting rural communities with supra-regional networks. *Journal of Rural Studies*. DOI: 10.1016/j.jrurstud.2017.12.005

Santos, F. M. (2012). A positive theory of social entrepreneurship. *Journal of Business Ethics*, 111(3), 335–351.

Sayer, A. (1992). *Method in Social Science: A Realist Approach*. London: Routledge.

Schuetze, F. (1977). *Die Technik des narrativen Interviews in Interaktionsfeldstudien: dargestellt an einem Projekt zur Erforschung von kommunalen Machtstrukturen [The Technique of Narrative Inquiry in Interaction Field Studies]*, Arbeitsberichte und Forschungsmaterialien No. 1. Bielefeld: Fakultät für Soziologie, Universität Bielefeld.

Steinerowski, A. and Steinerowska-Streb, I. (2012). Can social enterprise contribute to creating sustainable rural communities? Using the lens of structuration theory to analyze the emergence of rural social enterprise. *Local Economy*, 27, 167–182. DOI: 10.1177/0269094211429650

Strauss, A. and Corbin, J. (1990). *Basics of Qualitative Research: Grounded Theory Procedures and Techniques*. Thousand Oaks, CA: Sage.

Szreter, S. and Woolcock, M. (2004). Health by association? Social capital, social theory, and the political economy of public health. *International Journal of Epidemiology*, 33, 650–667. DOI: 10.1093/ije/dyh013

Thuesen, A. A. and Rasmussen, H. B. (2015). Danish rural areas' readiness for joint action as a proxy for the potential for co-production. *Journal of Rural and Community Development*, 10, 32–55.

Tilly, C. (1984). *Big Structures, Large Processes, Huge Comparisons*. New York, NY: Russell Sage Foundation.

Welter, F. (2011). Conceptual challenges and ways forward. *Entrepreneurship Theory & Practice, 35*(1), 165–184.

Wimmer, A. and Glick-Schiller, N. (2002). Methodological nationalism and beyond: Nation-state building, migration and the social sciences. *Global Networks, 2*(4), 301–334.

Yin, R. K. (2009). *Case Study Research: Design and Methods.* Thousand Oaks, CA: Sage.

Zografos, C. (2007). Rurality discourses and the role of the social enterprise in regenerating rural. *Journal of Rural Studies, 23,* 38–51. DOI: 10.1016/j.jrurstud. 2006.04.002

3 Rural Social Enterprise
An Emerging Strategic Action Field

In this third chapter, we engage in a cross-case analysis to identify similarities and differences among the four cases. Therefore, we initially return to the findings from the analyses in the previous chapters. It leads us to the insight that all four case organizations are characterized by some degree of institutional hybridity, as they simultaneously operate in different fields (e.g. state, market, third sector), which have their own institutional logics. Thus, social enterprises, as hybrid organizations, are especially vulnerable to legitimacy challenges from their external environment. On the one hand, they need to conform with values and practices of different organizational spheres. On the other hand, they also need to distinguish themselves from these other fields and carve out room for strategic action in order to survive (Macmillan et al., 2013; McInerney, 2013). Against this background, this chapter continues and deepens the action perspective of networks from Chapter 2, but applies a different theoretical lens, i.e. the Strategic Action Field Theory (Fligstein & McAdam, 2011, 2012), to explore the field positioning strategies of our case social enterprises.

The case descriptions from the perspective of an insider presented in Chapter 1 suggest that the four case organizations can be considered social enterprises in a broader sense according to key criteria outlined in the EMES framework (Defourny & Nyssens, 2013). They are presented to us as independent organizations pursuing social goals, i.e. an explicit aim to benefit the community, by applying entrepreneurial approaches and involving stakeholders in the decision-making.

If we take a closer look at the social dimension, we find that the Austrian social enterprise aims to develop solutions to counteract the brain drain of well-educated young people in rural areas. The Greek agricultural cooperative ultimately aims to strengthen the local community and economy, which was badly hit by a government-debt crisis. In the Irish case, we identify a social enterprise that aims to deliver core public services to local communities, enhancing employability, supporting small businesses, and promoting the region as a tourist destination. The objective of the Polish case organization is to support the development of the region primarily by facilitating civic and professional engagement of people and increasing its attractiveness for locals and tourists.

Additionally, in all our case studies, the social mission is complemented by economic activity and an entrepreneurial mindset, especially the reliance on paid work over voluntary work. The cases also reflect different degrees of economic risk taken by those involved and continuous efforts to market products and services.

Finally, our case enterprises report to practice participatory governance and thus broadly match the third EMES criterion of an ideal-typical social enterprise. Depending on their legal status, they either put a focus on the involvement of internal or external stakeholders. While the Austrian and the Greek cooperatives primarily appear to involve members and employees in organizational decision-making, the Irish charity and the Polish foundation mainly invite local authorities and communities to participate in the governance (Richter, 2018).

For a moment, let us move away from the label social enterprise. In light of the above outlined insights from Chapter 1, we hypothesize that the four case organizations are all characterized by some degree of institutional hybridity, reflected in their objectives, income sources, and governance arrangements. Thus, they operate in the same social domain together with a larger group of organizations, which has been labelled the third sector. More precisely, we refer to the European definition of the third sector, which is an analytical approach and based on the conceptualization of different types of associations, including both non-profit organizations (such as charities, voluntary organizations, and advocacy associations) and social economy organizations (such as cooperatives and mutual aid societies) (Evers & Laville, 2004).

In contrast to the European tradition, the US conception of the third sector has traditionally relied on a simple classification of organizations regarding the distribution of profit. Thus, it basically equates the third sector with the non-profit sector by excluding all organizations that violate the criterion of non-distribution of profits, e.g. cooperatives (Salamon & Anheier, 1995; Evers & Laville, 2004). However, as Evers and Laville (2004) convincingly argue, both non-profit and social economy organizations follow the same fundamental principle, which is not maximizing return on private, individual investment, but acting in the collective interest (whether it is general or mutual interest). Furthermore, one also needs to keep in mind that cooperatives and mutuals have never played an important role in the US society comparable to European countries.

An appropriate way to graphically display the hybridity in third sector organizations is the "welfare triangle" (Evers, 1990) or "welfare mix" (Pestoff, 1992), which is displayed in Figure 3.1. It refers to welfare provision as the interaction of four different social domains and respective institutional forms that can be positioned in a triangle.

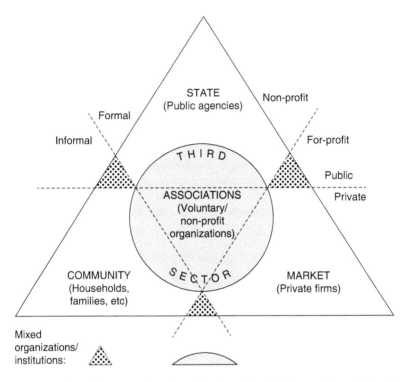

Figure 3.1 The welfare triangle and positioning of the third sector (Evers & Laville, 2004, p. 17)

The four social domains are state, market, the third sector, and community. The corresponding ideal-typical institutions are public agencies, private firms, associations, and households/families. The positioning of an organization in the triangle relates to institutional characteristics, i.e. the differences between public and private, for- and non-profit as well as formal and informal organization (Pestoff, 1992).

As indicated in Figure 3.1, third sector welfare providers operate in the intermediate area embedded by state, market, and community provision. However, its boundaries with the other sectors are blurred. Although voluntary associations are usually depicted as a private, formal non-profit organization, in Europe, they have traditionally co-produced public services with the state sector. Likewise, cooperatives have traditionally also been involved in the production of market goods (Defourny & Nyssens, 2006). What Figure 3.1 also suggests then is that in contrast to organizations in the other three domains, third sector organizations are characterized by a hybridity of the 'pure' guiding principles of the other three domains—profit (market), redistribution (state) or personal responsibility (community)—which results in a balancing act for the individual third sector organization (Evers & Laville, 2004).

While it has been argued that the third sector does refer to a discrete domain and pure organizational form (Billis, 2010), we rather concur with authors describing this space as a tension field with fuzzy borders to other organizational forms (e.g. Evers, 1990; Brandsen et al., 2005; Doherty et al., 2014). Tensions derive from the competing principles and values inherent in third sector organizations.

Social enterprise then refers to particular entrepreneurial and innovation dynamics with the third sector and can thus be seen as one of its sub-domains. These dynamics have resulted in the creation of a new set of organizations, but have also taken place among existing and more traditional third sector organizations, such as larger non-profit organizations (Defourny & Nyssens, 2006). In social enterprises, we find a particular configuration of hybridity, but nevertheless they operate within a larger social domain where all organizations display some degree of hybridity.

Zooming into the third sector, social enterprise represents a bridge between the domains of non-profit and social economy organizations, as displayed in Figure 3.2.

The social enterprise domain, in particular, combines two sets of organizations from both the social economy and the non-profit organizational camp. On the one hand, it attracts those production-oriented non-profit organizations that represent substantial entrepreneurial orientation and more economic risk-taking than advocacy non-profit organizations. On the other hand, there is a group of cooperative organizations that is more

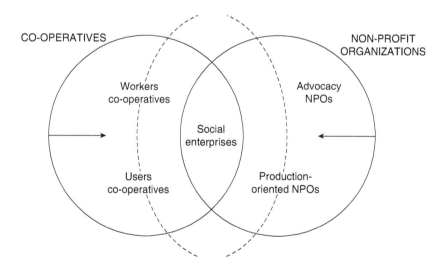

Figure 3.2 Social enterprise bridging the third sector sub-domains of non-profit and cooperative organizations (Defourny & Nyssens, 2006, p. 8)

oriented towards community (e.g. users cooperatives), or even the general interest, than just its membership (e.g. traditional workers cooperatives) (Defourny & Nyssens, 2006; Hatak et al., 2016).

Furthermore, social enterprises tend to adopt multi-stakeholder governance and thus aim to combine advantages from traditional member-focused cooperatives and advocacy non-profit organizations in terms of opportunity identification and search for information. While the involvement of internal stakeholders (members, employees) appears to be beneficial for developing novel solutions, the involvement of external stakeholders in decision-making is beneficial concerning the safeguard of community interests and the legitimization of social enterprise activities (Richter, 2018).

However, as social enterprise refers to a dynamic rather than a stable domain within the third sector, it is difficult to pin down the exact position of this group of organizations, which the dotted line in Figure 3.2 indicates. Due to differences in availability and purpose of certain legal forms across Europe, we have to use the term cooperative, as well as other organizational labels, with some caution. In fact, social enterprises exist in various legal forms and thus the dynamic indicated in Figure 3.2 goes beyond the two spheres of cooperatives and non-profit organizations (Defourny & Nyssens, 2006).

Returning to the findings of Chapter 1 in this book, we notice that each of our case organizations displays a specific configuration of hybridity, which should make it possible to determine its approximate position in the triangle. We can distinguish different sets of indicators to classify social enterprises (Crossan & Van Til, 2009, p. 8; Czischke et al., 2012). First, one could draw on *"descriptor values,"* i.e. formal institutional characteristics, such as the legal structure, profit orientation or governance. Second, there are so-called *"motivator values,"* which come down to the organization's objectives and social aims. We can easily recognize that these two sets of indicators broadly match the EMES pillars and indicators analyzed and discussed in Chapter 1. If we draw on selected descriptor and motivator values, the comparison in Table 3.1 strengthens the assumption that our case organizations occupy slightly different positions in Figures 3.1 and 3.2.

In general, all our case organizations represent private and formal third sector organizations. This means they are positioned in the space below the 'public/private line' and right of the 'formal/informal line' (see Figure 3.3). Their legal form and respective profit orientation can tell us even more about their approximate position within this area. From Chapter 1 we know that from a formal, legal point of view, the Austrian and the Greek cases are both for-profit cooperatives as their main goal is the promotion of a member's economic activity. Therefore, they should be positioned in the striped area within the third sector, i.e. right of the 'for-profit/non-profit line' (see Figure 3.3). In contrast, the Irish and the

Table 3.1 Analysis of hybridity by selected descriptor and motivator values in case social enterprises

Cases	Hybridity indicators			
	Descriptor values			*Motivator values*
	Legal form	*Profit orientation (legal definition)*	*Stakeholder participation (formal)*	*Objectives and social mission*
Irish	Limited company with charity status	Non-profit	Mainly external (communities, public authorities, local businesses)	Community benefits
Greek	Cooperative	For-profit	Mainly internal (members)	Focus on member and community benefits
Austrian	Cooperative	For-profit	Mainly internal (members, employees)	Focus on member and community benefits
Polish	Foundation	Non-profit	Internal and external (public authorities, local businesses, NGOs, employees)	Community benefits

Source: Based on Crossan & Van Til, 2009; Richter, 2018.

Polish cases have adopted non-profit legal forms. Therefore, they should be positioned left of the for-profit/non-profit line, in the squared triangle within the third sector circle (see Figure 3.3).

Based on the information gathered in Chapter 1, we consider another descriptor value relating to governance, the nature of stakeholder participation. In line with the concept of traditional cooperatives (such as workers cooperatives), in both the Greek and the Austrian case, the cooperative members are the dominant actors in the formal governance bodies of the organization (see also Table 3.1). In the Greek cooperative, the decision-making follows the principal of one member, one vote. The general assembly appoints the members of the board of directors and takes all key decisions such as the termination or merger of the cooperative, and it dis/approves the annual financial report. The Greek cooperative has recently started to take members on board who do not have a farming background, but who are concerned with the stevia business in some other way.

In the next step, we zoom into the identified approximate position of our case enterprises in the triangle (see Figure 3.4).

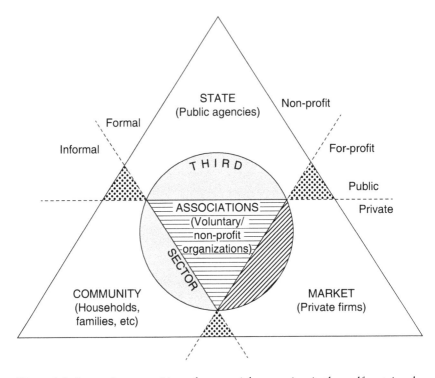

Figure 3.3 Approximate position of case social enterprises in the welfare triangle (based on Evers & Laville, 2004, p. 17)

In the Austrian case organization, the sociocratic governance approach allows all employed members of the cooperative to engage in the decision-making process. However, the participatory nature of the enterprise does not extend to external shareholders, such as local communities, authorities, and customers. Therefore, based on all the selected descriptor values (see Table 3.1), we would position the Greek and the Austrian cases in the left circle 'cooperatives' but outside the dotted line (see Figure 3.4), as they seem more similar to traditional cooperatives than to community cooperatives. We recall that the latter type of cooperatives reflects the dynamic towards social enterprise (inside the dotted line in Figure 3.4) in terms of clearly adopting multi-stakeholder governance.

However, we have not yet brought into the analysis the self-declared objectives of our case organizations. The analytical perspective of an insider in Chapter 1 suggests that both the Greek and the Austrian cases pursue a social mission that goes beyond social responsibility for their members. The management of the Greek cooperative is convinced that the cooperative is a way to address many problems that the local community faces such as (youth) unemployment and low rural incomes. It

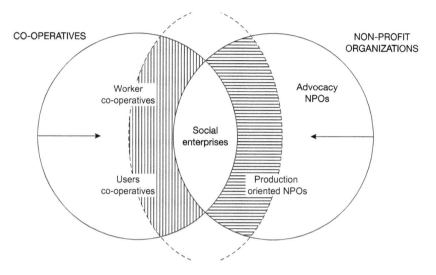

Figure 3.4 Approximate position of case social enterprises in the overlap of cooperative and non-profit organizations (based on Defourny & Nyssens, 2006, p. 8)

also expects that there will be more job opportunities and income for the local community as the business grows. Currently, however, most of the cooperative's profits are reinvested in the growth of the operation, especially in production and processing facilities and the entry in new markets. In the Austrian case, Chapter 1 presented evidence that the social enterprise shows social responsibility for the rural society and not just their members. In particular, their open technology labs should enable people to stay in or come back to their rural communities. In light of this, we would recognize the movement (see the arrow and the vertically striped area in Figure 3.4) towards the area demarcated by the left dotted line that represents the social enterprise dynamic within the cooperative sphere.

Looking at the nature of participatory governance in the Irish case, the description in Chapter 1 indicates that the boards of the company clearly represent the local communities affected by the activities of the regional development company. These external stakeholders have decision-making power regardless of capital ownership in the company. Regarding the involvement of internal stakeholders, however, there is no institutionalized form of internal participation in the Irish case. Such a governance structure resembles more the typical advocacy non-profit organization, which is not surprising given its predominant social mission of improving local communities. But we need to contrast this evidence with the pronounced entrepreneurial dimension in the Irish case. Besides the provision of services on the market, the entrepreneurial dimension of social enterprises manifests in the significant level of economic risk associated with their core activity, such as the risk of failure in competitive tendering for national and EU funds among local development companies.

We find a similar strong external accountability in the Polish case organization, which is accountable to its council representing 16 different stakeholders from public, private, and civil society organizations. Whereas a representative of the internal staff is also sitting on the board, the Polish foundation is characterized by the strong leadership of a chairman and low aspirations of, in particular, internal stakeholders to take responsibility. Taking into account the entrepreneurial mindset of the CEO and the mixed service portfolio of the Polish case enterprise, as described in Chapter 1, we would place it in the social enterprise area demarcated by the right dotted line within the circle 'non-profit organizations' (see the horizontally striped area in Figure 3.4) as well as the Irish case organization.

Descriptor values, i.e. formal institutional characteristics, as well as motivator values, i.e. the organization's objectives, only tell part of the story and do not necessarily mean that the organization in question actually acts according to those values.

In contrast to the first two domains of classification variables, a third set of indicators, the "*behaviour variables*," refer to the actual activities of social enterprises in meeting their goals (Crossan & Van Til, 2009, p. 8). For our analysis, this action view means exploring entrepreneurial strategies of our case organizations to fulfill their objectives, leading to an actual positioning in the triangle ("analytical perspective of the researchers").

Hybridity from the behavioral perspective is not so much defined by stable structural characteristics of the organizations, but it emerges from the strategic interaction of an organization with other organizations in a dynamic and changing environment (Brandsen et al., 2005; Doherty et al., 2014). Therefore, it makes sense to think of organizations as operating in *fields* that generally refer to meso-level social orders where actors compete over resources to gain positioning advantage relative to each other (Bourdieu & Wacquant, 1992; Emirbayer & Johnson, 2008). These fields are overlapping and they can be nested, and constituted at different levels (Fligstein & McAdam, 2012; Macmillan et al., 2013). For instance, an organization can be seen as a field in its own right, but it can also be part of a regional field of actors.

Thus, third sector organizations normally operate in multiple fields at the same time (Macmillan et al., 2013). We would think of the social enterprise field as nested within the broader field of the third sector and overlapping with the fields of cooperatives and non-profit organizations (see Figures 3.3 and 3.4), but also with the state, the market and the community field (Evers & Laville, 2004). In terms of third sector organizations, it is also important to distinguish between 'horizontal' and 'vertical fields' (Kendall, 2005). In this respect the horizontal view refers to all third sector organizations regardless of their service focus. In 'vertical' fields, in contrast, we can group organizations that are relevant to a particular policy area, such as health care, housing or regional development. From the policy and practitioner side, this 'vertical' field view is in fact very common and has a long tradition in many countries (Alcock, 2010).

The survival of social enterprises in the intermediate position of the triangle (see Figure 3.3) is influenced by the strategies of their stakeholders in all four social domains (e.g. through state legislation, private firm practices, civil society culture, and community needs) (Evers & Laville, 2004). These external influences result in legitimacy challenges (McInerney, 2013) that eventually manifest in the strategies and daily practices of the case organization (Czischke et al., 2012).

In light of this, the goal of the remainder of Chapter 3 is to *develop a comparative understanding of the positioning strategies of our cases in multiple fields*. Based on this understanding, we strive to answer the question *what we can learn about the field of rural social enterprises?*

The network analysis in Chapter 2 has already suggested that our case enterprises interact with stakeholders from all four social domains, the state, market, third sector, and community. However, each case displays a different kind of network. The Greek case, for instance, focuses most network activities on actors from the market sphere, while the Irish case is very much involved in networking with state actors.

In this respect, Chapter 3 continues and deepens the analysis of relationships from Chapter 2. In this chapter, however, we apply a different theoretical lens, which is a specific field theoretical approach, i.e. the Strategic Action Field Theory (Fligstein & McAdam, 2011, 2012). We believe that this approach particularly suits the analysis of social enterprises. As described above, social enterprise refers to entrepreneurial and innovation dynamics with fuzzy borders situated within more institutionalized and clearly demarcated areas of the third sector. This provides a good match with the focus of the Strategic Action Field framework on dynamics in and of fields (Barman, 2016). Moreover, the focus on strategic agency in Fligstein and McAdam's theory reflects our overall action focus in the analysis of rural social entrepreneurship in this book, which has already been outlined in the introductory chapter. The next section will introduce the Strategic Action Field Theory in more detail, before we engage in the empirical field analysis.

Strategic Action Fields

A Strategic Action Field is understood as "*a constructed mesolevel social order in which actors (who can be individual or collective) are attuned to and interact with one another on the basis of shared (which is not to say consensual) understandings about the purposes of the field, relationships to others in the field (including who has power and why), and the rules governing legitimate action in the field"* (Fligstein & McAdam, 2012, p. 9). The Strategic Action Field framework (Fligstein & McAdam, 2011, 2012) claims to synthesize the Bourdieusian and new institutionalist approaches and to address their perceived weakness of passive conception of actors by stressing the role of agency and field dynamics, such as formation or crisis (Swartz, 2014).

In the new institutionalist understanding, organizational fields "constitute recognized areas of institutional life [. . .] that produce similar services or products" (DiMaggio & Powell, 1983, p. 148). As Emirbayer and Johnson (2008) point out, this approach has been appealing to scholars in organizational studies. It makes it easier to group organizations according to a certain industry or product and thus appears to be a welcome pragmatic approach in research endeavors. However, besides its passive conception of actors in fields, institutional theory often failed to explain field dynamics such as formation or crisis (Fligstein & McAdam, 2012). Furthermore, it does not stress the issue of strategic boundary work in fields as a conscious process by actors (Emirbayer & Johnson, 2008). We have already highlighted that the fields of third sector organizations and social enterprises are actually characterized by fuzzy and dynamic borders (Macmillan et al., 2013).

Another key insight for our study is that Strategic Action Fields are overlapping and nested. Thus, the third sector and social enterprises can be seen as Strategic Action Fields of their own but at the same time the organizations active within these Strategic Action Fields also operate in other fields. The social enterprise field is nested within the broader field of the third sector and overlaps with fields such as those of cooperatives, non-profit organizations, and voluntary organizations, but also with the market and the state field. According to Fligstein and McAdam (2012), relationships with the state field are crucial for the existence of every Strategic Action Field, given the state's unique role in granting legitimacy.

Moreover, in fields individuals and organizations compete over resources to gain positioning advantage relative to each other (Bourdieu & Wacquant, 1992). This leads to the conception of "incumbents" and "challengers" in Strategic Action Fields who can be distinguished according to their resource access (Fligstein & McAdam, 2011, p. 5f). The incumbents shape the rules of the game, and the "governance units" in Strategic Action Fields are crucial to reproduce the dominant field logic. In contrast, challengers are not favored by the status quo and thus more likely to mobilize coalitions to enact change.

Different theoretical traditions suggest analytical dimensions that help us study the role of strategic actors in fields. One such dimension is the architecture of the *field environment*. Positioning strategies only make sense in relation to particular fields in which the case organizations are embedded, as well as in relation to respective actors. Thus, an initial step is to understand the particular *configuration of fields* in which our case organizations are positioned. We want to understand why our case organizations occupy a particular field space. Events in the external environment can make field boundaries shift and due to such dynamics organizations have to reposition (Fligstein & McAdam, 2011; Barman, 2016). Such events are often linked to the state field and can take the form of legislative changes and the provision of resources, which organizations see as opportunities. 'Empty' social spaces, for instance, can be the result of boundary changes of existing third sector fields but also the state field (Gorski, 2012). When established actors cede their field positions, actors from adjacent fields or newly emerging actors are likely to move into empty field spaces, for instance, because they promise to provide new niches. Fields can also be in a state of crisis when the rules that governed interaction no longer work, and actors are consequently looking for a new consensus to consolidate the field (Armstrong, 2005). Thus, we also need to engage, to a certain degree, in an historically informed analysis to identify both structural and contingent factors in the external environment as triggers for field changes (Domaradzka, 2018).

Based on an understanding of the field environment, we can analyze the *positioning strategies* of our case enterprises. It requires "social skill" to read social situations and enact new entrepreneurial opportunities in a field (Fligstein & McAdam, 2011, p. 7). An important tool of socially skilled actors is the framing of issues and compromise identities to which other field actors can agree (e.g. community groups, more formalized non-profit organizations, and state actors). This enables successful intermediation between an opportunity in the external environment and collective action (Snow & Benford, 1992). Social skill also involves linking local issues with existing frames and related actor networks. Part of the entrepreneurial activity of socially skilled actors is to provide practical and convincing solutions to local problems which shows how things can be done in a different way (Domaradzka & Wijkström, 2016). Arising opportunities in the policy environment, such as a new legislation or funding stream, also have to be met with actor-driven governance innovations. Mediating organizations and platforms are an institutionalized form of social skill and can stabilize the necessary bridging across organizational boundaries in fields (McQuarrie & Krumholz, 2011). Due to their own resource limitations, however, actors always face the strategic decision to push either their own or wider group interests in fields (Fligstein & McAdam, 2011).

As McInerney (2013) points out social enterprises, as hybrid organizations, are especially vulnerable to legitimacy challenges from their external environment as they simultaneously operate in different fields, which have their own institutional logics. Although the values and practices of the state, market, and community sphere are not necessarily compatible, social entrepreneurs need to "[. . .] present their organizations to members of diverse institutional environments as cohesive, coherent wholes" (Battilana & Dorado, 2010; McInerney, 2013, p. 242). At the same time, social enterprises aim to distinguish themselves from other fields and carve out room for strategic action in order to survive (Macmillan et al., 2013; McInerney, 2013).

Coming back to the positioning strategies of actors in fields, there is a range of rather short-term strategies that organizations apply in response to external shocks, e.g. financial constraints or new regulations from national funding agencies. Thus the legitimacy of social enterprises is threatened and they could for instance respond with a strategy of justification (McInerney, 2013), staff redundancies, organizational restructuring or even a merger strategy with other organizations in the field (Macmillan et al., 2013).

However, in this chapter, we are primarily interested in (re-)positioning, which is a longer-term strategy of actors in fields. Like the aforementioned short-term strategies, positioning is also triggered by events in the external environment but usually represents a pre-emptive move. In general, positioning always aims at affiliating with and differentiating from peer organizations (Macmillan et al., 2013). According to the Strategic Action Field theory, there is indeed constant positional jockeying going on in fields. This is linked to the social skill of actors, i.e. "a highly developed cognitive capacity for reading people and environments, framing lines of action, and mobilizing people" (Fligstein & McAdam, 2011, p. 7).

Inspired by Bourdieu's theories, we can further distinguish actual from symbolic positioning in fields (Gorski, 2012; Macmillan et al., 2013). In this chapter, we draw on two main indicators for *"actual" positioning* as a social enterprise. First, it refers to the organization's service or activity portfolio, which would need to be representative for social enterprise models in the respective country contexts. And second, actual positioning is indicated by the balance of pursuing both social and economic goals in strategic action. In contrast, *"symbolic" positioning* takes place when the strategic focus is on the perception of the organization as a social enterprise, or more precisely its brand, by others. The two types of positioning should not be regarded as mutually exclusive but often overlap in organizational life.

Positioning Strategies of the Case Organizations

In this section, we engage in a concise theoretically informed comparative analysis of our four case studies. The question we will explore is how the case organizations have positioned themselves in their fields and especially in relation to the field of social enterprises. In the field analysis, we combine three steps. First, we briefly sketch the historical development of the case organizations. Second, we describe their activities and strategies. And third, we analyze their positioning in respective fields putting a focus on the issue whether it is actual or symbolic positioning.

The Irish Regional Development Company

Looking back, the 1980s was a decade of extremely high unemployment and rural decline in Ireland. A series of governments and sequent elections contributed to further undermine the economic development. The initiative for founding the Irish case company started in 1987 when the local branch of the state tourism body convened a meeting to explore the future of the area. Participants in this meeting were representatives from agricultural tourism, farmers, and community platforms located in the region. In the following years, more and more local coordinating groups came on board throughout Mid-West Ireland. The first manager of the company was experienced in agritourism and was the driving force behind an integrated service approach to support communities in developing action plans and identifying a range of projects that deliver economic diversification and enhance quality of life in the region. The shift from a tourism initiative to a regional development organization was also influenced by the emergence of the LEADER program and respective funding. Right from the start, the first manager built strong partnerships with local, regional, national, and international actors. She and her successor have been able to generate income from the successful implementation of European and national funding programs very effectively.

In summary, the business models of the Irish case organization focus on the provision of core public services in local communities based on regional, national, and EU funding programs. The core areas of services are community development (social, economic, and environmental development), enterprise support (especially micro-sized and small businesses), employment (enhancing employability among the unemployed), as well as promoting the region as a tourist destination.

While these different activity areas represent fields in their own right, we argue that our case organization has primarily positioned itself in the Strategic Action Field of regional development which, as described above, represents a "vertical policy field" (Kendall, 2005, p. 3). In general, the existence of regional development as a Strategic Action Field in Ireland is very much linked to the state field. First, this Strategic Action Field initially emerged because state authorities were only marginally present on the regional level to deliver core public services. Thus, this empty strategic space was filled with a concrete service offer by the founder of our case organization who had already been a business developer with substantial "social skill" (Fligstein & McAdam, 2011, p. 7). Furthermore, the Strategic Action Field has been connected to another international Strategic Action Field made up of actors involved in the LEADER program. The first manager of the Irish case organization quickly seized the opportunities offered by the provision of LEADER resources to position in a niche within the regional development field in Ireland. When access to LEADER resources became more limited, the interactions with the state field increased through applications for crucial national funding schemes, such as the Local Community Development Programme (LCDP) or the Rural Social Scheme (RSS).

Both national and European programs exercise strong regulative power on organizations, such as our case enterprise, in this Strategic Action Field. Therefore, our case organization needs to implement and adapt services as well as branding according to the respective regulations in order to secure funding and thus survive in its strategic niche. The case organization's community development approach has always been based on entrepreneurial and market-based thinking when tackling social issues. This clearly reflects characteristics of the liberal welfare model in Ireland. So, when 'social enterprise' became a dominant discourse within the EU policy context in the mid-1990s (European Commission, 1995), the Strategic Action Field of regional development in Ireland had already been characterized by substantial entrepreneurial and innovation dynamics. Nevertheless, recent policy changes in Ireland towards more decentralization as well as limited access to LEADER resources led our case organization to re-position within the Strategic Action Field of regional development. In this respect, the strategic focus of the organization shifted from a community development to social inclusion and social cohesion in order to access respective funding. But this was not a case of symbolic positioning. Its service portfolio has always matched core dimensions of social enterprise conceptualization in both EU and national policy discourses, such as the foci on work integration and social cohesion, because it offers services and promotes employment opportunities to disadvantaged groups (O'Hara & O'Shaughnessy, 2017).

In a nutshell, there are two ways to look at the Irish case organization as positioned in Strategic Action Fields. First, from the vertical perspective of policy fields (Kendall, 2005), we were able to identify regional development as the main Strategic Action Field where the enterprise operates. This Strategic Action Field actually represents an umbrella field with nested policy fields, such as employment, enterprise support or tourism. Second, the case organization is also positioned in the Strategic Action Field of social enterprises, which represents a horizontal field (Alcock, 2010) as it groups third sector organizations active in a range of policy areas. The latter is an actual positioning strategy of the case organization, which matches the service portfolio of social enterprise defined by both EU and national policy (work integration, poverty reduction, social cohesion, and SME support), and it also enacts the self-declared objectives and social mission of the organization.

The Greek Agricultural Cooperative

The Greek agricultural cooperative provides us with a contrasting case to the field positioning strategies observed in the Irish case. In order to understand the specific field configuration in the Greek case, we need to go back to the situation before the cooperative was actually founded in 2012. Now and then, our case organization has been embedded in the overarching Strategic Action Field of agriculture. However, before 2012, the individual farmers from the cooperative had mostly been active in the nested Strategic Action Field of tobacco leaves farming. This used to be a highly institutionalized Strategic Action Field in Greece before it came into crisis.

A field comes into crisis when the rules that govern interaction no longer work. In our case study, the tobacco industry was restricted by national and EU rules and thus could no longer deliver enough profits for the individual producers. So, according to the Strategic Action Field theory, field actors—especially state actors—initially respond by looking for a new consensus to consolidate the field again (Fligstein & McAdam, 2011). However, the more intense such a field crisis plays out, the less likely it is that the old order can be re-established because the process of achieving field settlement will be contentious (Armstrong, 2005). This was exactly what happened in our case. The crisis of the tobacco farming field led to the crystallization of a new niche within the ecological agriculture field, stevia farming. The crisis of an existing field provides the opportunity for a social entrepreneur to come up with a viable project and the right frames in the right place to build a coalition of actors from different existing fields in order to produce a new Strategic Action Field. In our case study from Greece, we are able to identify the almost ideal-typical socially skilled entrepreneur described by Fligstein and McAdam (2011) in their Strategic Action Field theory. Although the initiative for Greek cooperative came from a group of farmers, the CEO of the Greek cooperative embodies social skill in that he recognized this opportunity, appealed to common interests and managed to professionalize a coalition of actors (producers, distributors, customers, researchers, public authorities etc), which is necessary for a new Strategic Action Field to emerge.

The CEO of the cooperative always considered himself to be a corporate entrepreneur with a portfolio of start-ups. And that is exactly how his business partners in the region describe him. Part of his field positioning strategy for the Greek cooperative involved establishing links to national government but also EU institutions, so that the cooperative can participate in national and international fairs as well as in international research projects. Such networking experiences convinced the CEO that through branding himself as a social entrepreneur and his cooperative as a social enterprise, he was able to distinguish his business even more from competitors (other cooperatives, agricultural companies etc). Highlighting the regional community benefits of the cooperative has become part of this branding strategy. In this way, the CEO has managed to position the cooperative in an already existing international Strategic Action Field together with work integration social enterprises and also community-development organizations, such as our Irish case organization.

In summary, from the vertical perspective of industry and policy fields (Kendall, 2005), we were able to identify healthy food production as the main Strategic Action Field of the Greek case organization. This reflects the actual product and service portfolio of the organization. Due to the value chain integration, the organization was able to position itself in a niche field of the food industry, instead of just staying in a nested field within the declining overall agricultural field. Furthermore, the case organization also positions itself in the Strategic Action Field of social enterprises, mainly on the national and international levels evidenced through the networking activities of the CEO. However, the self-declared social mission of developing the local community (see Chapter 1) is in contrast to its primary production activities of food production which might only have an indirect effect on community development (see Chapter 2). Thus, we would conclude that in this case, social enterprise refers to a rather symbolic positioning strategy, which helps the positioning efforts of the cooperative in its primary Strategic Action Field of healthy food production.

The Austrian Technology Cooperative

The positioning strategy of our third case shows similarities with the two previous ones discussed. The Austrian enterprise is positioned in a cooperative and also in a regional development field Strategic Action Field. Again, it makes sense to go back to the situation before the cooperative was founded to develop a better understanding of the field positioning strategies of the case organization. The social entrepreneur who eventually drove the foundation process of the Austrian cooperative used to work as a consultant in a public regional development agency. The knowledge and network he had developed during this period of work eventually helped him to build consensus among a group of actors to position himself as "challenger" (Fligstein & McAdam, 2011, p. 5f) within a highly institutionalized Strategic Action Field. In Austria, the regional development Strategic Action Field receives relatively strong state support through public funding. Thus, in this field, we find public development agencies operating as "incumbents" (Fligstein & McAdam, 2011, p. 5f) in every region of the country. They are faced with a range of private companies—the challengers—offering their service portfolio to local communities. However, to a large extent these private companies are also pushed into a position where they operate as subcontractors to public agencies. The rules of the game in this Strategic Action Field are therefore clearly stacked in favor of public development agencies. The dependency of challengers on these state-supported incumbents provides a degree of stability to the Strategic Action Field (Fligstein & McAdam, 2011).

However, a Strategic Action Field can never be entirely stable. There is constant maneuvering going on with new challengers entering the field and carving out niches, and incumbents doing their best to protect their dominant field position (Fligstein & McAdam, 2011). The social entrepreneur in our case study has indeed managed to position the social enterprise as a challenger and in a niche within the regional development Strategic Action Field. More precisely, he has positioned the social enterprise at the intersection with the Strategic Action Field of technology education, which has emerged in Austria over the last decade. The latter field is not as institutionalized as the regional development field in Austria but also linked to the state field through certain resource streams, such as the ones provided by the Regional Government of Upper Austria ("Innovatives Oberösterreich 2020") or by the Federal Ministry of Education ("Jugend forscht"). These funding streams mainly target private companies, such as small and large consultancies, whereas public organizations are hardly present in the actual service delivery. Moreover, some larger technology-oriented companies invest in this Strategic Action Field aiming to build a future labor market and social acceptance for new technologies.

The positioning strategy of our Austrian case organization needs to be seen against this background and is all about differentiating the enterprise from peer organizations in both the regional development and technology education Strategic Action Field. While its core service portfolio, e.g. open technology labs or the program "kids experience technology," clearly fit into the Strategic Action Field of technology education, it is a niche within the Strategic Action Field of regional development, hardly contested by neither public development agencies nor private consultancies. Furthermore, the framing as 'employment cooperative' and especially as rural social enterprise strengthens this differentiation strategy. Access to schools for technology education is much easier when you represent a social enterprise compared to a commercial enterprise. Furthermore, one needs to keep in mind that the field of social enterprise is still marginal in Austria and mainly exists in urban centers (Anastasiadis & Lang, 2016; Anastasiadis et al., 2018). As observed in the Greek case, social enterprise also represents a branding strategy for the Austrian cooperative that makes it possible to participate in an international field that is funded by foundations (e.g. Ashoka) and Europe-wide research programs.

In a nutshell, from a field theoretical perspective, the Austrian case organization represents social enterprise as both an actual and symbolic positioning strategy. Part of the cooperative's service portfolio, e.g. open technology labs or the program "kids experience technology," match with the self-declared social and community development objectives. However, we were also able to identify symbolic aspects in the positioning strategy. In the field of technology education—which is not a typical social enterprise field in Austria—it is the label social enterprise that helps the case organization to differentiate itself from their private and state competitors when it comes to providing the service and access funding.

The Polish Regional Development Foundation

Sometimes the magnitude of a crisis can be so high that it causes many proximate fields to destabilize. One can imagine the chaotic effects of a severe crisis of the state field, as almost any Strategic Action Field is linked to the state in one way or another (Fligstein & McAdam, 2011). Our case study from Poland tells the story of what happens to different Strategic Action Fields when the state field undergoes a historically unparalleled transition from central planning to a liberal democratic order. This external shock in Poland caused existing fields to establish new rules of the game, such as the Strategic Action Fields of education or agriculture, and it also created entirely new Strategic Action Fields, such as entrepreneurship.

It is not surprising that such a state of crisis and the disappearance of incumbent actors in many fields represents a unique opportunity for social entrepreneurs "to create a new cultural frame that reorganizes interests and identities" (Fligstein & McAdam, 2011, p. 18). Rural communities in particular represent a nexus of different interconnected issues and fields with blurring borders. This appears to be a perfect context to apply a hybrid and rather holistic positioning strategy (Steiner & Teasdale, 2018), which materializes in a diverse service portfolio as offered by our case organization. This portfolio ranges from (social) enterprise support, education—including entrepreneurial education, which is a relatively young Strategic Action Field that did not exist before the 1990s) and work integration. In light of this, the social enterprise frame should not be seen as a branding strategy, i.e. symbolic positioning. Similar to the Irish case, the Polish organization is clearly positioned in two sub-fields of social entrepreneurship in Poland, both already institutionalized. The first sub-field is the "entrepreneurial non-profit organization" field (Ciepielewska-Kowalik et al., 2015, p. 15), which involves public service delivery, drawing on mixed income and on volunteering as well as paid staff. The emergence and institutionalizations of this Strategic Action Field were linked to Poland's EU accession and impact of EU legislation, which led to more acceptance of an entrepreneurial orientation of non-profit organizations and respective funding streams. The second sub-field where our case enterprise is positioned refers to "work and social integration social enterprises" (Ciepielewska-Kowalik et al., 2015, p. 19).

Organizations in this Strategic Action Field target problems of labor market integration and have been supported by the Polish central government and the EU through receiving legal recognition and funding streams. We can conclude that the Polish case organization positions itself in the Strategic Action Field social enterprise that emerged and gained legal recognition and resources in Poland following the EU accession. Our case organization could increasingly benefit from its positioning in this Strategic Action Field through the influence of EU programs, such as EQUAL, in Poland (Ciepielewska-Kowalik et al., 2015). Accordingly, the Polish case organization offers a market portfolio that addresses the pressing social needs of the local population. With being active in the Strategic Action Field of social enterprise, the Polish case organization has actively contributed to the emergence and the further development of this Strategic Action Field in Poland and—due to the regional focus of the activities—especially in rural Poland. The activities of the CEO on the international level also contributed the Polish voice to the emergence and development of this Strategic Action Field on the international level.

Cross-Case Patterns

In this section, we compare key results of the individual case analysis and draw conclusions on the characteristics of the field of rural social enterprise.

The field positioning activities of all our cases are linked to some form of crisis in a field, especially in the agriculture Strategic Action Field in the 1980s and 1990s in Poland and Ireland, and in Greece where it lasted until the 2000s. This has led to a socio-economic and identity crisis among the local population. In the Austrian case, the positioning activities might already be located in a context of a post-industrial crisis. The respective socio-technical transition has challenged the governing rules in the Strategic Action Field of education in rural areas of Austria. The education system and the curriculums cannot keep up with the speed of transformation towards a digital society. Nevertheless schools need to prepare the children for the challenges in the digital age. Therefore, a strategic field space emerged around innovative educational approaches, such as the one that the Austrian case enterprise offers in rural communities.

We recall that third sector organizations are typically active in a number of Strategic Action Fields in parallel (Alcock, 2010; Macmillan et al., 2013). The analysis in this chapter suggests that 'social enterprise' is not necessarily the central Strategic Action Field where our case organizations operate. In terms of the actual service offer, the Polish and Irish cases are genuinely positioned in social enterprise fields that we can identify on the national level. These fields are already institutionalized and characterized by a certain degree of autonomy and field-specific capital, including the generation of sustainable resource and funding streams for its member organizations (Gorski, 2012).

In the Greek case, however, our analysis points to social enterprise as a symbolic positioning, or branding strategy. The actual service portfolio offered by the Greek case organization mainly targets economic goals and contrasts the self-declared social mission of developing the local community because it might only have an indirect effect on community development. In the Austrian case, we find a mix of actual and symbolic positioning. The Austrian cooperative strategically uses the label social enterprise to differentiate itself from private and state competitors when it comes to providing services and access funding. Our case evidence suggests that the relevance of such symbolic positioning as a social enterprise should not be underestimated. It gives organizations additional room to survive in strategic niches in their primary fields (such as in education and agriculture) due to differentiation from peer organizations and positioning advantages for national funding.

Furthermore, in all our four cases, we observe an affiliation with an internationally structured Strategic Action Field of social entrepreneurship which provides the case organizations with additional resource access (e.g. EU funding) and legitimacy for their national activities, e.g. through participation in research activities. Thus, the membership in this international Strategic Action Field helps the case organizations secure room to survive in niches in other Strategic Action Fields on the national level (e.g. technology education and healthy food production). The EU emerges as a driver of the establishment of this international field of social enterprise, including nested Strategic Action Fields such as *rural social enterprise*.

In a nutshell, our case enterprises are operating in Strategic Action Fields of social enterprise on different spatial levels. Their positioning on the international level appears more radical compared to the regional level where pragmatism guides their activities and strategies. This is because the explicit use of the label social enterprise in the rural regions is limited. The importance of traditional values, practices, and concepts reduces the legitimacy of new Strategic Action Fields such as social enterprise in rural areas. The spatial perspective on Strategic Action Fields actually highlights the limited institutionalization of social enterprise fields on the national level and especially regional and local level.

We believe that the field perspective helps to explore the dynamics taking place in rural social enterprises and goes beyond an analysis that only focuses on structural characteristics of these organizations. A field approach helps us to make sense of the complexity in organizational life where actors usually operate in multiple and nested strategic arenas (Macmillan et al., 2013).

In line with Steiner and Teasdale (2018), our case findings also suggest that rural social enterprises are very much influenced by the state field through different policies. This is partly because the case social enterprises are active in traditional policy domains, such as community development, work integration or education. Moreover, regional and rural development is a key policy area in the countries studied, which we believe has advantages for strategic field positioning. Rural communities in particular represent a nexus of different interconnected policy domains with blurring borders. This appears to be a perfect context in which to apply a hybrid and rather holistic positioning strategy (Steiner & Teasdale, 2018), which materializes in the diverse service portfolio as displayed by three of our case organizations.

Finally, it seems important to reflect on our own role in this Strategic Action Field of rural social enterprise. As academics, we have been part of EU wide research programs on this topic and thus we are participants in this field too. Our research projects and respective publications support the self-identification of our case organizations as social enterprises and help to create a shared understanding of actors in an international field. In any case, as authors we are highly conscious of this book and the underlying research program also being strategic action and strategic positioning efforts that help us strengthen our footing in the academic field.

Contrasting the findings of Chapters 1, 2, and 3, Table 3.2 compares the findings on the different dimensions of hybridity in our cases. In a nutshell, we compare the structural characteristics of the case organizations with their actual activities and strategies. Thus, we contrast key findings of our field analysis (behavioral dimension) in Chapter 3 with the findings of the network analysis in Chapter 2 (also behavioral dimension), and the findings on the descriptor and motivator dimensions earlier in Chapter 3 (drawing on evidence developed in Chapter 1 of this book).

In the Irish and Polish cases, both the network and the field analysis provide evidence that the actual activities of the organization match with the self-declared social mission and structural characteristics as a non-profit organization with an entrepreneurial orientation. The network analysis in Chapter 2 shows that the value of the activity of the social enterprises in the two cases on the community level lies in its intermediary role. In the Polish case, however, the social enterprise adopts a top-down linking approach, whereas in the Irish case, we find a bottom-up linking practice. It is reflected by a change in the place that improves the lives of the locals, because it satisfies a need that has not been addressed before or that has not been addressed in this quality so far. In the Irish case, this change unfolds among those active in the community during the participative process of developing the strategy and implementing the new solution addressing the need. As soon as the new solution has been implemented the change also reaches other locals who have not been involved in the project but enjoy the benefits of its outcome. Typical for a non-profit organization, the Irish regional development company lobbies the initiatives emerging on the community level among regime level actors, who to a large extent design the institutional framework conditions that represent the boundaries for rural development in the place.

Table 3.2 Analysis of hybridity by selected descriptor, motivator and behavior values in case social enterprises

| Cases | Hybridity indicators | | | | | |
| | Descriptor values | | | Motivator values | Behaviorial values | |
	Legal form	Profit orientation (legal definition)	Stakeholder participation (formal)	Social mission	Networking strategies	Field strategies
Irish	Limited company with charity status	Non-profit	Mainly external (communities, public authorities, local businesses)	Community benefits	Intermediary role addressing community concerns and lobbying with regime actors for local change (bottom-up linking)	SE as actual positioning strategy in the SAF of regional development; consistent on different spatial levels
Greek	Cooperative	For-profit	Mainly internal (members)	Focus on community and member benefits	CEO as entrepreneurial role model motivating local cooperative members but not yet local community	SE as symbolic positioning strategy on the national and especially international level to position in the healthy food production SAF
Austrian	Cooperative	For-profit	Mainly internal (members, employees)	Focus on community and member benefits	Social entrepreneur acts as entrepreneurial role model motivating local community members	SE as actual and symbolic positioning strategy on the national and especially international level in the technology education SAF
Polish	Foundation	Non-profit	Internal and external (public authorities, local businesses, NGOs, employees)	Community benefits	Intermediary role addressing community concerns and lobbying with regime actors for local change (top-down linking)	SE as actual positioning strategy in the SAF of regional development, consistent on different spatial levels

Source: Based on Crossan & Van Til, 2009; Richter, 2018).

In the Polish case, the president of the social enterprise maintains close contact with different actors on the regime level, such as with representatives of the national government and members of parliament. These contacts provide the president with access to national and European funding structures and opportunities to support a sustainable development in the home county of the Polish social enterprise.

In the Greek and the Austrian case, comparing different structural characteristics and the actual activities of the organizations does not deliver a coherent picture of social enterprise. The network analysis in Chapter 2 shows that the CEO of the Greek cooperative acts as an intermediary, but mainly between the cooperative members and the regime actors. The CEO motivates and activates the members of the cooperative towards an entrepreneurial mindset. In contrast, the Austrian cooperative also reaches out to members of the wider community through their local interest groups. But these community members as well as regime level stakeholders are not formally represented in the governance structure of the cooperative. In both cases, the social entrepreneurs and CEO respectively act as a role model for locals to unfold entrepreneurial activities, which eventually results in the delivery of offers that are new and valuable for the locals and thus helps fight the local community's main challenges: unemployment and outmigration. But in the Greek case, the self-declared social mission has not yet materialized according to our evidence and thus we would question the actual positioning as a social enterprise. The field analysis in this chapter supports this conclusion. In the Austrian case, the field analysis provides a less contradictory picture. Although the cooperative clearly pursues social goals, it also deliberately uses the label social enterprise to differentiate itself from private and state competitors when it comes to providing services and access funding. Therefore, in both cases, but to different degrees, our analysis shows social enterprise as a symbolic positioning.

Summarizing our findings, we can also draw on a recently published framework of institutional trajectories of social enterprise models (Defourny & Nyssens, 2017), see Figure 3.5. The assumption hereby is that not all of our cases have been initially and genuinely positioned in the SE field, which is the intermediate area of hybrid resources in the triangle.

Figure 3.5 shows different institutional trajectories that can generate social enterprise models. There are three interest principles in the corners of the triangle that represent the starting points for the evolution of social enterprise models. In light of our case evidence, we see the "capital interest" converging with 'individual interest'. In principle, the trajectories come down to two different moves. First, "an 'upward' move of mutual or capital interest organizations," so that the social mission and pursuing community and general interest becomes more important. Second, there is a " 'downward' move of general interest organizations [. . .] towards

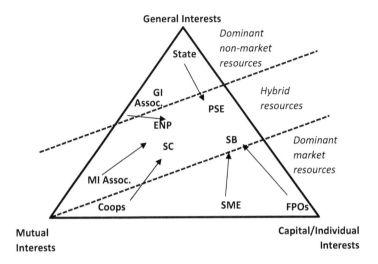

Figure 3.5 Institutional trajectories and resulting social enterprise models (based on Defourny & Nyssens, 2017)

more market-oriented activities" to sustain the social mission with market income (Defourny & Nyssens, 2017, pp. 2479–2480). As already mentioned above with regard to Strategic Actions Fields, these models are also dynamic and not necessarily stable.

Applying the model to our case evidence, we see that the Irish and the Polish cases come close to the Entrepreneurial Non-profit (ENP) Model and the Public-Sector Social Enterprise (PSE) Model. For these models, income from commercial activities sustains their core social mission and general interest activity. The Strategic Action Field where these organizations are embedded also represents clear policy domains, e.g. regional development, work integration, which somehow supports their general interest orientation. Nevertheless, we do not find much evidence of an institutional trajectory in our cases from state and general interest non-profit organizations towards the Entrepreneurial Non-profit (ENP) Model and the Public-Sector Social Enterprise (PSE) Model.

In contrast, we could identify trajectories in the Austrian and the Greek cases. The Austrian social entrepreneur started his career in a public regional development agency (PSE Model), moving left towards the mutual interest corner when initially founding a mutual interest association and eventually a cooperative. The Greek case started in the mutual interest corner, represented by the farmers' cooperative before the social entrepreneur eventually engaged in this cooperative strategy, thus moving it a bit towards the lower right 'individual interest' corner. But in order to position themselves in the social enterprise (middle) zone, they needed to signal to the external environment that they are also acting in a general interest to some degree, thus moving a bit upwards in the triangle. Both organizations brand themselves as Social Cooperatives (SC), cooperatives acting in the general interest, and also as Social Businesses (SB), social mission driven commercial enterprises, depending on the context. Our data suggests that they are successful as being perceived as social enterprises by key stakeholders on the national and international level.

References

Alcock, P. (2010). A strategic unity: Defining the third sector in the UK. *Voluntary Sector Review*, 1(1), 5–24.

Anastasiadis, M., Gspurnig, W. and Lang, R. (2018). *A Map of Social Enterprises and Their Eco-Systems in Europe. Country Report: Austria*. Brussels: European Commission.

Anastasiadis, M. and Lang, R. (2016). *Social Enterprise in Austria: A Contextual Approach to Understand an Ambiguous Concept*, ICSEM Working Papers, No. 26, Liege: The International Comparative Social Enterprise Models (ICSEM) Project.

Armstrong, E. (2005). From struggle to settlement: The crystallization of a field of lesbian/gay organizations in San Francisco, 1969–1973. In G. Davis, D. McAdam, W. R. Scott, and M. N. Zald (Eds.): *Social Movements and Organization Theory* (161–187). Cambridge: Cambridge University Press.

Barman, E. (2016). Varieties of field theory and the sociology of the non-profit sector. *Sociology Compass*, 10(6), 442–458.

Battilana, J. and Dorado, S. (2010). Building sustainable hybrid organizations: The case of commercial microfinance organizations. *Academy of Management Journal*, 53(6), 1419–1440.

Billis, D. (2010). Towards a theory of hybrid organisations. In D. Billis (Ed.): *Hybrid Organizations and the Third Sector: Challenges for Practice, Theory and Policy*, Chapter 3 (46–69). London: Palgrave Macmillan.

Bourdieu, P. and Wacquant, L. (1992). *Invitation to a Reflexive Sociology*. Chicago: University of Chicago Press.

Brandsen, T., van de Donk, W. and Putters, K. (2005). Griffins or chameleons? Hybridity as a permanent and inevitable characteristic of the Third Sector. *International Journal of Public Administration*, 28, 749–765.

Ciepielewska-Kowalik, A., Pieliński, B., Starnawska, M. and Szymańska, A. (2015). *Social Enterprise in Poland: Institutional and Historical Context*, ICSEM Working Papers, No. 11, Liege: The International Comparative Social Enterprise Models (ICSEM) Project.

Crossan, D. and Van Til, J. (2009). *Towards a Classification Framework for Not-For-Profit Organisations: The Importance of Measurement Indicators*, EMES Selected Conference Paper Series. EMES.

Czischke, D., Gruis, V. and Mullins, D. (2012). Conceptualising social enterprise in housing organisations. *Housing Studies*, 27(4), 418–437.

Defourny, J. and Nyssens, M. (2006). Defining social enterprise. In M. Nyssens (Ed.): *Social Enterprise: At the Crossroads of Market, Public Policies and Civil Society* (3–26). London and New York: Routledge.

Defourny, J. and Nyssens, M. (2013). Social innovation, social economy and social enterprise: What can the European debate tell us? In F. Moulaert, D. MacCallum, A. Mehmood, and A. Hamdouch (Eds.): *International Handbook on Social Innovation* (40–52). Cheltenham, UK and Northampton, USA: Edward Elgar.

Defourny, J. and Nyssens, M. (2017). Fundamentals for an international typology of social enterprise models. *Voluntas: International Journal of Voluntary and Nonprofit Organizations*, 28(6), 2469–2497.

DiMaggio, P. J. and Powell, W. P. (1983). The ironic cage revisited: Institutional isomorphism and collective rationality in organizational fields. *American Sociological Review*, 48, 147–160.

Doherty, B., Haugh, H. and Lyon, F. (2014). Social enterprises as hybrid organizations: A review and research agenda. *British Academy of Management, 16*, 417–436.

Domaradzka, A. (2018). Urban social movements and the right to the city: An introduction to the special issue on Urban mobilization. *Voluntas: International Journal of Voluntary and Nonprofit Organizations*, 29(4), 607–620.

Domaradzka, A. and Wijkström, F. (2016). Game of the city re-negotiated: The Polish urban re-generation movement as an emerging actor of a strategic action field. *Polish Sociological Review, 195*, 291.

Emirbayer, M. and Johnson, V. (2008). Bourdieu and organizational analysis. *Theory and Society, 37*(1), 1–44.

European Commission (EC). (1995). *Local Development and Employment Initiatives: An Investigation in the European Union*. Brussels: European Commission.

Evers, A. (1990). Im intermediären Bereich: Soziale Träger und Projekte zwischen Haushalt, Staat und Markt' [In the intermediary zone: Social actors and projects between household, state and market]. *Journal für Sozialforschung*, 2(30), 189–210.

Evers, A. and Laville, J-L. (2004). Defining the third sector in Europe. In A. Evers and J-L. Laville (Eds.): *The Third Sector in Europe* (11–42). Cheltenham: Edward Elgar.

Fligstein, N. and McAdam, D. (2011). Toward a general theory of strategic action fields. *Sociological Theory, 29*(1), 1–26.

Fligstein, N. and McAdam, D. (2012). *A Theory of Fields*. London: Oxford University Press.

Gorski, P. S. (2012). Bourdieusian theory and historical analysis: Maps, mechanisms, and methods. In P. S. Gorski (Ed.): *Bourdieu and Historical Analysis* (327–367). Chapel Hill: Duke University Press.

Hatak, I., Lang, R. and Roessl, D. (2016). Trust, social capital, and the coordination of relationships between the members of cooperatives: A comparison between member-focused cooperatives and third-party-focused cooperatives. *Voluntas, 27*, 1218–1241. https://doi.org/10.1007/s11266-015-9663-2

Kendall, J. (2005). *Third Sector European Policy: Organisations Between Market and State, the Policy Process and the EU*, Third Sector European Policy Working Paper 1, London: LSE.

Macmillan, R., Taylor, R., Arvidson, M., Soteri-Proctor, A. and Teasdale, S. (2013). *The Third Sector in Unsettled Times: A Field Guide*, Third Sector Research Centre Working Paper 109, University of Birmingham.

McInerney, P-B. (2013). From endogenization to justification: Strategic responses to legitimacy challenges in contentious organizational fields. *Organization Management Journal*, 10(4), 240–253.

McQuarrie, M. and Krumholz, N. (2011). Institutionalized social skill and the rise of mediating organizations in urban governance: The case of the Cleveland housing network. *Housing Policy Debate*, 21(3), 421–442.

O'Hara, P. and O'Shaughnessy, M. (2017). *Social Enterprise in Ireland: WISE, the Dominant Model of Irish Social Enterprise*, ICSEM Working Papers, No. 41, Liege: The International Comparative Social Enterprise Models (ICSEM) Project.

Pestoff, V. A. (1992). Third sector and co-operative services: An alternative to privatisation. *Journal of Consumer Policy*, 15, 21–45.

Richter, R. (2018). The Janus face of participatory governance: How inclusive governance benefits and limits the social innovativeness of social enterprises. *Journal of Entrepreneurial and Organizational Diversity*, 7(1), 61–87.

Salamon, L. M. and Anheier, H. K. (1995). *Defining the Nonprofit Sector*. Manchester: Manchester University Press.

Snow, D. A. and Benford, R. D. (1992). Master frames and cycles of protest. In A. Morris and C. Mueller (Eds.): *Frontiers of Social Movement Theory* (133–155). New Haven, CT: Yale University Press.

Steiner, A. and Teasdale, S. (2018). Unlocking the potential of rural Social Enterprise. *Journal of Rural Studies*. https://doi.org/10.1016/j.jrurstud.2017.12.021

Swartz, D. L. (2014). Theorizing fields. *Theory and Society*, 43(6), 675–682.

4 Practitioner's Voice

Reflections on the Relevance of the Identified Measures for Rural Social Entrepreneurship Practice

This book builds on the idea of a conversation between researchers and practitioners. It provides and links the researchers' and practitioners' perspectives on social enterprise. The present chapter gives the floor to the involved rural social enterprises. In four interviews the social entrepreneurs respond to guiding questions and provide a vivid impression of what motivates and challenges social entrepreneurs. Together with the researchers' analysis in previous chapters the practitioners' points of view enable the comparison of inside and outside perspectives. One after another, the representatives of the Irish, the Greek, the Austrian, and the Polish social enterprise have their say. Each section begins with a short introduction of the social entrepreneur, thus providing a view on the different life paths that lead to the role as a rural social entrepreneur. A similar set of questions makes it possible to compare the positions of the practitioners to issues such as self-perception as social enterprise and possible tensions between social and entrepreneurial mission. Thus the interviews close a loop. We set out with case descriptions from the perspective of the practitioners in Chapter 1 and analyze the cases in Chapters 2 and 3. Now we return to the practitioners' view and how they reflect on the guiding questions of this research endeavor. The insights from this conversation between the practitioners' and researchers' perspective on social enterprise are subsequently discussed in Chapter 5.

Social Entrepreneur Behind the Irish Regional Development Company

Born and raised in Mid-West Ireland, the family father worked in Germany before he engaged in regional development in his home region. The keen sportsman loves the countryside for its tight social fabric and strong community feeling as well as for the vast opportunities for outdoor activities such as hiking and mountain biking. He joined the regional development company more than a decade ago and made his internal career in the areas of tourism and regional development before he was appointed CEO of the regional development company in 2016.

Authors: What makes your organization a social enterprise?

Social entrepreneur: The label *social enterprise* is not that prevalent in Ireland at present. While many of the activities that the organization engages in are entrepreneurial and lead to social innovation, the organization would use the label 'community led local development' more than social enterprise. The business model of the organization is that of community led local development. It is a dynamic process by facilitating community and citizen development through an inter-active process of animation, capacity building, engagement, partner-ship, planning, review, and evaluation. The social mission is core to activities and the organization works in partnership, across multiple levels, to develop empowered and inclusive communities that inspire and embrace new opportunities, drive positive sustainable social and economic change, and reduce inequalities. However, the organiza-tion also needs to be sustainable economically in order to progress its vision. Remaining relevant for over 30 years has required entre-preneurial thinking to constantly adapt to the changing environment and to optimize emerging opportunities. Throughout its history it has been innovative in identifying the needs of its communities and creating solutions to these gaps from within the communities themselves.

Authors: Who are the dominant advocates of the social and entrepre-neurial mission?

Social entrepreneur: The approach of the organization involves the active participation of the residents of rural communities in developing responses to the key economic, environmental, and social challenges identified in their areas. The organization focuses on facilitating and building the capacity of communities, individuals, and businesses to participate in community led local development through three key aims: Community Development, Economic Development, and Envi-ronmental Development. Local residents are key advocates for the social and entrepreneurial mission. Board members lead the organi-zation and understand their role as being critical to the social and economic life opportunities of local communities and citizens. The Board, comprised of Local Government, Social Partners, Community and Voluntary, and Statutory agency representatives, devises the over-all strategy based on identifying local needs through stakeholder con-sultations and responding based on development of local solutions. Responsibility for managing implementation and meeting the organi-zation's objectives is delegated to an executive team and implemented through experienced and dedicated teams working across focused development programs, projects, and initiatives. The management and employee teams deliver on the three core aims through delivery of services across six thematic areas: 1) Training and Lifelong Learning, 2) Children, Families and Well Being, 3) Community Development, 4) Environmental Development, 5) Tourism, Recreation and Culture, and 6) Economic Development. The combination of engaged communities, a dedicated Board and a professional team of management and staff ensures that the organization remains focused on its social and entrepreneurial mission.

Authors: Are there any tensions between the social and the entrepreneurial mission? how do you handle these tensions?

Social entrepreneur: Tension may always arise within an organization that has a triple focus on social development, economic development, and environmental sustainability. While resources are allocated on a program by program or project by project basis, with varying degrees of focus, the organization manages the balance by approaching all of its activities as interdependent of each other. For example, a social inclusion strategy may be developed around personal development and progression of individuals and households. However, a holistic solution may not be achieved in the absence of economic supports like progression into employment or enterprise supports. Expenditure on a community landscaping project may be viewed as inefficient in financial terms, however, the non-financial indicators of such an activity may be an improved living environment and closer community cooperation and engagement, which in turn create the necessary conditions for proving opportunities for the promotion of the other services such as enterprise supports.

Authors: Your social enterprise operates in a rural region with distinct cultural and institutional features. Does your organization build on established structures, trends, routines or cultural elements?

Social entrepreneur: Communities within the area first came together in 1989, in response to the continued decline of services and employment opportunities in the area. Since then, the organization's experience of designing and implementing solutions to facilitate the development of local communities has placed it to the fore in evolving and developing innovative community participation methodologies, networking fora, and collective implementation plans. The organization has played a number of different but complementary roles in the local development process. These have included supporting research, identifying needs and service gaps, supporting and facilitating project plans, and implementing innovative solutions in partnership with local communities. All of these activities have centered on supporting empowered citizens through capacity building, advocacy, and meaningful participation, complemented by real decision making at local level.

This partnership-based, locally-led process continually evolves, taking account of social, cultural, environmental, and economic changes. This process of innovation ensures that supports are targeted, inclusive, market-led, and quality focused and add value to established structures and processes.

Authors: How do social routines in the region and beyond legitimize your organization and its activities?

Social entrepreneur: Understanding how local communities work and consistently listening and responding to local needs is crucial in the work of the organization. The communities across the area broadly break down into peri urban communities, traditional market towns, and their hinterlands and remote rural areas. Each of these area types has its own opportunities and challenges and the organization service delivery model reflects local needs. Recessions consistently reveal underlying and persistent weaknesses and disadvantages across the area. This is evidenced by higher than average un- and underemployment rates and increased out-migration levels. The area also has pockets of concentrated inter-generational disadvantage along with hidden social exclusion in more spatially dispersed rural areas. The geographic area covered by the organization evolved in line with local social and cultural connections and while the area crosses local government administrative boundaries, the geography reflects activity between local communities and also reflects functional economic areas as evidence by where people live and work.

Authors: How do current trends in the region and beyond legitimize your organization and its activities?

Social entrepreneur: The need for increased social inclusion, improved economic diversification and a sustainable environment all continue to provide challenges for the area. Opportunities exist in line with national and EU policy to strengthen local participation through increased citizen engagement and capacity building. The organization continues to actively engage and animate communities to improve their input to local social and economic planning processes and identify local priorities for investment. This socio economic planning model is core to the work of the organization as it underpins the work in communities across the area. A national policy focus on rural communities, rural towns and villages, the rural economy, and the environment are opening up improved opportunities for rural communities. The organization *focuses* on rural tourism, outdoor recreation, local artisan food, and the bio and circular economy continues to evolve, however, the economic, social, and environmental impact of these opportunities have yet to be fully realized.

Authors: Does your organization moderate between the interests of the communities/groups you work with and powerful agents in the broader society, such as central government and large corporations? If so, please describe your role as intermediary between these parties?

Social entrepreneur: The organization has evolved excellent competencies in engaging, animating and supporting individuals, communities, and businesses in the design and development of locally led strategies through collaborating on the planning, management, and delivery of national and EU funded community, social, and rural development programs since its establishment in 1989. This locally led process continually evolves, taking account of social, cultural, environmental, and economic changes. Delivery to clients centers on supporting progression from initial engagement, through personal development, education, training, employment, and enterprise supports to both full community and civic participation. This takes account of clients' skills, experience, learning, and social needs, with engagement facilitated at locations and times that respect the diversity of client needs. Activities are overseen by the Board to a comprehensive set of standards, procedures, and policies that cover governance, program requirements, financial, HR, and health & safety management, to comply with public funding requirements on program delivery, procurement, financial management, monitoring, evaluation, processing of data, and funding apportionment.

Authors: How does your organization interact with local communities?

Social entrepreneur: The organization supports the principle that people who live and work in rural communities are best placed to understand the local challenges and decide what support is needed to facilitate the development of their communities. Engagement, animation, and capacity building are critical to local interaction. The coaching, guidance, and support to individuals and communities so as to enhance and empower their potential contribution to the development of the area is delivered through individualized support, group training, and facilitate networking opportunities. The emphasis of the model is pre-development training, animation, capacity building, and networking. District Fora are keys to this engagement and provide an opportunity for communities and groups in a local area to meet and share experiences. Networking events facilitate the transfer of learning from one community to another and communities become more informed and empowered to participate more actively in their own communities and in decision-making processes more widely. The networking also ensures that the communities have an increased knowledge of the activities and interventions being implemented and considered by the organization.

The development of strategic priorities for the organization evolves through local consultations with a broad range of stakeholders, to develop a Community Led Local Development Strategy. Stakeholder feedback and analysis of the available evidence aim to create a clear understanding of the key challenges and determine the priority activity areas. The organization then focuses on creating partnerships and achieving solutions to enhance the development and potential for local social, community, economic, and environment development.

Authors: Which resources does your organization receive from the local community?

Social entrepreneur: In accordance with our mission to develop, empower, and include communities, understanding the needs of communities and groups is critical. Information and knowledge from the communities is an important resource for the organization. The close connections and exchange of information with communities facilitates a two-way communication flow. In addition, there are also eight elected community members on the board of the organization where their experience and on-the-ground knowledge is invaluable to the strategic planning and operational delivery. Information enables the organization to adapt and evolve and continue to provide relevant services based on understanding community needs.

Authors: Did your organization change the way local people live, work and/or interact?

Social entrepreneur: Since its foundation in 1989, the organization has contributed to the social, economic, and environmental change in the area. The contribution may be accounted for in financial terms by the many millions of Euros brokered by and invested through the organization in the area. However, such a purely accounting procedure would ignore the real added value of the organization. By following an integrated, partnership based, community led local development strategy, the organization has contributed far beyond the financial investment. A more accurate picture of the changes is gained by examining the levels of engagement such as the numbers of people encouraged to engage in education, training, and employment related activities, the level of community pride in the area, the increased visitors to the area to participate in a variety of authentic heritage experiences and world class recreation activities. The emergence of new economic sectors and the social innovation that has driven new service delivery mechanisms such as elder care using social economy models. The area today is one where communities have a strong sense of ownership for their area and feel they can influence economic and social change in their relevant communities.

Authors: Which are the major challenges your organization faces?

Social entrepreneur: The organization is confronted with several challenges; some affect the enterprise, others the rural communities that we serve. First off, how the organization adopts constantly evolving new technologies to continue to support increased awareness of and improved access to services and how it can effectively and efficiently communicate the value and impact of its work is a key challenge. Of importance, also, are the changing fund allocation models, both nationally and on the EU-level, with a move toward more competitive calls and tendering processes and increased fragmentation of the available funding. This requires the organization to devote an increased amount of resources on brokering funding on behalf of local communities to support the community led local development process. There is no guarantee of continuity in delivery of services. This in turn may impact on future development of the region. A second challenge is the cost of meeting increased governance and compliance requirements as required by agencies in charge of public funding and regulators. The increased costs put pressure on us because they reduce the funds available for front line services.

Authors: What are the challenges for the next five to ten years and how does your organization address them?

Social entrepreneur: The finalization of the EU 2021–2027 plan and in particular its Rural Development Policy along with the recent developments in Ireland of an integrated plan for Local and Community Development and the development of a Policy and Strategy for Social Enterprise are likely to determine how the challenges and opportunities evolve over the next five to ten years for the organization. In the delivery of these strategies there is a need to affirm the contribution of the community led local development approach to building a more just and prosperous society and acknowledge that the process provides human, social, and community services that impact across all key areas of life. To prepare for future challenges the organization needs to strengthen its relationship with key partners, build new partnerships and continue to provide support that the area needs to ensure the continued valuable contribution of the organization to local communities. The challenge is to ensure that all residents in local communities, including those individuals and groups who are experiencing the highest levels of inequality, are facilitated to come together to identify their own needs and issues and have their voices heard in the decision making processes that affect them and their community.

Authors: Provide a sketch of how you think your organization and its activities in the region will look like in five years?

Social entrepreneur: The organization will continue to focus on its vision of 'empowered inclusive communities and a diversified economy' by continuing to support communities across the area and by working in partnership. The three core aims of community development, economic development, and environmental development will continue to be key to the delivery of services and supports. All communities will be engaged in shorter cycles of social economic planning and review so that plans are relevant and in tune with the external environment and changing opportunities. The organization will have continued to evolve and grow to adapt to the external environment and continue to be a leader in community led local development by optimizing social innovation processes to provide new services of need to local communities. The organization will have a greater focus on integrating environmental sustainability across all of its services with local economic sectors increasingly taking advantage of opportunities in the circular and bio economy. The organization will be increasingly using technology to create inspiring local success stories that engage an increased number of individual and communities in the community led development process.

Authors: How did the relevance of social enterprises as a type of organization change in your country in the last decade? How do you see the future prospects?

Social entrepreneur: While there is growing awareness of social enterprise, social entrepreneurship, and social innovation the emergence in 2019 of a Social Enterprise Policy and Strategy will facilitate the major focus that is required for the sector to grow stronger and achieve sustainability. Especially, there is likely to be more awareness over the coming years of social enterprise. Currently, few of the organization's stakeholders would describe the organization as a social enterprise. Growth can be increasingly facilitated by new forms of social enterprises that are operating in the market and competing with the private sector to generate a return that is subsequently invested in the social mission. New opportunities will emerge through inclusion of social clauses in public procurement to deliver increased levels of public services through the social enterprise model. Gaps in service provision exist in rural Ireland, given much of the country will not be of economic interest to the commercial sector and there will be increased openings for the social enterprise model to engage in social innovation and design, develop, and deliver services. Technology and increased availability of broadband across the country will provide opportunities for the social enterprise sector to engage in online solutions and services to a broader market. Opportunities also exist for intensified partnerships with the private sector to optimize corporate social responsibility.

Social Entrepreneur Behind the Greek Stevia Cooperative

Born and raised in a mid-sized town in Central Greece the energetic and smart businessman has returned to his hometown with his family a decade ago after having worked in Asia for some years. He is now in his late 40s. The trained mechanical engineer with a strong background in renewable energy and project management has developed a successful international career in the finance and banking business and is founder of two innovative startups in the agri-food sector.

Authors: What makes your organization a social enterprise?

Social entrepreneur: The term social enterprise is still new in our country although cooperatives and in our case agricultural cooperatives have been operating for many decades. The last few years, cooperatives are regaining respect and consumers are more willing to buy a cooperative product due to the social background as well. That is to say that beyond quality and environmental issues, consumers nowadays are paying attention to the social approach of producing and trading. The stated consumers feel the need to support products that are made by a social enterprise as a cooperative. Thus, it is important that all our members describe the organization as a cooperative. This is very clear in their minds.

Actually, we are a social cooperative, but we usually use the label "Agricultural Cooperative." By statute it is part of the organization's brand name. It is used in all kinds of official documents but also in our everyday communication. Social cooperatives are a special type of organization that consists of two layers: One layer is the layer with the farmers and the other layer is the layer with business people. Most of the farmers do not have an entrepreneurial mindset: Thirty percent at maximum. It is the business people who bring the ideas, but all the important decisions need the green lights from the members. This combination of a group of farmers with my entrepreneurial mindset is the innovation of our cooperative. In combination we are a social enterprise. But to be clear: I have not built a social movement, but a business that is based on an entrepreneurial business model. When it works out well, in a few years, the farmers will make good business in our cooperative. So, the cooperative is good for them—it is social.

Authors: Who are the dominant advocates of the social/entrepreneurial mission?

Social entrepreneur: The dominant advocates of the social mission are the members of the cooperative. From the very beginning, we tried to convince the opinion leaders in the region to participate in the cooperative, the kind of people others would ask, for example, what they thought about stevia. The cooperative's founder—a former leader of the tobacco cooperatives—strongly believes that we can only be successful by working together in the cooperative and by remembering the common good for society, and this is the social mission he promotes. The management team and I reflect the entrepreneurial mission of the cooperative, as it aims to address matters in an entrepreneurial, economically profitable way. As CEO, I represent this mission. I am certainly not a philanthropist, someone who gives money to help people in the region. But I am an entrepreneur, and by setting up and running the business I help them. The board of directors tries to combine the two missions so that each mission is fulfilled to a satisfying degree. Interestingly, I feel that our cooperative established a way to keep away the influence of local, regional and national government, and other powerful groups. We are working in a parallel system far away from powerful players.

Authors: You talk about combining the social and the entrepreneurial mission. Are there any tensions between the social and the entrepreneurial mission? How do you handle these tensions?

Social entrepreneur: Whenever we see tensions between the social and the entrepreneurial mission, we try to solve them in accordance with the cooperative's principles. We try to come up with a solution and then discuss the advantages and disadvantages related to this solution. This procedure either takes place at the level of the board of directors or even at the level of the general assembly. A recent example for such tensions was the question whether the cooperative should provide credit to its members to enable them to buy supplies. On the one side, a lot of members were facing difficult economic times and we thought that the cooperative should support them. On the other side, however, the financial situation of the cooperative had to be considered as well. The board of directors discussed this issue and finally decided to grant credit to the cooperative's members. One of the difficulties in this respect is that as soon as the general assembly is involved, we have to discuss any issues with the members of the cooperative, who are farmers and mostly do not have an entrepreneurial mindset. They have a completely different way of thinking than the management team. It often takes a lot of time to explain why things need to be done in a specific way, and this can cause considerable delay. When we wanted to build the storage and office space, for example, we had to describe and explain in detail how we wanted to set everything up and illustrate it with pictures and graphs so that everybody had an idea why having the space was important. So, overall, there are a lot of internal discussions to address any tensions resulting from the dual mission of the cooperative. When we look at the question how to represent the social and the entrepreneurial mission to people outside the cooperative, we tend to emphasize one of the missions depending on who and why we meet. If we meet business partners, we focus on our entrepreneurial mission. If, however, we meet other social entrepreneurs, we focus on our social mission. I think you can compare us to the moon that has a dark side and a bright side.

Authors: Your social enterprise operates in a rural region with distinct cultural and institutional features. Does your organization build on established structures, trends, routines or cultural elements?

Social entrepreneur: The region is characterized by its agricultural production. Some of the agricultural goods that are produced here are cotton, corn, wheat, olives, cherries, pistachios, and walnuts. For many years, tobacco was produced in this region as well. A lot of members of the cooperative are former tobacco growers. Due to the decline of the European tobacco industry, they had to look for different crops. Today, they cultivate the stevia plant, which is quite similar to tobacco growing and processing in terms of crop management. In addition, the financial crisis has changed the way in which people think in this country. I think that it forced them to think in a more entrepreneurial way.

Authors: How do social routines in the region and beyond that legitimize your organization and its activities?

Social entrepreneur: During the economic crisis, a lot of cooperatives were established. They are the traditional way to organize agricultural activities in rural regions and allow the wellbeing of their members and the development of the region to be taken into consideration. In our case the crisis helped us to realize that we need to exploit the entire value chain instead of just selling dried stevia leaves and that we need to work together. We therefore thought that a cooperative would be the perfect organizational form for us.

Authors: How do current trends in the region and beyond that legitimize your organization and its activities?

Social entrepreneur: I think there are three main trends that our organization relates to: First, health is an extremely important topic both at national and at European level. Stevia is a natural sugar substitute that is 300 times sweeter than sugar with no calories and therefore suitable for diabetics' use. However, the product is not only targeted at people with diabetes, but also at people with obesity and at young people who like to be fit. We also try to develop products for children. Second, cooperatives are trendy forms of organizations. A lot of consumers want to buy products from cooperatives, not necessarily only from European cooperatives, but also from cooperatives from other parts of the world. So even though our main aim was to set up an organizational structure that allows us to take decisions in a more democratic way, by choosing a cooperative we were also able to attract additional customers who prefer to buy from these types of organization. This also relates to the third trend, which is that agricultural production needs to become more sustainable and independent. Farmers currently search for new methods of cultivation and new products that enable them to reap the benefits of their work and to offer value-added products to their customers. We therefore try to cover the whole value chain. We do not only produce dry leaves and sell them, but we aim at producing the final product and try to be as close to the customer as possible. Hence, we either market our products directly or sell them to supermarkets so that we cover everything from the field to the shelf.

Authors: You talked about how the members of the cooperative interact. How does your organization interact with the local community?

Social entrepreneur: We offer knowledge and information on different topics regarding our region to the local community. We also highlight opportunities where we and the local community can work together and create new businesses or cooperatives. For example, back in 2013 we organized a workshop to introduce the idea to establish a new energy production cooperative and showed successful examples of such cooperatives in the EU. Together with the municipality and the University of Thessaly we talked about the possibility of producing pellets by using municipal pruning. Currently, we collaborate with Greenpeace to produce pellets and provide them to schools in the region. All these initiatives lead to more job opportunities for the local community as our cooperative grows.

Authors: Which resources does your organization receive from the local community?

Social entrepreneur: Our organization occasionally uses the public spaces of the local community for meetings and educational purposes. One recent example is a small conference on agro-energy that we organized in a theater here in town. Approximately 250 people attended this conference and we talked about how to use the energy that farmers produce. In addition to that, we also organized some meetings where all people of our region could participate. This helps us to exchange ideas, learn about the concerns that locals have, and receive feedback for example on our packaging. A lot of shops here in the local community support us by selling our product.

Authors: Did your organization change the way local people live, work and/or interact?

Social entrepreneur: I do not think that there have been a lot of changes regarding the economic situation of the people in the region. Even the members of our cooperative have not received much profit yet as we are still in the process of entering the market. Nevertheless, I think a lot of the people here in the region have changed the way in which they collaborate and the way they think about farming and agriculture. They have learned about new methods of cultivation, such as new fertilizers or how to reduce pesticides, and how to reduce production costs. By organizing meetings and conferences, we foster an exchange of ideas within the local community. It also helps to work together with other companies and local public authorities on topics such as monitoring the micro-climate of our cultivations. We also collaborate with the Diabetics Association of the region and held a joint event on World Diabetes Day to inform people about diabetes and how to live with it. Overall, I think that we may not be able to completely change the entire region, but by starting fires in different places, we hope that they become bigger and bigger and eventually change people's lives.

Authors: Which are the major challenges your organization faces?

Social entrepreneur: I have talked about the mindset of the members of the cooperative before. So, even though some of them have become more entrepreneurial over the past years, the majority of them still want to concentrate on the production of stevia leaves and is not ready to take any risks. This implies that we always have to go the slowest possible way because the members do not want to invest additional money. Instead of transporting the leaves abroad to extract pure stevia, we could build a factory here in Greece. By doing so, we would be able to increase our margin considerably, but nobody wants to take the risk. It is not even possible to invest money in machines that collect the stevia leaves directly. To date, the farmers still defoliate the leaves from the stems by hand. Within less than a year the money saved for this manual process would exceed the cost of the machine needed. The same is true for funding. We cannot apply for EU funding, because the majority of applications is not successful and our application would thus present a risk that the cooperative members do not want to accept. The members also decided that they do not want a loan or to take an investor on board, because they were afraid to lose their voice in the company. Another challenge is the difficulty of finding qualified staff. The region currently suffers from a brain drain, as a lot of bright people are leaving.

Authors: What are the challenges for the next five to ten years and how does your organization address them?

Social entrepreneur: I think that one of the main challenges will be to build a bigger team that takes care of sales and marketing. But this would require investments from the members of the cooperative and the problem is that they do not understand that if you want to sell something you need to invest first. They want to earn a lot of money from day one. This is just not possible! It would also be good if we could improve the structure of the organization and employ more people. Regarding the stevia plant, we will have to address cultivation issues, such as possible pests and diseases. Last but not least, another challenge will be to reduce production costs. We will therefore have to look for practical and yet economic ways to harvest, dry, defoliate, and transport the stevia leaves.

Authors: Provide a sketch of how you think your organization and its activities in the region will look like in five years?

Social entrepreneur: I believe that the members of the cooperative, its employees and the local community will actively support the organization, just as the organization will support the community for example by setting up new businesses or providing job opportunities. I think that we will also have new collaborations to develop agricultural products and with new cooperatives that foster economic and cultural development.

Authors: How did the relevance of social enterprises as a type of organization change in your country in the last decade? How do you see the future prospects?

Social entrepreneur: The social economy officially appeared in Greece with the Law 2646/1998, that led to the creation of Protected Productive Laboratories, in which at least three-fifths of the staff have to be employees with special requirements. The key role of this new legal form was to integrate people with psychosocial issues into the labor market. The Social Economy was legally introduced by Law 2716/1999, which defined a new legal form: the Social Cooperatives of Limited Liability. Later in 2011, the government issued the Law 4019/2011 entitled "Social Economy and Social Entrepreneurship and Other Provisions." This law updated the legislation regulating the social economy and social entrepreneurship. In this update the government could realize significant improvements of the regulations for Social Cooperative Companies. Lately there is a lot of interest in social enterprises, perhaps due to the recent update of the legislation that replaced and improved the technical aspects and reduced obstacles for the development of social enterprises. As far as the agricultural cooperatives are concerned, there is also a positive view regarding their development due to Greek rural specifics and market demands, but also due to the Common Agricultural Policy that leads farmers in rural areas to organize their production through cooperation and cooperatives.

Social Entrepreneur Behind the Austrian Brain Gainers

The father of three is married, currently in his late 40s and well networked in the international scene of social entrepreneurs. He is trained in social and vocational pedagogy and IT engineering and has extensive experience as a consultant for regional development and planning. He is a serial entrepreneur with a focus on delivering education and consulting on digital transformation to public and private customers. Besides, he is a part-time university lecturer. In his main career he is the initiator and a founding member of the Austrian case enterprise.

Authors: What makes your organization a social enterprise?

Social entrepreneur: Our intentions and business model correspond with well-known definitions of social entrepreneurship, such as put forward by Ashoka. Our social mission refers to bringing change and promoting empowerment in society with a range of consulting services. We consult, for instance, on social and environmental sustainability as well as resilience in regional development. One target group for these services is municipalities. Another key consulting area refers to new employment models to achieve a balance between work and personal life. This includes workplace design as well as knowledge distribution regarding suitable company forms, including the promotion of new types of cooperatives. Our social enterprise also promotes resident participation on the local and regional level through networking activities and know-how transfer on participatory processes. Furthermore, we engage in the redesign and restructuring of public space by providing "nodes" for innovation that are accessible to everyone. These "nodes" are based on a culture of networking and open hosting. We are keen to mobilize and scale local resources for the development of new ideas, strategies, and models. Our organization also promotes digital literacy for people of all ages and initiatives where people can reflect on new technologies, such as 3D printing or virtual reality. The social mission is also reflected in our very own cooperative culture. The cooperative is designed as a solidarity-based organization where individual members can live up to their capabilities and full potential through cooperation with others. At the same time the cooperative embodies a specific entrepreneurial mission. It aims to facilitate employment for persons with entrepreneurial competence who would like to work both independently and in teams, and also for non-profit aims. Employed members have their own product portfolio and thus generate their self-determined salaries, as well as represent their own cost centers. But they can also access a collective pool of funding and income possibilities as well as shared knowledge in the above-mentioned product and service areas.

Authors: Who are the dominant advocates of the social/entrepreneurial mission?

Social entrepreneur: All cooperative members are employees and also entrepreneurs. They share vision, mission, and objectives as well as the sociocratic and self-administered structure of the cooperative. The fundamental idea of a cooperative is that the social and entrepreneurial mission should support and strengthen each other. In our case, the mission is additionally based on the concept of sociocracy, referring to a circle organization and consent decisions, ensuring transparency, identification, and commitment. Then we have certain working groups (WG), which guarantee that both missions are carried out appropriately. The WGs Finance and Public Relation have a good view on entrepreneurial objectives, whereas the WGs Staff and Organization put an emphasis on social objectives (in relation to employees and fields of activities).

Authors: Typically, social enterprises combine a social with an entrepreneurial mission. Are there any tensions between the social and the entrepreneurial mission? How do you handle these tensions?

Social entrepreneur: With regard to non-profit activities, for instance, it has turned out that the customers (non-profit organizations, public institutions etc) often have limited budget available. This makes it challenging to meet the customers' needs, but also to implement entrepreneurial objectives. Employed members try to compensate for this by acquiring new orders and also by convincing financially strong clients to invest in non-profit projects.

Authors: On which occasions do you use the label "social enterprise" for your organization?

Social entrepreneur: We use the term "social enterprise" only in the context of other "social enterprises" or vis-à-vis funding agencies. Sometimes we also use this term in the context of stakeholder meetings or lectures.

Authors: Which of your stakeholders describe your organization as a social enterprise?

Social entrepreneur: In particular, funding agencies such as the Public Employment Service, the Chamber of Commerce or public bodies. Non-profit foundations or organizations such as Ashoka also call us a social enterprise.

Authors: Is it useful to be perceived of as a social enterprise?

Social entrepreneur: For us, this is mainly relevant for subsidies. Otherwise, we prefer to appear as a "normal" company. In Austria, the term social enterprise is too closely associated with "semi-governmental" organizations such as BFI or Wifi [institutions of education run by the Austrian Chambers of Commerce and Labor]. In any case, in Austria this term primarily implies 100 percent of publicly funded institutions and organizations.

Authors: Your social enterprise operates in a rural region with rich history. Does your organization build on established structures, trends, routines or cultural elements?

Social entrepreneur: There were two crucial inspirations for our organization. The first came from the social philosopher Professor Frithjof Bergmann and his theories of "Neue Arbeit—Neue Kultur" ["New Work—New Culture"]. The constructive but also critical exchange with Frithjof Bergmann influenced the actual implementation of his approach in our organization. Bergmann is also known for his question: "Was ist das, was du wirklich, wirklich willst?" ["What is it you really, really desire?"] and his critical view on the "Lohnarbeitsparadigma" [paradigm of paid labor], which he describes as "milde Krankheit" [light illness]. A second inspiration came from the neurologist Gerald Hüther with his keywords "Potenzialentfaltung" [development of potential], "dazugehören und wachsen dürfen" [integrate and being allowed grow], and "inspirieren, begeistern, ermöglichen" [inspire, excite, make it possible]. More generally, our enterprise was based on the idea of how to redesign work in the future and to analyze how this change can be successful. Our cooperatives are locations with a welcoming structure, offering locals the possibility to develop their potential in an interdisciplinary and low-threshold way. Interested groups ("Nodes") are formed and a Community Education Program is created by citizens for citizens.

Authors: How does the way locals are used to thinking and acting in the region and beyond enhance the acceptance of your organization and its activities?

Social entrepreneur: The issue of restructuring paid labor in the region has been raised repeatedly. It was linked to the salt mines, the summer retreats of the aristocracy or the decline of agriculture. In locations where we initially established our "Nodes" (as associations), bottom-up citizens' initiatives had already existed in the areas of culture, social cohabitation, and design of change for some years, and had actually achieved an impact. One could say that in regions where our organization is active, you will find a comparatively well-established culture of self-organization and self-empowerment.

Authors: How do current trends in the region and beyond legitimize your organization and its activities?

Social entrepreneur: In light of the economic crises, cooperatives have recently become an attractive alternative to the limited company—not only for non-profit initiatives. Thus, our business model of an employment cooperative attracts increasing attention. We also served as a role model enterprise for citizen involvement in the energy sector and the newly founded cooperative umbrella and audit association "Rückenwind." So you see there are interesting developments in the area of cooperatives in Austria. Business ideas for new coops range from the preservation of a local bakery, the re-organization of a design work group to a municipal cooperative for local supply—all of them aiming at the improvement of the local job market and the integration of migrants. It seems that many people think about the economy from the perspective of cooperation and also start living accordingly. We are certain that the establishment of new local associations and their achievements will further increase target group acceptance.

Authors: Does your organization moderate between the interests of the communities/groups you work with and powerful agents in the broader society, such as central government and large corporations? If so, please describe your role as intermediary between these parties?

Social entrepreneur: We primarily act as intermediaries at a regional level. We are currently, for example, in the process design of future regional development structures. This is where we bring in our experience from the voluntary innovation network. In addition, we increasingly cooperate with national and international organizations. Here we are mainly asked for topics such as regional innovation capability or the development of innovation cultures.

Authors: You mention the collaboration with authorities and companies. How does your organization interact with the local community?

Social entrepreneur: Our employed members are active members in their local communities and live there according to our enterprise values. As an organization, we have managed to increase the number of local projects, such as with schools and cultural associations. Furthermore, we implemented co-working areas in some of our locations, which are used by our cooperative employees as well as the public. In general, acceptance of our local associations has increased considerably, also among more conservative target groups (men's circles and of course Repair Cafés), which is also reflected in actual attendance figures. Our locations are probably seen as a "neutral" space where people and also institutions, which normally do not interact, can freely exchange ideas and work together. In such an atmosphere, the integration of asylum seekers is also easier (nobody has the right to "send them away") since the facilities are used by local residents and use is free of charge. In a nutshell, it has become more normal for community members to accept our locations as a suitable environment for exchanging ideas or organizing events.

Authors: Which resources does your organization receive from the local community?

Social entrepreneur: Most employed members also work voluntarily for our local associations contributing their knowhow and experience. This includes project development, team leading, communication, moderation, project management, but also networking, which results in sponsorships. In addition, they support our community projects and events (partly voluntary, partly in conjunction with their job at the cooperative). They often pro-actively address certain topics, organize events or create structures to allow new target groups to engage with our social enterprise. Furthermore, employed cooperative members also join broader cooperations with companies or local schools to strengthen the community. Employed members are hosting visits to our locations and events. They also make an effort to raise public funds for networking activities to improve knowledge transfer within the cooperative, but also with external partners.

Authors: How does your organization motivate community members to contribute?

Social entrepreneur: We organise events on interesting and timely topics. Then we have presentations and workshops to enhance sensibility for our company form, the employment cooperative. Finally, our employees encourage various networking activities.

Authors: Did your organization change the way local people live, work and/or interact?

Social entrepreneur: Our locations are meeting points for engaged residents and our employees working on projects, joint interests, and events. Our enterprise is deliberately positioned in-between institutions such as politics, education, economy, media, and social partners. It takes over the role of a catalyst between systems that normally would not work together smoothly. We offer neutral ground to discuss delicate topics and this might lead to improvements in the local community. Our activities also trigger reflexivity among local initiatives and private companies who often find it hard to express their values and objectives. Internally, for our employees, the membership in this type of employment cooperative is seen as a major improvement to operating in a sole proprietorship. Compared with the previous working environment, there is a situation as a single company where the social work situation has improved tremendously. More team experience, cooperation with a high level of mutual trust and transparency. Economically, they can simply reach out to more potential clients and attract more business, which certainly improves their financial security.

Authors: Thinking of the region, how did your organization change the economic and social situation?

Social entrepreneur: Local companies have become interested in cooperative work because they can see the advantages and want to benefit from the business model. This might be possible if a company's understanding of profit is not simply defined as monetary. The employment cooperative is closely monitored. The business form "cooperative" is well established in Austria but the employment cooperative is relatively unknown. Other cooperatives (banking or agricultural coops) are reminded of their original objectives so it makes sense to focus on employees and their development and not only on the stakeholders. Our social enterprise contributes to expanding awareness locally and regionally so that the economy can be designed differently. Our ideas and initiatives result in specific projects and activities in the sphere of local politics or in the education sector. We also try to empower individuals to stand up for their ideas in public and in political arenas. Apart from bringing people with different work backgrounds together, we present political decision makers with new options, which were not evident before. This can refer to propositions such as recognizing the connection between sharing knowledge and its attractiveness for leisure. In exchange for free of charge overnight stays, a local authority could make the visitor's knowledge accessible for local residents and strengthen the community as a whole.

Authors: Which are the major challenges your organization faces? What are the challenges for the next five to ten years and how does your organization address them?

Social entrepreneur: One of our biggest challenges refers to distance and sense of community. This challenge arises from the geographical distribution of our activities. We do not have a central or joint office but locations spread all over the region. Now we even have some international offices. Joint projects are still rare and the company image is unclear. Furthermore, many prototypes are constructed but we still lack the ability to make them scalable and reproducible. Some of our members also lack management know-how. Another challenge is the handling of reproducible management processes, such as distribution and reimbursement. Finally, we are facing the challenge of going for growth or facing stagnation in our activities.

Authors: Can you sketch your organization and its activities in the region in five years time?

Social entrepreneur: After founding the enterprise, we were mainly inward looking and focused on routines in areas where we had already been very active. Now we are progressively developing innovative projects and offers. This includes the promotion of new cooperatives, which are based on our business model. We have also become aware of better interpersonal communication, this will result in more frequent face-to-face meetings, co-working and co-creating and hence the challenge of missing a joint office location will be resolved.

Authors: How did the relevance of social enterprises as a type of organizations change in Austria in the last decade?

Social entrepreneur: The initiative of Ashoka and other foundations has led to an increasing clarification of the term and thus to a distinction between social enterprises according to the Ashoka definition and publicly funded institutions. In some cases, the distinction is not very easy to make, but the discussion process that has begun has already led to its own funding programs that are primarily aimed at social enterprises.

Authors: How do you see the future prospects of social enterprises in Austria over the next decade?

Social entrepreneur: I think that Austria, due to its strong social partnership structures, still has a long way to go in terms of cultural development. Social enterprises are still viewed very critically because they often use hybrid approaches in order to be able to operate economically successfully and at the same time pursue their social mission. Up to now, there has been a very strict separation—also in the area of funding. This requires further development and networking within the social enterprise scene.

Social Entrepreneur Behind the Polish Mind Changers

The president of the Polish social enterprise is a trained economist and teacher. Now in his 60s, he took the leading role in the organization some 25 years ago after he had stepped down as a mayor of the provincial town. During these years he has built up significant expertise in regional development, social entrepreneurship and entrepreneurship support and has authored several books on these topics. He is a member of the local support fund as well as Ashoka and he has a strong national and international network to rely on in his manifold activities. For his social entrepreneurship activities he has been presented awards by the European Union, the Polish government, and international media.

Authors: What makes your organization a social enterprise?

Social entrepreneur: The mission of the organization is to support local development. The organization has the status "non-for-profit," which implies that any profits have to be reinvested in order to develop the organization and realize its mission. To do that, the organization supports the establishment of start-up companies as well as social enterprises, the development of civil society organizations and the education of children and young adults who live in rural areas. We want to use our cultural and historic heritage as well as natural resources to create sustainable development. This means that our activities aim to preserve regional traditions and protect the environment. At the same time, we also account for the needs of the people who live in this region as well as the needs of local companies, public authorities, and other social enterprises. We thus have a social as well as an entrepreneurial mission that is also reflected in the organization's funding. Approximately 75 percent of funds stem from public funding from the EU as well as from Polish public authorities. These funds are used for social projects. The remaining 25 percent of funds result to a large extent from our business activities such as the theme village and to a minor extent from donations. I think that our approach really fosters change. Back in the 1990s, we were the poorest commune in the region with the highest rate of unemployment. Today, in the same region, more than 2,000 small companies operate and the rate of unemployment is very low.

Authors: Who are the dominant advocates of the social/entrepreneurial mission?

Social entrepreneur: My wife and I were teachers before we started the foundation and I was the mayor here. We would always be involved in activities for the community, such as setting up a committee that made sure that everyone had access to a phone line and a gas connection. Everybody knew us, which made it easier for us, I think. It was easy to get support from local companies and public authorities because we were already friends. I still have a lot of contact with local, regional, and national authorities. I have also engaged in the activities of the Ministry of Labor, the Polish parliament, and the president. It was nice to participate in a process in which you can create something and offer new solutions. With regard to the foundation I think that my relations to local and regional companies, social enterprises and public authorities are most important.

Authors: Are you a social enterprise?

Social entrepreneur: I have to be clear: We are a social enterprise. Labor market and social assistance institutions, non-governmental organizations, and unemployed people, in particular, address us as a social enterprise.

Authors: Typically, social enterprises combine a social with an entrepreneurial mission. Are there any tensions between the social and the entrepreneurial mission? How do you handle these tensions?

Social entrepreneur: Well, the term *social enterprise* is still rather unrecognized in Poland. Thus, it is hard to say if it is useful for us. Anyway, we pursue social objectives and use business tools to achieve revenues for the implementation of social activities. I do not think that there is a conflict between the social and the entrepreneurial mission. We have separate organizations and keep separate books for them. The Local Fund Organization, for example, promotes the social mission by supporting the education of young adults, whereas the Theme Village focuses on the entrepreneurial mission by attracting tourists and offering tailored programs to companies. Each field of activities has its own objectives and a specific audience. They are also managed separately.

Authors: Your social enterprise operates in a rural region with a rich history. Does your organization build on established structures, trends, routines or cultural elements?

Social entrepreneur: Both the culture and the organizational structure of the foundation are based on our experience regarding the legal regulations in Poland. Some of the programs explicitly relate to traditions here in this region. The Theme Village, for example, is based on the fact that our town was a center of ceramics in former East Prussia. Here, the most famous Mazurian tiles were made. For a long time after the war, pottery and bricks were still produced in this region. For this reason, craft traditions are extremely important. The choice to build the Theme Village was thus dictated by these traditions. Also, with regard to our activities in the field of tourism, we rely on our heritage and the cultural diversity of the region.

Authors: How does the way locals are used to think and act in the region and beyond enhance the acceptance of your organization and its activities?

Social entrepreneur: After 1990, we were confronted with a new political system to which social routines had to adapt. The challenge was to change the mentality of the people and to activate them. They had to learn that they should not wait for externals to take the decision, but to be proactive and ask what they could do. I think it is important that we focus on long-term activities, impact, and influence. And on building and shaping the awareness among the locals that they are responsible for themselves.

Authors: How do current trends in the region and beyond legitimize your organization and its activities?

Social entrepreneur: I think there are a number of trends that legitimize our organization. First, theme villages were already known in, for example, Germany, Austria, and Ireland, but not in Poland in 2007. So, we traveled around Poland to introduce this idea. We met people from companies as well as public authorities and explained how important local collaboration was in order to set up a theme village. We showed them that even in regions without major tourist attractions it was possible to create something nice that would provide work for the locals and the possibility to have a good life. Afterwards, similar initiatives were started in many places. Second, people today want to relax. It is important to show them that they can find calmness and inner peace in rural areas. We do not have a lake and sunbeds that we can charge money for, but we create opportunities for active relaxation, like the theme village and our Paradise Garden. Third, there is also a need to establish micro enterprises. We support this development by providing individuals or organized groups of people with grants, loans, and credit guarantees.

Authors: Does your organization moderate between the interests of the communities/groups you work with and powerful agents in broader society, such as central government and large corporations? If so, please describe your role as intermediary between these parties?

Social entrepreneur: Absolutely! I think we actually play the role of an intermediary in the region. For example, we obtain public funds and distribute them as subsidies for social cooperatives. They create businesses and jobs. Thus, we translate public funds into subsidies and loans for actual creation and development of small businesses. We are also organizers of events and initiatives with the participation of residents, which are supported by commercial companies. We activate locals to become active members of the community.

Authors: You mention the collaboration with authorities and companies. How does your organization interact with the local community?

Social entrepreneur: There are a number of ways in which we interact with the local community. We have meetings, for example on specific thematic or environmental issues; we initiate and implement joint development programs, projects, and development strategies. We promote our activities in the bulletin "Theme Village." We make announcements in the press, on TV, and on radio, and we distribute leaflets and our annual report. Together with entrepreneurs, local authorities, and NGOs, we organize charity events, such as a charity ball for a scholarship fund for young people. During the summer, we also organize several events, such as festivals, concerts, and fairs in the theme village.

Authors: Which resources does your organization receive from the local community?

Social entrepreneur: The main resources we receive are donations and voluntary work. There are also several hundred people from the region who participate in activities in the Paradise Garden on a regular basis and provide funding for the scholarship program. Companies from the region also support social and cultural initiatives organized in the theme village, such as music festivals and concerts.

Authors: How does your organization motivate community members to contribute?

Social entrepreneur: We offer, for instance, a card called "Friends of the Paradise Garden." This card entitles its owner to unlimited and free visits to the Paradise Garden, whereas everybody else has to buy tickets. Another way of motivating people to contribute is to put their name on promotional and information materials and to emphasize their support for upcoming events. The use of the internet has made it easier to make our activities visible. We can promote them on our Facebook page or our blog and this does not only help us to get more customers, but also to motivate community members to donate their time or money to our organization.

Authors: Did your organization change the way local people live, work and/or interact?

Social entrepreneur: Our organization implements partnership projects and thereby activates the locals and leads to social and economic development. The Local Fund Organization is a good example of this. It grants scholarships for talented young people in difficult financial situations. The main criteria for getting a scholarship are good grades and social activities, like involvement in charities, volunteering or extra classes. The aim of the Local Fund Organization is not only to allow children from the region to get a good education, but also to encourage former scholarship holders to return to the region. Some of them are teachers, doctors, and officials in local authorities. If someone wants to come back and asks us to help with finding a job here in the region, we speak to the owners of local businesses and recommend the respective scholarship holders. There is at least one of our scholarship holders working in nearly every company here. By offering good education and the possibility for former scholarship holders to get a job in the region we are able to foster social and economic development. For people who want to develop as entrepreneurs we have support in the form of free training and financial support.

Authors: Thinking of the region, how did your organization change the economic and social situation?

Social entrepreneur: Over time, the foundation has awarded micro-loans, guarantees, and grants that helped more than 800 start-up companies. Within 10 years of our work, these companies have created over 1,000 new jobs. The companies generate revenues and invest in the development and appearance of the villages in the region. Several dozens of new social enterprises were created. Overall, the standard of living has improved considerably for many inhabitants. People's readiness to engage in charitable causes also increased. Our activities also help to change the social situation through what I call the effect of reverse education. A lot of young people participate in our programs, who then informally educate their parents and grandparents. This is extremely important because the generation of the former state farm workers often has a rather passive attitude. However, through their children and grandchildren they learn that it is important, for example, to engage and to take care of the environment.

Authors: Which are the major challenges your organization faces?

Social entrepreneur: The main challenges that we see at the moment are to obtain enough funding to ensuring the financial stability of the organization in the long term. Having enough savings for a rainy day so to say. In order to reduce our dependence on EU funding for projects, we are trying to diversify our sources of funding. Therefore, we run our own business activity, the income from which we use for investments in the theme village and for improving the skills of our employees. Another challenge is to build social capital in the local environment and among our partners from economic and social programs and projects. This goal is also served by our actions and cooperation with companies in the field of corporate social responsibility. It is very important to ensure an educated staff in the foundation, which will carry out the foundation's activity in the future.

Authors: What are the challenges for the next five to ten years and how does your organization address them?

Social entrepreneur: Rather short term we would like to improve the technical infrastructure of our theme village to function all year round. In addition, we would like to build a Centre for Social Innovation with an overall investment volume of approximately 2 million Złoty. Over the next ten years, the organization has the goal to become independent from public funding. Instead, we aim to create revenues from diversified business activities, such as services for businesses, government or social enterprises, tourism activities, and activities in the Paradise Garden. To realize these objectives, we continuously invest in staff training and the infrastructure. We also find it important to cooperate with other businesses and implement joint projects. We would also like to set up a tourist agency.

Authors: Provide a sketch of how you think your organization and its activities in the region will look like in five years?

Social entrepreneur: In five years, the foundation will employ a dozen people and pursue permanent, long-term programs, such as the Centre for Social Innovation, the English Teaching Program, the Centre for Supporting Social Enterprises, loans programs and the Laboratory of Nature. In addition, we will run the theme village. However, to do so we need to build a better infrastructure, which requires additional funding and skilled employees. The services that the foundation provides to businesses, governments, and other social enterprises will further strengthen the foundation's brand in the region and the country.

Authors: How did the relevance of social enterprises as a type of organization change in Poland in the last decade? What are the future prospects?

Social entrepreneur: There are still too few social enterprises to be able to bring about change at the national level. Local change is noticeable in the form of increased activity of inhabitants, creation of new jobs, development of social initiatives. This perspective highly depends on state policy and regional strategies and attitudes of local authorities. Unemployment-friendly instruments and forms of support as well as access to funds for the creation and development of social enterprises are necessary. Currently, funds are available for the creation of social cooperatives and such new businesses will be created in the next three years. However, it is difficult to determine the future prospects today.

5 Key Takeaways

Implications for Social Entrepreneurship and Innovation in Rural Europe

This book highlights that rural social enterprises are a specific type of organization. Like other social enterprises, they combine a social mission with an entrepreneurial spirit and participatory governance—even though they vary in the extent to which they share these characteristics. We call them *rural* if they operate to the benefit of rural regions and the people living in these areas. Rural social enterprises counteract challenges occurring in rural regions and often develop innovative solutions that allow these challenges to be faced in a different way than was possible with established solutions. This leads to the question: How do rural social enterprises succeed with developing and implementing novel solutions? Our analyses suggest that the rural social enterprises' positioning as intermediary between otherwise less connected groups and domains enables them to develop and implement innovations. Rural social enterprises systematically cross the boundaries between various domains, such as the state, the market, and the civil society, or their sub-domains (e.g. the education system, the tourism sector). Crossing boundaries allows them to gain insights into different fields and to think outside the box, which is crucial for innovation. It also enables them to recontextualize ideas by transferring them from one domain to another. This recontextualization describes how the observed case companies have developed novel products and services, such as rural open technology labs, new field crops, community empowerment models, and theme villages.

However, the recontextualization of ideas as such would not be sufficient to implement innovative solutions in a sustainable way. This also requires resources, such as money, power, and legitimacy. The observed rural social enterprises are able to acquire these resources because they act as intermediaries in vertical networks. As intermediaries, they link communities with few resources, but with the power to act and regime-level actors with resources and ideas but limited possibilities to realize them. This intermediary position enables rural social enterprises to mobilize resources, such as public funds, free provision of infrastructure and volunteer work, on different hierarchical levels. The ability to skillfully recombine these resources is of particular importance for the business models of rural social enterprises because it allows these companies to offer services to, for example, unemployed people or children from disadvantaged families at reduced fees or free of charge.

The position between different hierarchical levels and in different fields of the society also supports our argument that rural social enterprises are hybrid organizations that share characteristics of public, business, and civil society organizations, and operate in each of these domains without fully belonging to any. This hybridity characterizes social enterprises as a contemporary type of actor. While the notion of hybridity was originally developed in postcolonial studies (Bhabha, 1994), it has found its way into discourses about contemporary societies. It emphasizes the avoidance of essential positions and clear identities, and describes the amalgamation and overlapping of formerly distinguished social practices and figures (Kneer, 2010; Hillebrandt, 2015). This is consistent with the observation that in postmodern societies the boundaries between functional areas are gradually blurring (Lash, 1990; Angermüller, 2008). While in classical modernity the dominant mode of modernization was to constantly differentiate functional areas, in late modernity politics, economy, and other spheres increasingly lost their uniqueness and clarity (Rosa et al., 2013). Following this line of arguments, the emergence of social enterprises would reflect the trend towards dedifferentiated societies and hybrid organizations that constantly cross boundaries.

Rural social enterprises are independent actors that use their power to act and create scope for innovative solutions. They are shaped by institutions but also retroact on the institutional environment. This power of action is also reflected in the important role of the social entrepreneurs in the case companies. Even though the companies are based on participatory governance structures, they have social entrepreneurs who have particular shaping power and authority and drive the innovation process. This highlights the deliberate strategic approach on which the activities of the social enterprises are based. However, this does not mean that institutional framework conditions can be neglected. In fact, we observe that a legal status appropriately reflecting the characteristics of social enterprises and their typical activities, a fiscal law that supports the integration of social and entrepreneurial activities, and political awareness for social enterprises and their potential for social and economic development, especially in rural regions, are important conditions that foster social enterprises and the domains in which they operate. Thus, for understanding rural social entrepreneurship it is important to account for both agency and structure and their mutual influence on social enterprise business models and fields. Our research provides empirical evidence that the emergence of social enterprises can neither be explained by focusing solely on entrepreneurial action and market mechanisms nor by focusing solely on the shaping power of the state and civil society.

Let us now take a closer look at some key findings of this research and their implications for future research. For this purpose, we will shed light on four topics, which directed our interest: (1) What characterizes the activities of rural social enterprises? (2) Which role does the rural environment play for their activities? (3) How do rural social enterprises innovate and foster social change? (4) What are the field positioning strategies of rural social enterprises between the main societal fields state, market, and civil society and how do they deal with the different institutional logics in these fields?

Rural Social Enterprises: The Difficulty of Balancing Different Orientations

To resolve the question what makes rural social enterprises a specific type of organization it is meaningful to look for similarities and differences between the investigated enterprises. At first glance, there seem to be more differences than similarities. The operational fields of the enterprises are diverse, ranging from technology education and regional development to agriculture and work integration. Likewise, the legal status—cooperative, foundation, limited company with charity status—and the organizational structures differ considerably. However, there are also a number of similarities. First, *rural* does not only indicate the location of the enterprises, but also the focus of their activities. They address challenges in rural regions and strive to improve the living conditions of the people in these areas. For this purpose, second, they mobilize resources available in the regions they are embedded in. Third, each of the rural social enterprises has a social mission and a participatory governance structure, and executes entrepreneurial activities. While rural social enterprises share general characteristics with the broader group of social enterprises they are specific in that their activities address challenges typical for rural regions. Thus, rural social enterprises are a distinct subgroup of social enterprises and not just social enterprises that happen to be located in rural regions.

Acknowledging that rural social enterprises follow a social and an entrepreneurial mission is not to say that both orientations coexist without tensions. In fact, our analyses reveals that following both orientations without a mission drift is a challenging task (Cornforth, 2004; Ometto et al., 2018). We identify three reasons for these challenges in our case companies and different strategies to cope with them. First, tensions between the social and the entrepreneurial mission emerge when the business model does not generate enough revenue for the business to be sustainable, as was the case at the beginning of the Austrian social enterprise. The solution to this dilemma was to separate the social mission from economic activities by establishing two organizational units, a more economically oriented cooperative and an affiliated network of independent open technology labs with the social mission at its center.

The Greek cooperative is another example of the organizational separation of social and entrepreneurial activities. In the Greek case, the reason for social and entrepreneurial tensions is different orientations among the involved persons with the CEO having a strong entrepreneurial mindset and the farmers defending social values and goals. Third, in the Irish social enterprise we could observe a mission drift caused by a growing dependence on public funding and a loss of autonomy, at the expense of entrepreneurial activities. The enterprise addressed this change by way of outsourcing the entrepreneurial function: The organization actively supports start-ups and small and medium sized enterprises while its own economic activities, such as producing goods and selling services, played a minor role.

Challenges may also occur when it comes to participatory governance. The description of how rural social enterprises involve stakeholders in their decision making (Chapter 1) has already shown that the concept of shared decision making may be undermined if single persons in the social enterprise are very powerful or influential. The Polish, the Greek, and the Austrian social enterprises are shaped by managers or influential members who exert more influence than they would be formally entitled to. Differences between the managers and other stakeholders became evident in interviews when the managers talked about their strategies regarding the company's future and their plans on how to persuade the stakeholders, whereas the stakeholders' orientation was less strategic and more focused on the present. A common strategy to balance the different expectations of managers and stakeholders is to establish formal decision-making rules, which ensure that the rights of stakeholders are considered (e.g. one member one vote, decision making in consent, weighted voting power). In practice, however, these rules are undermined because some social entrepreneurs are more influential due to their knowledge, skills or charisma. Interestingly, stakeholders typically accept the managers' influence because it advances the visibility of the social enterprise and its activities in public and among regime level actors. Thus, the charisma of the social entrepreneurs enhances resource excess for the social enterprise. On the individual level it also relieves stakeholders of the social enterprise from the pressure of taking responsibility in decisions. However, formal participatory governance arrangements are important because they ensure that the behavior of the charismatic social entrepreneurs can be restricted and guided towards a consensual strategy with the other stakeholders. In the Greek cooperative, for example, the CEO found it important to accelerate the growth of the business by taking loans, but could not convince the cooperative members, who ultimately decided against the plan. Thus, although participatory governance is often undermined in day-to-day practice, the implementation of formal decision-making rules helps to secure the rights of internal and external stakeholders when it comes to strategic decisions.

*Having Impact On and Being Shaped
by the Rural Environment*

Rural social enterprises can be regarded as a specific type of organization because they operate to the benefit of rural regions and because they are shaped by the rural environment. Our study reveals that rural social enterprises are interwoven with their rural environments in at least three respects: (1) they address challenges that occur in rural regions, (2) their activities benefit from regional resources that are typical to rural regions, and (3) they are shaped by institutional conditions and know how to use these conditions in rural settings to their benefit. Regarding the first criterion, all investigated rural social enterprises have the aim of benefitting rural regions and their inhabitants by addressing the challenges that occur in these regions. These challenges are often related to structural changes, which manifest themselves as lack of sustainable farming opportunities (Greece), structural poverty and unemployment (Poland), the continued absence of the state from providing public service (Ireland), and the brain drain of young and skilled people (Austria). Fighting these challenges in some cases requires that the needs of particular groups (as, for example, small farmers in Greece) are addressed, and in other cases the needs of entire communities or regions. Particularly in the latter case, rural social enterprises actively contribute to rural development to make the rural area "an attractive location in which to live, do business and visit."[1]

As to the second criterion, rural regions and their inhabitants provide resources that are crucial for the business model of rural social enterprises. One of the most important resources is volunteer work. All investigated social enterprises benefit from this resource but only in addition to paid work. Even though volunteer work plays a role in non-rural social enterprises as well, we argue that it is more easily available in rural regions due to the "culture of self-help" (Steinerowski & Steinerowska-Streb, 2012, p. 173) that prevails in these regions. Self-help and volunteer work are not only consequences of the lack of public and private services but also an integral part of being socialized in rural regions. Working together for everyone's benefit adds to social cohesion, particularly in sparsely populated areas. In their endeavor to provide social added value, rural social enterprises can build on this culture. Besides volunteer work, the social enterprises also benefit from the provision of buildings or land by the municipality at low cost or for free. These resources are also more likely to be available in rural regions than in urban areas.

Regarding the third criterion, rural social enterprises are shaped by and make use of the institutional conditions that prevail in rural areas. Rural social enterprises are hybrid organizations that systematically cross boundaries between otherwise separated domains. They often have a diverse product and service portfolio, including work integration courses, enterprise support, educational services, and touristic products. At the same time rural regions often have less distinct societal fields. Where in cities, for example, politics, economy, and civil life are distinct domains and businesses are highly specialized, in rural areas the boundaries are more fluid. As hybrid organizations, which require access to different domains, rural social enterprises benefit from blurred roles and domains. The existence of overlapping fields and less specialized businesses might cause institutionalized acceptance of this type of new enterprises in rural regions. Consequently, the holistic and integrated product portfolio of rural social enterprises can be understood as a form of isomorphism between social enterprises and their rural environment which ultimately helps to ensure the survival of the enterprise (DiMaggio & Powell, 1983). Rural social enterprises are socially embedded in and emotionally attached to the place. They are based on trust, which is crucial to access information and to gain the good will of decision makers.

From Innovation to Social Innovation: The Role Model Effect of Novel Products and Services

Rural social enterprises address needs that emerge in rural regions. To do so, they do not only rely on established solutions but often develop novel products and services that aim to address social challenges better than before. The innovative services, products, and processes are diverse. They range from cultivating new field crops and covering the whole value chain in an agricultural cooperative to the establishment of rural open technology labs and the operation of theme villages. The significant degree of innovation apparent in these offerings is highly interesting because the innovative power of social enterprises is a subject of academic discourses. While scholars from the EMES school of thought regard the ability to innovate as less important (Defourny & Nyssens, 2013; Pestoff, 2014), other researchers see the ability to come up with novel and valuable solutions as an important characteristic of social enterprises (Dees, 2001 [1998]; Martin & Osberg, 2007).

Another interesting result refers to the role of rural social enterprises as intermediaries, who connect communities and regime-level actors in vertical networks, as well as horizontally across different fields and domains. It is the rural social enterprises' position as intermediaries that enables them to develop and implement innovations. On the horizontal level, rural social enterprises have access to actors in different fields, such as to administrations and governments, commercial enterprises and civil society groups without being fully integrated in one of the domains. This hybrid position enables them to think outside the box, recontextualize ideas and combine previously separated elements, which may lead to innovative solutions. However, implementing an innovative idea also requires resources for developing ideas into marketable products and services and to make sure that they can be provided, especially as they are typically provided for low fees or for free. Here, the rural social enterprises' intermediary position in vertical networks comes into play. This intermediary position provides access to resources on different hierarchical levels and enables the enterprises to integrate them. The ability to mobilize different resources, such as public funds, political support, and volunteer work, and to combine them in one product or service that is new and valuable is a remarkable asset of successful rural social enterprises.

The intermediary position between rural communities and regime-level actors does not only help rural social enterprises to mobilize resources but also to gain legitimacy, which also fosters the development of innovative solutions. We observed two types of legitimization processes. In a *bottom-up process*, rural social enterprises gain legitimacy through their role as advocates of rural communities. Vertical linkages with these communities and the ability to address their needs make rural social enterprises legitimate advocates of rural communities in the eyes of regime-level actors. Consequently, rural social enterprises are more likely to get access to resources controlled by these actors. In a *top-down process*, rural social enterprises gain legitimacy through vertical linkages with regime-level actors. It is essential to first establish reliable contacts with regime level actors because they provide both important resources and legitimacy. Once acknowledged by regime level actors, rural social enterprises have the authority to mobilize additional resources, such as infrastructure and volunteer work, on lower hierarchical levels. The position as intermediaries in hierarchical networks makes rural social enterprises an attractive partner for both communities and regime-level actors because they seem to solve two problems: the action problem of regime-level actors, who have resources and strategies but limited possibilities to implement them, and the idea and resource problem of rural communities, who have the power to act but limited access to resources and know-how.

All efforts to counteract social challenges in innovative ways must ultimately be evaluated based on their impact and the social change they bring about. We find that rural social enterprises follow two different innovation strategies or, more often, a mixture of both. The first strategy can be called "in-house production strategy." In the in-house production strategy novel solutions are implemented by rural social enterprises themselves to counteract social challenges or to address the social needs of a specific group of people or in a specific area. The Polish social enterprise, for example, operates a theme village that aims to integrate long-term unemployed into work and combines, for this purpose, previously separated elements such as establishing a tourist attraction and providing cultural education. While the degree of novelty is comparatively high, we find that the social impact of the in-house production strategy is limited because the number of addressed persons is rather low. The second strategy can be called "spin-off strategy." Instead of realizing the innovative solution alone, the social enterprise that follows a spin-off strategy promotes the idea and provides support and know-how but leaves the realization to decentralized groups. Again, the Polish social enterprise can be taken as an example, because they not only operate a theme village themselves but also promote it as a role model and encourage other communities to adopt the idea. As a consequence, almost 50 new theme villages have been established across the country. While the degree of novelty of these additional villages might be rather low, the reproduction of the innovative idea creates much more social impact. The spin-off strategy thus encourages people to adopt the innovation, which can then lead to social innovation, i.e. to a change of practices in a social environment aimed at solving a social challenge better than it was possible before.

Three Domains for Positioning the Field of Rural Social Enterprises

In this section, we return to the image of our case organizations operating in fields, with social enterprise representing one important action field for them (see Chapter 3). Dealing with the phenomenon of *rural* social enterprises also means embracing a spatial perspective on social enterprise fields. Our analysis in Chapter 3 suggested that all case organizations are clearly positioned in national and international fields of social enterprise where they access crucial funding, such as through EU programs, and gain legitimacy for their activities. However, as one moves down the spatial hierarchy to rural regions and their local communities, our study found that the relevance of positioning as a social enterprise differs between the cases and even loses importance. This is clearly reflected in the interviews with our case social entrepreneurs (see Chapter 4) when they, for example, talk about their use of social enterprise terminology.

One possible explanation is that the relevance of social enterprise as a positioning strategy in the rural context corresponds with the legitimacy of this organizational form in the respective countries. Actors in the state field are crucial when it comes to granting legitimacy to social enterprise fields, such as through policies, discourse, and legislation (Fligstein & McAdam, 2012; Nicholls & Teasdale, 2017). We find specific social enterprise legislation, for instance, in the cases of Greece, Poland, and Ireland (see Chapter 4). However, our cross-country empirical evidence presented in this book suggests that rural social enterprise currently gains more legitimacy and resources from the EU-level, through its rural development framework, than from the national policy level—although EU funding has apparently become more competitive.

Indeed, the national 'eco-systems' for social enterprises look rather different in, for instance, Ireland versus Austria. In the Irish context, also reflected in our case study, rural social enterprises have received a certain level of recognition among regional and national policy makers. The idea of involving community-based enterprises in local development through partnerships with the public and private sector is more established than in other countries. In Austria, in contrast, social enterprise might be a growing sector, including new initiatives in rural areas, and gaining importance with the prospect of neo-liberal welfare-state reforms under the present right-wing-conservative government. However, the current eco-system is still underdeveloped, for instance, in terms of societal and political recognition and support, specific funding streams as well as legal and fiscal specifications (Anastasiadis et al., 2018).

Without downplaying contextual specificities of our case countries and particular rural areas within them, we can distinguish three general domains that are relevant to the development of rural social enterprises as a field (Steiner & Teasdale, 2018, pp. 7–9). These three domains thus also influence the potential for organizations when positioning themselves as rural social enterprise.

First, the *rural domain* offers both challenges and opportunities to social enterprises, which is also apparent from our case studies. In the digital age, the lack of adequate technology infrastructure, such as fast internet, is just one important challenge for social enterprises operating in rural areas which might limit their market access compared to urban businesses. The key thing is to turn the challenges in rural spaces into viable business opportunities. Our case social enterprises, for instance, translate the challenge of demographic change into business opportunities by addressing the needs of older people with their services. Or they translate the challenge of the remoteness of rural settings into opportunities by developing business models for tourism. Cultivating new crops for life-style products like stevia in organic farming is a way to translate the challenge of the downturn of traditional agriculture into a business opportunity.

Second, the *social enterprise domain* refers to organizational characteristics. The analyses in previous chapters of this book revealed that the hybrid character of social enterprises is again the source of both opportunities and challenges for these organizations. It enables them, for instance, to simultaneously tap resources in different fields and occupy market niches through offering tailored services to marginalized communities. At the same time, however, tensions result from their contradicting economic and social missions, and from the need to be accountable to various stakeholders who operate according to different institutional logics. Our case studies further tell the stories of rural hybrid organizations that more or less struggle to access sustainable financing and depend on public funding. In light of this, social enterprise and regional development policies need to accept and account for the diversity of social enterprise approaches in rural areas. Some rural social enterprises need permanent public funding while non-financial consulting support would be important for developing commercially viable business ideas (Steiner & Teasdale, 2018).

Apart from public support, the formation and institutionalization of a third sector field such as rural social entrepreneurship also needs to build on the self-help potential among relevant actors. In this respect, the creation of support networks, platforms and umbrella organizations helps stabilize collective action and at the same time supports the individual social enterprise (Finnemore & Sikkink, 1998; McQuarrie & Krumholz, 2011). This network building and intermediation is usually driven by "socially skilled" actors (Fligstein & McAdam, 2011, p. 7) and thus typically is part of the spectrum of activities of social entrepreneurs. Indeed, we observed that our case entrepreneurs operate as intermediaries between community initiatives and regime actors (see Chapter 2).

However, the institutionalization of rural social enterprise fields requires broader-based platforms and intermediaries that span across a range of policy domains, industries and also regions. Community-led housing in England represents a current example of such field building activities. With the stimulus of the Community Housing Fund and support from foundation funders, such as Power to Change and Nationwide Foundation, regional and local hubs have been set up across the country to stimulate community-led housing activity (Housing and Communities Research Group, 2018). Earlier examples of broader-based organizational platforms that have contributed to successful field building are secondary housing cooperatives, and umbrella bodies for community land trusts in England (Lang, 2019). Apart from servicing local community-based organizations, these regional and national platforms operate as intermediaries between conflicting institutional logics of community groups and government professionals. In a nutshell, such a 'bootstrapping-approach' could eventually lead to networks of smaller rural social enterprises that cooperate when bidding for and delivering public contracts. It could also help them with pooling when buying and selling their services on the market (Steiner & Teasdale, 2018).

Finally, we turn to the *policy domain* of rural social enterprise. In the field analysis in Chapter 3, we have already noted that rural communities represent a nexus of different interrelated policy issues, such as health care, cohesion, and employment. Against this backdrop, social enterprises as a hybrid organization appear perfectly positioned to simultaneously address different local challenges. In fact, the diverse service portfolio represented by three of our four case organizations—in Austria, Ireland, and Poland—speaks for the relevance and viability of this positioning strategy. It is this integrated approach to tackling socio-economic issues which represents an innovation that differentiates rural social enterprise from other types of organizations (Steiner & Teasdale, 2018). We need to keep in mind that organizations in the public and also third sector have traditionally operated in specific policy areas (Kendall, 2005), thus potentially missing out on making the connections needed to address 'wicked' local development problems. We also believe that the integrated approach is more typical of rural than urban social enterprise, given the characteristics of the policy environment in rural settings versus cities.

Nevertheless, policy makers still need to recognize the important benefits of social enterprises for integrated rural development. This has to materialize in local and national policies that support rural social enterprise to effectively complement the work of public bodies, private companies, and non-profit and voluntary organizations. However, rural social enterprises can support this process by being pro-active and engaging with relevant but often abstract rural policies and presenting themselves as practical solutions to policy needs (Obstfeld, 2005; Mullins, 2018).

Contributions, Implications, and Recommendations

Research that is funded with tax money also needs to give back to society. We believe that the research presented in this book offers a valuable contribution to research, practice, and politics concerned with social enterprises, innovation, and rural development.

Contributions to Research

The current state of the art in empirical research on social entrepreneurship does not provide a database with a sufficiently large number of contacts, which impedes a large-scale survey. Thus, the first challenge for this project was to design an empirical study that enables us to tackle the issue of generalizability of our insights in a qualitative research design. We therefore chose a multiple case study over a single case study design. Combined with a theoretical sampling approach we could assess the reach of the generalizability of our insights by comparing the similarities and differences between the four cases investigated in this book. The insights generated from this comparative approach will inform future research on social entrepreneurship. Especially, it provides rich information for sampling strategies and thus adds another stepping stone to paving the way towards much needed future quantitative studies.

We decided to take an action focus. This volitional decision stems from our belief that our study will only add to the scientific discourse if we avoid getting stuck in the definitional struggle of what is a social enterprise. Our starting point is the insight that it is the specific set of actions taken that is common across most individuals and organizations that are defined as social entrepreneurs, social entrepreneurships, and social enterprises respectively. Thus, the delineating aspects lie in the activities rather than the individuals or organizations. This insight not only provided a valuable starting point, but also led to the identification of the roots of these specificities of social entrepreneurial action: the challenges addressed by performing the action. As a consequence, it was the action focus that enabled us to realize that the specific rural of rural social entrepreneurship is rooted in the specific social and economic challenges that rural regions face. This insight contributes to scientific research on social entrepreneurship because it helps to define rural social entrepreneurship as a specific field of research in its own right.

For properly understanding cause and effect it is necessary to take a dynamic approach. While retrospective narrations can provide the data for analysis of chains of cause and effect, they suffer for example from biases of memory and over rationalization. When the past is translated into history, the validity of data is often lost. Thus, we decided to conduct a longitudinal data collection. We followed the case organizations over a period of nearly two years. During this time, we could capture social entrepreneurship activities and their effects in the place and beyond. The rich data helped us to attribute specific causes to specific effects. Thus, the longitudinal case study design enabled us to generate dynamic models of how the action taken by social enterprises enabled innovation in rural regions. These dynamic models of social enterprises mediating in multi-level networks and positioning in strategic action fields can provide a theoretical underpinning for future research. The models developed in this book can also help to integrate the different streams of research on social entrepreneurship by providing the action perspective as a common basis. We call for future empirical research, both qualitative and quantitative, that challenges and extends our theorizing and the proposed models.

Implications and Recommendations for Practice

One of the key performance indicators in management is firm growth. For social enterprises growth needs to be connected with both dimensions expressed in the concept of the double bottom line. These firms not only grow when their level of economic activity rises, but also when their impact becomes stronger. This implies that, compared to corporate firms, scaling of social enterprises follows a different logic. Drawing on the insight that social enterprises address societal challenges with new and valuable offers in the form of product/service and process innovation our analysis informs practitioners on the potential of scaling these innovations. We find that scaling product and service innovation is strongly limited because social enterprises are active in niches that are so small that they are attractive neither for state nor for corporate (Santos, 2012). For practice this implies that business models of social enterprises that are active mainly in product and service innovation need to be sustainable given the small market volume defined by the special needs of the target group (e.g. parents in a rural village who have the need for a playground or elderly inhabitants of a remote place who suffer from social isolation). Social entrepreneurs who build a business model of such a social enterprise on a growth strategy have to ask themselves if the addressed need is shared by a larger number of potential customers. If this is the case a growth strategy is an attractive option. However, this at the same time questions the decision to address this need with the establishment of a social enterprise.

For social entrepreneurs who pursue a business model that mainly builds on process innovation growth is an attractive option. The scaling of the new and valuable process either to new groups of the local population or to new geographical contexts can reinforce the legitimacy of the offer. Interestingly, the scaling activity does not have to be done by the innovator, but can be transferred to other independent social enterprises following the spin-off strategy discussed above. Even if there is no monetary benefit gained from such scaling strategies, the investment in supporting and consulting the newly emerging imitators can pay off indirectly through the enhanced visibility and legitimacy of the process. The enhanced legitimacy in turn enhances resource access for all social enterprises implementing this process and thus, also for the innovator. On a higher level, scaling social entrepreneurship activities also fosters the formation of social enterprises as an institutional field.

A major success factor for social enterprises is the handling of the tensions inherent in the duality of social and entrepreneurial missions. Only social enterprise business models that manage to synergetically use the energy emerging from the motivation to pursue the two missions can succeed in generating noticeable social impact on an economically sustainable basis. For pursuing conflicting goals within one business the ambidexterity literature suggests separation and integration strategies. Our analysis shows that both can work in the context of social enterprises. However, business models that actively and continuously work on the mutually exclusive goals of social and entrepreneurial missions that, at the same time, in their realization depend on each other deliver more valuable offers to their respective target group. It seems like in social enterprises a separation strategy rather generates product/service innovation whereas an integration strategy fosters process innovation. Practitioners should take a conscious decision which strategy they follow in order to avoid getting stuck in the middle. Without a volitional decision and a consequent implementation of the strategy in the design of the organization and the portfolio of market offers, the dilemma of pursuing a social and an entrepreneurial mission at the same time will lead to costly tensions in everyday business.

However, the best business model and organization design will not help social entrepreneurs out of a situation where they are facing a dual set of demands. They are expected to perform well economically in order to provide sufficient resources for realizing the activities that generate the intended social impact. At the same time they are not expected to earn too much in their role as a social entrepreneur, even if their workload justifies an income well above average. These conflicting roles and the imbalance between effort and reward (Siegrist, 1996) lead to strain and threaten social entrepreneurs to suffer from sustained stress (Kibler et al., 2018) with the typically negative consequences for physical and mental health (Rauch et al., 2018). Appropriate social enterprise business models that allow for an adequate compensation are thus not only in the interests of the social entrepreneur, but also in the interests of all stakeholders in the social enterprise.

Policy Recommendations

Our results have direct implications for policy. First, policy needs to assign social entrepreneurship a clear role in rural society and economy. Policy makers on the national and the European level need to decide which role social entrepreneurship has to play in rural society and the economy. Social entrepreneurship has great potential to contribute to society and the economy in many ways, but it is not a panacea that solves everything for everyone. We call for a responsible discussion and a reasoned political decision on which areas of social needs governments will allocate social businesses to cover. However, delegation must not result in the state withdrawing from the provision of core services in rural regions. A clear position on the role of social entrepreneurship in the delivery of answers to societal challenges would enable policy makers to formulate a consistent social entrepreneurship policy that provides stability and planning security for social entrepreneurs. This also includes the definition of legal forms for social enterprises that appropriately accommodate the specific characteristics of social entrepreneurial activity. This in turn is a prerequisite for a vivid and sustainable development of social entrepreneurship in rural Europe.

Second, policy needs to facilitate sustainable business models for social innovation. While social entrepreneurship is sometimes seen as a euphemism for the cost-driven outsourcing of public services to private contractors, at its core it is a social mission complemented by an entrepreneurial mission. Over and above the positive aspects of entrepreneurship, such as innovation and structural change, the business models of social entrepreneurs address societal challenges like unemployment, poverty, social exclusion, and marginalization. This extra contribution of social entrepreneurship justifies favorable institutional conditions such as simplified accounting procedures, social clauses in public procurement, access to funding schemes, or tax breaks. We call for support schemes for social entrepreneurship that utilize a pro-active and risk-taking mindset to facilitate innovative answers to societal challenges based on a sustainable business model. Social innovation can be reflected in a new means of service delivery or in the delivery of new services that address previously neglected societal challenges. The delivery of standardized public services, however, should not be subsidized beyond the value of the outsourced services.

Third, we call for policies that reinforce voluntarism in social entrepreneurship as a mechanism for social inclusion in rural Europe. Voluntary work remains a strong tradition in communities across rural Europe.
Social entrepreneurship draws heavily on this resource, as it not only
helps to deliver social services that would otherwise not cover their costs,
but more importantly enhances social inclusion. Particularly groups that
are threatened with marginalization in rural communities, such as unemployed, retired or disabled people, and also immigrants can build social
relationships by contributing their time to voluntary work for a social
enterprise in their local community. By involving volunteers, social entrepreneurship improves skills and enhances social inclusion. Moreover,
providing token payment and insurance protection is a sign of appreciation and reduces the threat of exploitation. However, many national
contexts hamper the contribution of volunteers in social enterprises due
to unfavorable legal regulations. The access to potential volunteers is
often blocked by privacy laws. We call for a regulatory environment that
is more supportive of the contributions of volunteers in social entrepreneurship and that enables governmental bodies to effectively link social
entrepreneurs with potential volunteers.

We hope that the book at hand can help to refocus research, practice, and politics towards an understanding of social enterprise that puts
action center stage. With an action focus research will be able to develop
a more consistent body of knowledge that allows for more concrete recommendations for practitioners and policy makers.

Note

1 Website of the Irish social enterprise (January 28, 2019).

References

Anastasiadis, M., Gspurnig, W. and Lang, R. (2018). *A Map of Social Enterprises
and Their Eco-Systems in Europe: Country Report: Austria*. Brussels: European Commission.
Angermüller, J. (2008). Postmoderne zwischen Repräsentationskrise und Entdifferenzierung [Postmodernism between the crisis of representation and dedifferentiation]. In S. Moebius and A. Reckwitz (Eds.): *Poststrukturalistische
Sozialwissenschaften* (245–260). Frankfurt am Main: Suhrkamp.
Bhabha, H. K. (1994). *The Location of Culture*. London: Routledge.
Cornforth, C. (2004). The governance of co-operatives and mutual associations:
A paradox perspective. *Annals of Public and Cooperative Economics*, *75*(1),
11–32.
Dees, J. G. (2001/1998). *The Meaning of "Social Entrepreneurship."* Retrieved
from https://centers.fuqua.duke.edu/case/wp-content/uploads/sites/7/2015/03/
Article_Dees_ MeaningofSocialEntrepreneurship_2001.pdf

Defourny, J. and Nyssens, M. (2013). Social innovation, social economy and social enterprise: What can the European debate tell us? In F. Moulaert, D. MacCallum, A. Mehmood, and A. Hamdouch (Eds.): *The International Handbook on Social Innovation* (40–52). Cheltenham, UK: Edward Elgar.

DiMaggio, P. J. and Powell, W. P. (1983). The ironic cage revisited: Institutional isomorphism and collective rationality in organizational fields. *American Sociological Review*, 48, 147–160.

Finnemore, M. and Sikkink, K. (1998). International norm dynamics and political change. *International Organization*, 52(4), 887–917.

Fligstein, N. and McAdam, D. (2011). Toward a general theory of strategic action fields. *Sociological Theory*, 29(1), 1–26.

Fligstein, N. and McAdam, D. (2012). *A Theory of Fields*. London: Oxford University Press.

HCRG (Housing and Communities Research Group) (Ed.). (2018). *Hope for Housing Conference Report*. University of Birmingham. Retrieved from www.birmingham.ac.uk/documents/college-social-sciences/social-policy/HCRN/hope-for-housing-conference/hrc-report-06-11-18.pdf. Accessed November 17, 2018.

Hillebrandt, F. (2015). Die hybride Praxis. In T. Kron (Ed.): *Soziale Hybridität—Hybride Sozialität* (151–170). Weilerswist: Velbrück.

Kendall, J. (2005). *Third Sector European Policy: Organisations Between Market and State, the Policy Process and the EU*, Third Sector European Policy Working Paper 1, London: LSE.

Kibler, E., Wincent, J., Kautonen, T., Cacciotti, G. and Obschonka, M. (2018). Why social entrepreneurs are so burned out. *Harvard Business Review*, online first.

Kneer, G. (2010). Der Hybride [The hybrid]. In S. Moebius and M. Schroer (Eds.): *Diven, Hacker, Spekulanten: Sozialfiguren der Gegenwart* (219–234). Berlin: Suhrkamp.

Lang, R. (2019). Social sustainability and collaborative housing: Lessons from an international comparative study. In M. R. Shirazi and R. Keivani (Eds.): *Urban Social Sustainability: Theory, Policy and Practice* (193–216). London: Routledge.

Lash, S. (1990). *The Sociology of Postmodernism*. London and New York: Routledge.

Martin, R. L. and Osberg, S. (2007). Social entrepreneurship: The case for definition. *Stanford Social Innovation Review*, 5(2), 28–39.

McQuarrie, M. and Krumholz, N. (2011). Institutionalized social skill and the rise of mediating organizations in urban governance: The case of the Cleveland housing network. *Housing Policy Debate*, 21(3), 421–442.

Mullins, D. (2018). Achieving policy recognition for community-based housing solutions: The case of self-help housing in England. *International Journal of Housing Policy*, 18(1), 143–155.

Nicholls, A. and Teasdale, S. (2017). Neoliberalism by stealth? Exploring continuity and change within the UK social enterprise policy paradigm. *Policy & Politics*, 45(3), 323–341.

Obstfeld, D. (2005). Social networks, the tertius iungens orientation, and involvement in innovation. *Administrative Science Quarterly*, 50(1), 100–130.

Ometto, M. P., Gegenhuber, T., Winter, J. and Greenwood, R. (2018). From balancing missions to mission drift: The role of the institutional context, spaces, and compartmentalization in the scaling of social enterprises. *Business & Society*. https://doi.org/10.1177/0007650318758329

Pestoff, V. (2014). The role of participatory governance in the EMES approach to social enterprise. *Journal of Entrepreneurial and Organizational Diversity*, 2(2), 48–60.

Rauch, A., Fink, M. and Hatak, I. (2018). Stress processes: An essential ingredient in the entrepreneurial process. *Academy of Management Perspectives*, 32(3), online first.

Rosa, H., Strecker, D. and Kottmann, A. (2013). *Soziologische Theorien [Sociological Theories]*. Konstanz and München: UVK.

Santos, F. M. (2012). A positive theory of social entrepreneurship. *Journal of Business Ethics*, 111(3), 335–351.

Siegrist, J. (1996). Adverse health effects of high-effort/low-reward conditions. *Journal of Occupational Health Psychology*, 1(1), 27–41.

Steiner, A. and Teasdale, S. (2018). Unlocking the potential of rural social enterprise. *Journal of Rural Studies*. https://doi.org/10.1016/j.jrurstud.2017.12.021

Steinerowski, A. and Steinerowska-Streb, I. (2012). Can social enterprise contribute to creating sustainable rural communities? Using the lens of structuration theory to analyze the emergence of rural social enterprise. *Local Economy*, 27, 167–182. DOI: 10.1177/0269094211429650

About the Authors

Matthias Fink is founding head of the Institute of Innovation Management at the Johannes Kepler University Linz, Austria and a Professor for Innovation and Entrepreneurship at ARU Cambridge, U.K. In addition he is academic director of two MBA programs at LIMAK Austrian Business School. Matthias holds a Ph.D. and a postdoctoral qualification (Habilitation) from WU Vienna University of Economics and Business and was a Visiting Professor at several universities, for example, Universitat Autònoma de Barcelona, Spain and University of Twente, The Netherlands. In research, Matthias' focus is on the role of innovation in new venture creation and small business management. His current interests include entrepreneurship as a driver of innovation and change in regional contexts, entrepreneurial finance, and ethical issues in business research. In his research designs, Matthias combines quantitative and qualitative methods. His research has been published in journals such as *Journal of Management Studies*, *Journal of Business Venturing*, *Entrepreneurship Theory & Practice*.

Richard Lang is Assistant Professor at the Institute of Innovation Management at Johannes Kepler University Linz, Austria, and an Honorary Senior Research Fellow at the School of Social Policy at University of Birmingham, U.K., where he previously held a Marie Curie Fellowship. Richard also holds a Ph.D. from WU Vienna University of Economics and Business. His current research focuses on social innovation and social enterprise models in urban and regional development, including collaborative housing models and the role of networks. His research has been published in scholarly journals such as *European Planning Studies*; *Housing, Theory and Society*; *International Small Business Journal*; *Journal of Rural Studies*; *Technological Forecasting and Social Change*, and *Voluntas*.

Daniela Maresch is an Associate Professor at the University of Southern Denmark (DK) and an Associate Senior Researcher at the Institute of Innovation Management (IFI) at the Johannes Kepler University Linz (A). She holds a Ph.D. in Business Administration and an LL.M.

(WU) in Business Law from WU Vienna University of Economics and Business. The focus of her research is on topics at the intersection of entrepreneurship, innovation, and finance, such as the role of trust in bank lending, social and refugee entrepreneurship as well as the social impact of disruptive technologies. The results of her work have been published both in scholarly journals such as *Technovation*, *Technology Forecasting and Social Change*, and *Entrepreneurship and Regional Development*, and in transfer publications such as the *European Central Bank Working Paper Series*.

Ralph Richter is a senior researcher and lecturer in Regional and Urban Sociology. At the Leibniz Institute for Research on Society and Space (IRS) in Erkner/Germany he has conducted research projects on social innovation and social enterprises in rural communities, among them the EU funded project "Social Innovation in Structurally Weak Rural Regions" (RurInno). Recent stages in his career were the Technical University of Darmstadt/Germany and the University of Leipzig/Germany where he worked on projects on regional identity and the intrinsic logic of cities. His Ph.D. thesis contributes to the discourse on place-related identity in shrinking cities. He studied Sociology and Communication and Media Science at the University of Leipzig and the University of Naples/Italy. The research focus of Ralph is on the spatial dimension of social change, social innovation, migration, social networks, social entrepreneurship, and identity and image processes.

Index

Note: Numbers in **bold** indicate a table. Numbers in *italics* indicate a figure.

For Product Safety Concerns and Information please contact our EU
representative GPSR@taylorandfrancis.com
Taylor & Francis Verlag GmbH, Kaufingerstraße 24, 80331 München, Germany

www.ingramcontent.com/pod-product-compliance
Ingram Content Group UK Ltd.
Pitfield, Milton Keynes, MK11 3LW, UK
UKHW020941180425
457613UK00019B/493